Palgrave Executive Essentials

Today's complex and changing business environment brings with it a number of pressing challenges. To be successful, business professionals are increasingly required to leverage and spot future trends, be masters of strategy, all while leading responsibly, inspiring others, mastering financial techniques and driving innovation.

Palgrave Executive Essentials empowers you to take your skills to the next level. Offering a suite of resources to support you on your executive journey and written by renowned experts from top business schools, the series is designed to support professionals as they embark on executive education courses, but it is equally applicable to practicing leaders and managers. Each book brings you in-depth case studies, accompanying video resources, reflective questions, practical tools and core concepts that can be easily applied to your organization, all written in an engaging, easy to read style.

Ronan McIvor

Digital Transformation

Strategies for Management Success

Ronan McIvor
Ulster University
Belfast, UK

ISSN 2731-5614   ISSN 2731-5622 (electronic)
Palgrave Executive Essentials
ISBN 978-3-031-99257-5   ISBN 978-3-031-99258-2 (eBook)
https://doi.org/10.1007/978-3-031-99258-2

© The Editor(s) (if applicable) and The Author(s), under exclusive license to Springer Nature Switzerland AG 2025, corrected publication 2025

This work is subject to copyright. All rights are solely and exclusively licensed by the Publisher, whether the whole or part of the material is concerned, specifically the rights of translation, reprinting, reuse of illustrations, recitation, broadcasting, reproduction on microfilms or in any other physical way, and transmission or information storage and retrieval, electronic adaptation, computer software, or by similar or dissimilar methodology now known or hereafter developed.

The use of general descriptive names, registered names, trademarks, service marks, etc. in this publication does not imply, even in the absence of a specific statement, that such names are exempt from the relevant protective laws and regulations and therefore free for general use.

The publisher, the authors and the editors are safe to assume that the advice and information in this book are believed to be true and accurate at the date of publication. Neither the publisher nor the authors or the editors give a warranty, expressed or implied, with respect to the material contained herein or for any errors or omissions that may have been made. The publisher remains neutral with regard to jurisdictional claims in published maps and institutional affiliations.

Cover figure: b7a | Shutterstock

This Palgrave Macmillan imprint is published by the registered company Springer Nature Switzerland AG.
The registered company address is: Gewerbestrasse 11, 6330 Cham, Switzerland

If disposing of this product, please recycle the paper.

Preface

Digital technologies such as social media, data analytics, artificial intelligence (AI), the internet of things (IoT) and cloud computing are profoundly transforming business and society. These digital technologies have eliminated traditional boundaries of time and geography, created virtual communities of employees, customers and suppliers, and allowed firms to do things not possible in the physical world. The challenges brought about by the COVID-19 pandemic have further spurred firms to accelerate the use of digital technologies. Many firms have become digital innovators, creating new product and process innovations with digital technologies.

The increasing prominence of digital technologies and the exponential growth in data from digital applications and devices have been forcing many firms to embark on digital transformation. Digital transformation involves employing digital technologies to drive significant changes in processes, products and business models. It can involve changing established organisational structures and work practices to allow firms to react more quickly to the disruptions brought about by digital technologies.

Digital transformation can bring benefits in a range of areas, including using data analytics to collect and analyse customer data to provide more personalised products and services, and employing AI to predict trends and customer behaviour. Digital sensors in cars allow automakers to access performance data to support the continuous development of the car and inform future new product development activities. Digital transformation allows firms to experiment with new ideas, products and services more quickly and at lower costs. Scaling up digital sales channels has lower marginal costs than the direct costs of scaling up physical channels, which involves recruiting additional people and renting or purchasing more buildings.

Digital transformation is challenging as it involves changing existing processes, systems and structures. Established firms often have ineffective legacy systems, firm silos and people who are resistant to change, making it difficult to fully exploit the benefits of digital technologies. Firms are fearful of introducing digital technologies as they challenge existing business practices and established ways of creating value for customers. Digital transformation occurs in an environment where digital technologies have accelerated the pace of change, leading to more disruption, uncertainty and complexity. For example, ChatGPT, the generative AI application, attracted over 100 million users just two months after its launch, whereas it took Facebook over four years to reach that number of users.

This book provides an understanding of digital transformation in a range of organisational contexts and highlights how digital technologies are employed in the context of digital transformation. The book focuses on the following key issues:

- Careful attention is given to understanding how digital technologies disrupt industries by transforming business processes, products and business models. Much of the attention on digital transformation has focused on born-digital exemplars such as Amazon, Google and Netflix. These firms have disrupted sectors such as retail, media and technology, and created innovative business models to generate significant returns. The analysis in this book highlights how established firms can learn from these born-digital companies and achieve the benefits of digital transformation by combining digital technologies with their existing assets to strengthen their competitive position.
- Significant emphasis is placed on understanding the management capabilities required for digital transformation and exploiting the opportunities that digital technologies offer (Chap. 1). The value of employing digital technologies comes from transforming products, processes and business models, which is consistent with the view that technology is seen as an opportunity for the business, rather than as an opportunity for technology.
- The book incorporates important concepts associated with digital transformation, including digital platforms (Chap. 2), digital innovation (Chap. 6) and business model innovation (Chap. 7). Consideration is given to the issues involved in implementing key digital technologies

related to digital transformation, including the IoT (Chap 3), AI (Chap. 4) and data analytics tools (Chap. 5).
- The book considers key issues around implementing digital transformation, including formulating a strategy (Chap. 8), building a digital core (Chap. 9) and leading change in digital transformation (Chap. 10). For example, a framework is outlined, which proposes a typology of digital transformation strategies based on the level of disruption in the business environment and the strength of a firm's digital capabilities. The analysis highlights how digital transformation can involve radical change over a short time period, whereas in other instances, it involves gradual change over a longer time period. Leading change focuses on issues such as the importance of understanding the changes in organisational and people capabilities required to drive digital transformation.
- The book includes practical management frameworks that provide an understanding of digital transformation and how digital technologies can be employed in this context. It shows how these frameworks can be applied across a range of business settings by providing real-world business examples.
- Illustrations from practice are included in each chapter to enrich the analysis and provide support for the frameworks proposed. The book is strengthened through references to contemporary research on digital transformation from a range of leading international journals, including Sloan Management Review, Harvard Business Review, MIS Quarterly Executive, Long Range Planning and the Global Strategy Journal.

The book is aimed primarily at the postgraduate market and management programmes such as MBAs. It can be used on executive management programmes to give both middle and senior managers an awareness of the issues surrounding digital transformation. It can also be used on business technology programmes by technical specialists who need to understand the management issues related to digital transformation. The book is suitable for higher-level undergraduate modules on digital transformation in business or business technology courses, where significant attention is given to digital transformation.

Much of the content of the book is relevant to practitioner management development programmes on digital transformation. The book is based on contemporary research, which has focused on examining the benefits and challenges of digital transformation. Integrating contemporary practice and frameworks stimulates a deeper understanding of digital transformation and alerts practitioners to the key issues that must be addressed if they are approaching the problem themselves. The book will help to develop competencies around making effective decisions regarding planning and implementing digital transformation in a practical setting. The book is structured as follows:

Chapter 1, Introducing Digital Technologies and Digital Transformation, provides an overview of digital technologies; outlines the transformational impact of digital technologies; provides an overview of the challenges of digital transformation; and presents a framework for understanding digital transformation capabilities, outcomes and customer value at the process, product and business model levels.

Chapter 2, Digital Platforms, presents an overview of the types and key elements of digital platforms; contrasts value chain firms with digital platform firms; outlines how value is created and measured on digital platforms; highlights the risks for firms dependent on digital platforms; considers why digital platforms fail; and outlines strategies for reducing the threat to digital platforms.

Chapter 3, The IoT and Digital Transformation, outlines the key building blocks and capabilities of the IoT; considers the transformational impact on business functions, customer relationships and supply chains; outlines the privacy and security issues surrounding the IoT; and highlights the key issues involved in IoT implementation in digital transformation.

Chapter 4, Artificial Intelligence in Digital Transformation: Capabilities, Risks and Ethics, outlines how AI capabilities can enhance business performance; highlights the risks of AI implementation; and outlines the key practices required for effectively managing the business, technical and ethical issues involved in implementing AI in digital transformation.

Chapter 5, Managing Data for Business Value in Digital Transformation, provides an understanding of how firms should manage data for digital transformation, including the 3 V's of volume, velocity and variety in big data; the digital data streams concept; data network effects; data management challenges; data analytics applications; and how trust and transparency can be integrated into managing data.

Chapter 6, Digital Innovation, highlights the relationship between innovation, creativity and design; outlines how digital technologies drive innovation and transform the design process; considers how data drive digital innovation; and provides a framework for understanding the stages and enablers in the digital innovation process.

Chapter 7, Business Model Innovation, provides an overview of the business model concept, disruptive innovation and its impact on business models, and business model innovation; outlines how digital technologies drive business model innovation; and highlights how the business model canvas and design thinking can be used in business model innovation.

Chapter 8, *Digital Transformation Strategy,* presents a digital transformation strategy framework that generates potential strategy options based on the link between business strategy, the influence of digital technologies on disruption in the business environment and the importance of digital resources and capabilities; and highlights the key issues involved in implementing a digital transformation strategy.

Chapter 9, *Building a Digital Core for Digital Transformation,* outlines common causes of poor information technology performance; considers digital maturity frameworks and the transition to building a digital core; and highlights the key practices required for building a digital core, including process improvement, organisational redesign, sourcing strategy, customer experience and operational efficiency pathway choice, and cybersecurity and resilience management.

Chapter 10, *Leading Change in Digital Transformation,* considers digital transformation contextual change factors, including scope, speed, preservation, cultural diversity, capability and capacity; highlights digital transformation change paths, including *revolution*, *evolution* and *adaptive*; outlines the key issues involved in leading change, including the importance of changing organisational structures, building employee collaboration, developing digital skills and capabilities, and driving change through leadership.

Acknowledgements I would like to thank the many people who have helped in the writing of this book. The rationale and structure of the book were greatly influenced by empirical research, knowledge transfer activities and numerous discussions with academics. In particular, colleagues including Trevor Cadden, Paul Humphreys and Martin McCracken provided valuable feedback on the structure and early versions of certain chapters of the book. Many of the frameworks and concepts in this book are based on a number of literature streams, including digital transformation, business strategy, economics, operations management and organisational behaviour. I would like to thank those academics and researchers whose work I have cited throughout the book. I am also grateful to Gillian Armstrong, Danielle McWall and Christine Wightman, who gave me the opportunity to teach digital transformation to students at Ulster University from leading firms such as Deloitte and PwC. These students provided valuable feedback on various ideas and concepts in the book. I am also indebted to the firms that allowed me to carry out case studies to validate some of the ideas and concepts introduced. The three anonymous reviewers of the proposal for the book provided valuable guidance and suggestions for improvement. Additionally, Alec Selwyn at Palgrave provided helpful advice and useful comments at various stages in the writing process. Finally, I would like to thank my family, and in particular Deirdre and Nathan, who contributed support and encouragement throughout the preparation of this book.

May 2025	Ronan McIvor

Competing Interests The author has no competing interests to declare that are relevant to the content of this manuscript.

Contents

1 Introducing Digital Technologies and Digital Transformation   1
   1.1 Introduction   1
   1.2 An Overview of Digital Technologies   2
   1.3 The Evolution of Computing and Digital Technologies   3
   1.4 How Digital Technologies Increase Scale and Productivity   4
   1.5 The Transformational Impact of Digital Technologies   7
   1.6 The Digital Transformation Phenomenon   14
   1.7 Why Digital Transformation is Challenging   16
   1.8 A Framework for Understanding Digital Transformation   20
   References   27

2 Digital Platforms   29
   2.1 Introduction   29
   2.2 Types of Digital Platforms   30
   2.3 Key Elements of Digital Platforms   35
   2.4 Why Some Digital Platforms Dominate Markets   36
   2.5 Digital Platforms Versus Value Chain Firms   39
   2.6 Why Managers Struggle With Digital Platform Strategy   39
   2.7 How to Create Value on Digital Platforms   41
   2.8 How to Measure Value on Digital Platforms   44
   2.9 Risks for Firms Dependent on Digital Platforms   45
   2.10 Why Digital Platforms Fail   47
   2.11 Strategies for Reducing the Threats to Digital Platforms   50
   References   52

xiv Contents

3 The Internet of Things and Digital Transformation   55
- 3.1 Introduction   55
- 3.2 The Power of the IoT   56
- 3.3 The Key Building Blocks of the IoT   57
- 3.4 The Capabilities of the IoT   58
- 3.5 How the IoT Impacts Business Functions   60
- 3.6 How the IoT Transforms Customer Relationships   62
- 3.7 How the IoT Transforms Supply Chains   65
- 3.8 The IoT and Servitised Business Models   67
- 3.9 Privacy and Security Implications Around the IoT   69
- 3.10 Challenges Around Implementing the IoT   71
- 3.11 A Framework for Implementing the IoT in Digital Transformation   72
- References   79

4 Artificial Intelligence in Digital Transformation: Capabilities, Risks and Ethics   81
- 4.1 Introduction   81
- 4.2 AI Overview   82
- 4.3 Machine Learning   85
- 4.4 Fixed and Adaptive Algorithms   86
- 4.5 How AI Capabilities Transform Business Performance   87
- 4.6 How AI Transforms Process and Product Capabilities   90
- 4.7 Risks of Applying AI   92
- 4.8 Practices for Integrating Business, Ethics and Technical Issues Into AI Implementation   95
- References   106

5 Managing Data for Business Value in Digital Transformation   109
- 5.1 Introduction   109
- 5.2 Business Intelligence, Business Analytics and Data Analytics   110
- 5.3 Big Data   111
- 5.4 The Concept of Digital Data Streams   112
- 5.5 Data Analytics and the Time Dimension   113
- 5.6 Data Network Effects   114
- 5.7 Data Management Challenges   115
- 5.8 A Framework for Managing and Analysing Data to Create Value   116

	5.9 Data Analytics Tools for Unstructured Data	121
	5.10 Data Analytics Tools for Social Media	123
	5.11 Practices for Building Trust and Transparency in Managing Data	124
	References	130
6	**Digital Innovation**	**131**
	6.1 Introduction	131
	6.2 Innovation	132
	6.3 How Digital Technologies Drive Innovation	133
	6.4 How Digital Technologies Transform the Design Process	135
	6.5 An Overview of Digital Innovation	138
	6.6 How Data Drives Digital Innovation	138
	6.7 Challenges of Digital Innovation	140
	6.8 A Framework for Understanding the Digital Innovation Process	141
	References	150
7	**Business Model Innovation**	**153**
	7.1 Introduction	153
	7.2 The Business Model Concept	154
	7.3 Disruptive Innovation	156
	7.4 Business Model Innovation	158
	7.5 How Digital Technologies Drive Business Model Innovation	162
	7.6 Barriers to Employing Digital Technologies in Business Model Innovation	164
	7.7 How the Business Model Canvas Can be Employed in Business Model Innovation	165
	7.8 How Design Thinking Can be Employed in Business Model Innovation	168
	References	172
8	**Digital Transformation Strategy**	**175**
	8.1 Introduction	175
	8.2 Why Digital Transformation Should be Linked with Business Strategy	176
	8.3 Digital Transformation and the Strategy Process	177
	8.4 A Framework for Understanding Digital Transformation Strategy	178

8.5	Stage 1 Digital Disruption Analysis	179
8.6	Stage 2 Digital Capability Analysis	183
8.7	Stage 3 Digital Transformation Strategy Choice	190
8.8	Stage 4 Implementation, Evaluation and Adaptation	199
References		204

9 Building a Digital Core for Digital Transformation — 207

9.1	Introduction	207
9.2	Common Causes of Poor IT Performance	208
9.3	The Digital Core Concept	211
9.4	Digital Maturity Frameworks and the Transition to the Digital Core	212
9.5	The Importance of Modular Architectures in the Digital Core	215
9.6	Practices for Building a Digital Core for Digital Transformation	216
References		229

10 Leading Change in Digital Transformation — 231

10.1	Introduction	231
10.2	Leading Change in Digital Transformation	232
10.3	Contextual Change Factors in Digital Transformation	232
10.4	Change Paths in Digital Transformation	238
10.5	Practices for Embedding Change in Digital Transformation	243
References		251

Correction to: Digital Transformation — C1

Glossary — 253

Index — 257

List of Figures

Fig. 1.1	How digital technologies drive productivity [4]	6
Fig. 1.2	How digital technologies influence service job automation	14
Fig. 1.3	A framework for understanding digital transformation	21
Fig. 2.1	Types of digital platforms [1]	30
Fig. 2.2	Platform players [6]	35
Fig. 2.3	Strategies for reducing the threats to digital platforms [26]	50
Fig. 3.1	A framework for implementing the IoT in digital transformation	72
Fig. 4.1	Levels of AI [3]	83
Fig. 4.2	The transformational impact of AI on firm capabilities [13]	90
Fig. 4.3	A framework for integrating business, technical and ethical issues into AI implementation	95
Fig. 5.1	A framework for managing and analysing data to create value	117
Fig. 6.1	The relationship between creativity, innovation and design [2]	133
Fig. 6.2	A framework for understanding the digital innovation process	142
Fig. 7.1	Diagnosing disruption threats to business models	162
Fig. 7.2	The business model canvas and the impact of digital technologies	166
Fig. 7.3	The business model canvas for Google	167
Fig. 8.1	A framework for understanding digital transformation strategy	179
Fig. 8.2	The digital resources and capabilities matrix	184
Fig. 8.3	Digital transformation project resource requirements and impact matrix	201
Fig. 8.4	Implementation, evaluation and adaptation in the digital transformation strategy process	202
Fig. 9.1	Key practices for building a digital core for digital transformation	216
Fig. 9.2	The relationship between customer experience and operational efficiency [17]	223

List of Tables

Table 2.1	Characteristics of innovation and transaction digital platforms [4]	33
Table 2.2	Contradictory impacts of digital platforms [9]	37
Table 2.3	How the principles of strategy differ between digital platforms and value chain firms	41
Table 2.4	Value drivers in digital platforms [18]	43
Table 3.1	Examples of IoT applications in business functions [7]	61
Table 3.2	Potential benefits of the IoT for firms [25]	74
Table 3.3	Common elements of the IoT technology infrastructure [28]	77
Table 4.1	AI technologies and application areas [4]	84
Table 5.1	Data variety examples	112
Table 6.1	Innovation from data versus innovation as data [8]	139
Table 8.1	Key elements and strategic actions in each digital transformation strategy option	191
Table 9.1	Business issue and performance impact (included in shaded grey above)	211
Table 9.2	Suggested conditions for each sourcing improvement option	221
Table 10.1	Contextual change factors and change paths in digital transformation	239

1

Introducing Digital Technologies and Digital Transformation

1.1 Introduction

The increasing prominence of digital technologies has fundamentally changed the expectations and behaviours of consumers, increased competition for many firms and disrupted a range of industries. Digital technologies have allowed new digital start-up firms to rapidly spring up and disrupt the strategic position of many established firms. Consumers now have a range of digital channels to trade with firms, whilst at the same time being able to communicate with other consumers via social media channels. Dealing with digital transformation has become a strategic imperative for firms across a range of business sectors.

Digital transformation can mean different things to different people, which can lead to misunderstandings around the phenomenon. In some sectors, such as media and retail, it has involved considerable disruption, with the displacement of established players and the entry of new start-ups. Whilst in other sectors, digital transformation has involved incremental change, where firms have employed digital technologies such as artificial intelligence (AI) to automate certain knowledge-based tasks. Moreover, some erroneously believe digital transformation is primarily about digital technologies, without fully considering the business implications of digital transformation.

This chapter highlights the reality of digital transformation and differentiates between digital technologies and digital transformation. It outlines the transformational impact of digital technologies for firms and provides an overview of the challenges of digital transformation. A framework for understanding digital transformation is then presented.

> **Learning Outcomes**
> - Understand common digital technologies associated with digital transformation.
> - Understand the evolution of computing and digital technologies.
> - Understand how digital technologies drive scale and productivity.
> - Understand the transformational impact of digital technologies on customer experience, competition, operations and employee roles.
> - Understand the digital transformation concept.
> - Understand the challenges of digital transformation.
> - Understand digital transformation capabilities, outcomes and customer value at the process, product and business model levels.

1.2 An Overview of Digital Technologies

The emergence of innovative digital technologies, such as social media, data analytics tools and cloud computing, has been key to driving digital transformation. Products such as wearables and smartwatches are connected digitally to generate data that allow firms to respond to and anticipate consumer needs, using data analytics to deliver more targeted advertising. Similarly, digital technologies have been used in manufacturing to connect equipment, transmit and analyse data to improve quality, enhance traceability and better predict faults. An overview of the most prominent digital technologies associated with digital transformation is outlined below:

- *Social media* includes websites and applications that are designed to allow people to share content quickly, efficiently and in real time via apps on their smartphone, tablet or other electronic devices. Social media can be used to seek career opportunities, find people across the globe with similar interests to share their thoughts and feelings.
- *Mobile device technologies* are multi-functional devices capable of hosting a broad range of applications for both business and consumer use. Smartphones and tablets allow people to use instant messaging, text messaging, and web browsing, as well as work on documents, manage contact lists, and more.

- *Data analytics* involves analysing data to make predictions and conclusions. Data analytics techniques and processes can be automated through processes and algorithms that analyse data for human decision-making.
- *The internet of things (IoT)* refers to the concept of connecting devices, such as cars and fitness devices, to the internet and to other connected devices, all of which collect and share data about the way they are used and the environment around them.
- *Cloud computing* involves using a network of remote servers hosted on the internet to store, manage and process data. It provides users with a series of functions, including email, storage, data backup, data retrieval, creating and testing apps, analysing data, audio and video streaming and delivering software on demand.
- *AI technologies* perform tasks that require human intelligence, such as visual perception, speech recognition, decision-making and translation between languages. AI allows human intelligence to be defined in a way that a machine can replicate and execute tasks, ranging from simple to more complex ones.

Other digital technologies sometimes considered along with digital transformation include blockchain, augmented reality and virtual reality technologies. Blockchain technology is a shared digital ledger that securely records transactions across a distributed computer network. Once a transaction is recorded on the blockchain, it is difficult to alter, thus making transactions more secure, reliable, transparent, irreversible and traceable. Augmented reality technology enhances the real-world environment by overlaying digital content, such as images or videos, allowing users to interact with both the real-world and the superimposed digital content. Virtual reality technology immerses users in an entirely new digital environment, providing an interactive experience through the use of headsets or glasses.

1.3 The Evolution of Computing and Digital Technologies

Developments in computing and digital technologies have led to significant improvements in firm performance. Advances in computer hardware and software over time have significantly enhanced the capabilities of these technologies, whilst at the same time, the cost of hardware has reduced—sometimes referred to as Moore's Law.

Early applications of information technology (IT) in the 1960s and 1970s focused on automating previously manual-based business processes such as payroll processing, order processing and manufacturing resource planning. These applications led to increases in firm productivity and the capture and analysis of large amounts of data.

The rise of the internet, along with low-cost and ubiquitous connectivity, led to further productivity gains for firms in the 1980s and 1990s, allowing firms to coordinate and integrate business processes both internally and externally with suppliers and customers, and across different geographic locations [1].

More recently, further advances in computing power, data storage via cloud computing and data analytics have led to further increases in productivity for firms [2]. For example, smartphones have far more processing power, data storage and access capabilities than early computers, along with widespread ownership across much of the world's population. Computers can fit in a person's pocket or on their wrist, with apps that automate tasks traditionally done by humans, leading to more personalised products and services.

A further advance is that digital technologies have now become an integral part of the product itself. Sensors, software and connectivity in products, along with cloud computing that allows product data to be stored and analysed, are driving significant improvements in product functionality and performance. For example, smartwatches have sensors that can gather real-time data on sound and images, light, proximity, rotation, movement, magnetic field, temperature, humidity, atmospheric pressure and location. Computing and digital technologies are no longer the sole concern of IT specialists but are being applied to every part of a firm's operations and supply chain.

1.4 How Digital Technologies Increase Scale and Productivity

Digital technologies can boost firm performance by increasing scale and productivity, as outlined below.

Scale—Digital technologies can be a key driver in enabling a firm to scale up its business. There are three properties of digital technologies that drive scale [3]:

- Digital signals can be transmitted perfectly without error, which contrasts with non-digital signals. For example, a web page will look the same when it is generated in one location as it does when a consumer accesses it in another location, regardless of geography.
- Digital signals can be replicated indefinitely; for example, the same web page can be accessible to billions of customers globally without any degradation.
- Once the investment in the technology infrastructure has been made, the web page can be communicated to additional customers at zero, or almost zero, marginal cost. For example, many high street retailers and banks have transitioned to web channels, as it is more efficient to add more customers online than with their high street operations.

Achieving scale often involves significant upfront costs when implementing digital technology. However, the increased availability of cloud computing allows firms to scale up or down their infrastructure. Many cloud service providers offer software, infrastructure and platforms that allow firms to rapidly adjust their digital resources in response to changes in customer demand.

Productivity refers to the measure of efficiency of a person, firm or technology in converting inputs into outputs. Increased productivity has long been considered an important driver for employing digital technologies, and this relationship is outlined in Fig. 1.1. Productivity can be improved by either increasing outputs, reducing inputs or doing both, and clearly, digital technologies have a significant role to play. For example, on the output side, digital technologies can be employed to offer additional services to customers and, at the same time, make labour more efficient in the operations process, thus increasing outputs. On the input side, digital technologies such as AI technologies can act as a substitute for knowledge workers, thus decreasing input costs.

Productivity and the impact of digital technologies can also be influenced by the following factors:

- The level of competition in the business environment and product and service characteristics can influence the level of productivity. Digital technologies are more likely to lead to higher productivity in industries where there is strong competition, and the potential for product and service digitisation is significant. For example, publishing industries such as newspapers and books, with high competitive rivalry and ease of digitisation, have been radically transformed by digital technologies. This contrasts with many public sector contexts, where the absence of competition has led to less pressure on organisations to innovate through digital technologies.

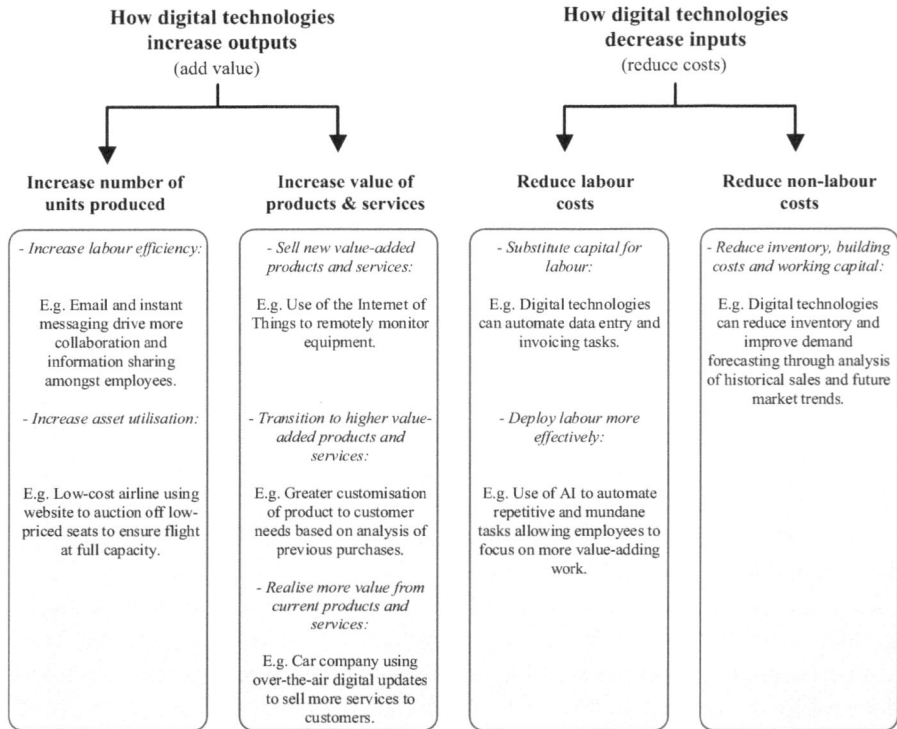

Fig. 1.1 How digital technologies drive productivity [4]

- Digital technologies alone do not deliver productivity gains and must be combined with investments in developing people's skills and designing new business processes. For example, employees must be effectively trained in the use of digital technologies to enhance their performance.

> **Illustration 1.1 Digital Technologies and Entrepreneurship in the Medical Field**
>
> The transformative impact of digital technologies has had a significant influence on entrepreneurship, particularly in the case of new start-up firms. Digital businesses have been able to deploy widely available technologies at a low cost to quickly establish global reach. The medical services field

has seen the emergence of new start-ups offering medical-related services enabled by digital technologies. Advances in technology have allowed new manufacturers of wearable devices, smartwatches and other digital devices to measure blood pressure, pulse rates and monitor conditions such as sleep patterns. Moreover, the COVID-19 pandemic highlighted the need for digital tools with capabilities to support and monitor patient healthcare remotely.

New start-ups in the medical field have established digital platforms to allow individuals to share data with peers, employers and trainers in return for healthcare services. The emergence of medical services firms is likely to accelerate as advances in AI allow early diagnosis of health conditions through the analysis of an individual's conditions in real time. AI technologies have enabled firms to create health treatment recommendation apps with tailored care plans for patients based on their health status and previous treatments. Apps have been developed to manage conditions such as insomnia, tinnitus, obesity and osteoarthritis. These apps can provide a wealth of data to healthcare organisations such as insurance providers and pharmaceutical firms. Rather than relying solely on randomised controlled trials, pharmaceutical firms now have access to real-world health data across a range of medical conditions.

Of course, entry into this market by start-up firms will be impacted by regulatory, data protection and security issues. In the European Union, some healthcare apps must be CE-certified as a medical product before being approved for use. Individuals will also have to give their consent to share sensitive data about their health conditions with these firms. However, individuals are more likely to give their consent to data sharing when they feel they are receiving value in return in the form of better health outcomes.

1.5 The Transformational Impact of Digital Technologies

Cloud computing, data analytics, social media and other digital technologies have had a more profound impact on firms than earlier information technologies. Many of these digital technologies are open, flexible and accessible to almost anyone, not just to firms. These technologies allow greater connectivity across firm boundaries and can be embedded in the product itself. They have had significant implications for firms in the areas of customer experience, operations, competition and employee roles. Each of these impacts is now outlined.

1.5.1 How Digital Technologies Transform Customer Experience

With online customers being more mobile in terms of choice, many firms have had to focus on improving the customer experience to lock-in customers to their offerings. Digital technologies have had an important impact on how firms manage customer experience across the following areas:

- *Product and service co-design*—social media and other digital technologies have allowed customers to be involved in designing and improving products and services by offering ideas for improvements or even being actively involved in the design process. Customer involvement in design has become an important strategy for firms as they encourage customers to be co-creators of the product [5]. For example, Lego uses the Lego Ideas function to encourage customers to suggest ideas for new designs and then allows other customers to vote on these designs. This provides Lego with insights into market trends and enables the generation of designs that are closely aligned with the demographics of the market.
- *More intensive and interactive relationships*—the trend toward product and service co-design requires a closer and more interactive relationship between the firm and its customers. These relationships are based on data sharing and analysis, which allow firms to develop a better understanding of each customer's needs and knowledge of how they can create better products and services to meet those needs [6]. For example, digital footprints can collect data on customer behaviour, and information inputs can be used for the design of new products [7]. Additionally, AI technologies can be employed to develop customer intelligence in real time, enabling highly personalised interactions in the form of recommendations for product purchases or personalised product offers.
- *Customer network approach*—in many instances, the firm is no longer the key influencer in persuading the customer to purchase its products and services. Customers now rely on customer-to-customer interactions on social media platforms, where customers share their product experiences through comments, videos or blog entries. Firms have had to reach out to customers via a network approach, where they manage a multi-channel customer experience approach that includes interacting with customers via social media, mobile apps and augmented reality [8].

1.5.2 How Digital Technologies Transform Operations

Developments in digital technologies are allowing firms to improve their operational capabilities in both product manufacturing and services in the following areas:

- *Internal and external traceability*—the increasing prevalence of sensor technologies and analytical tools is transforming many operations. Sensors can be embedded in robots, equipment, vehicles and operator wearable devices internally to allow firms to continuously transmit and analyse data in real time. These sensors, along with AI technologies, allow data to be collected and analysed to predict equipment failures, identify quality problems early in the production process and reduce overall quality and production costs. Externally, firms can exchange data in the supply chain to synchronise production with suppliers, reduce delivery times and be more responsive to customer demands.
- *Quicker decision-making*—connected devices allow data to be collected in real time from multiple sources and multiple points via sensor technologies, which means significant amounts of data can accumulate over time. Algorithms and other data analytics tools allow every source of data to be analysed to make quicker and more informed decisions. Consider the example of Schindler, a maker of elevators and escalators, and how it uses digital technologies to understand and manage traffic flows in real time. Through employing sensors and data analytics, it can optimise transportation across office buildings, anticipate when people will be moving from one location to another and respond to mechanical issues before they become faults [9].
- *Continuous product design*—the emergence of digital technologies has allowed manufacturers to continuously upgrade their products via software remotely. This has enabled firms to customise the product to the specific needs of the customer and address any performance problems. For example, industrial heating manufacturers have been able to tailor their products to specific customer categories through remote software updates. Firms can also monitor real-world performance data whilst the product is in use, which may help identify and address design problems that were not detected during product testing.
- *Sustainability*—despite digital technologies being responsible for significant carbon emissions, they can improve sustainability for firms by reducing waste, optimising energy consumption and extending the life cycle of

products. For example, AI technologies can schedule pre-emptive maintenance to identify any problems before they arise, and smart metering can optimise the use of renewable energy supply. Digital technologies can also track and manage the life cycle of components in products, which makes it more straightforward to recycle them at the end of their useful life.

1.5.3 How Digital Technologies Transform Competition

Digital technologies have led to changes in the competitive environment for many firms across the following dimensions:

- *Blurring and redefining of industry boundaries*—there has been a blurring and redefining of established industry boundaries. For example, before the emergence of the internet, firms in industries such as travel and financial services defined their industry boundaries based on direct competitors with similar profiles. However, technological disruption has led to the entry of new competitors from other industries and the emergence of start-up firms. Online retailers now offer travel and banking services, whilst digital start-ups such as Expedia have entered the travel sector, and challenger banks such as Revolut and Starling have entered the financial services sector.
- *Increasing competition for incumbent firms*—advances in digital technologies have led to increasing competition for incumbent firms in many markets. Digital channels have eroded the incumbents' traditional sources of advantage and increased competition by reducing entry barriers for new start-ups. For example, new start-ups can rapidly establish global operations with low investment by using cloud services. Digital technologies have also created greater information transparency and customer mobility, thus allowing customers to find the lowest price and thereby eroding the incumbents' competitive position in markets for standard products or services.
- *From product to platform competition*—the proliferation of digital platform businesses such as Amazon and Airbnb has had a major impact on competition across many product and service markets. Previously, firms in a range of markets competed on product features such as low price, variety and functionality. Automakers owned and controlled strategic resources such as manufacturing assets and design knowledge to compete by offering products superior to those of their competitors. However, the balance of power is shifting away from competing on products to

platforms, where firms such as Alibaba and eBay compete in multiple markets and extend their products and services to attract and retain customers, thus competing across related and unrelated markets. These platforms benefit from network effects, where the value of the platform increases as more users join the platform. For example, as eBay puts in place mechanisms for attracting more buyers to its platform, this is likely to attract more sellers, thus creating network effects.

- *Competing on data*—data have become a critical resource for firms that can be used as a competitive differentiator. Where a firm can access and analyse more and more data, it can create business intelligence [10]. For example, Google has built its dominance in search through accumulating and analysing more and more data on user searches to develop more tailored searches. Data can also be employed as a means of entering new markets. Consider an automaker that uses the IoT and data analytics to collect and analyse data on driver behaviour to develop different risk profiles. This capability can allow the automaker to enter the car insurance market and potentially offer lower premiums than incumbents due to a more detailed understanding of driver behaviour than established players in the insurance market.

1.5.4 How Digital Technologies Transform Employee Roles

Algorithms and software applications have been able to perform many tasks previously undertaken by employees. In some cases, digital technologies such as AI have been able to exceed human capabilities in areas such as pattern matching and learning. Digital technologies can either act as substitutes for employees, or augment and support employees in their tasks, as outlined below.

Employee substitution. Firms have been attracted to the greater use of technologies as a substitute for employees, as it allows them to scale up digital applications with low marginal costs, in contrast to the additional direct costs of recruiting more employees. Digital technologies have become substitutes for employees across the following tasks:

- *Physical tasks*—digital technologies have already digitised many customer contact services through online reservation systems and chatbots. Moreover, security employees in airports, railway stations and city centres have been replaced by digital surveillance applications with sensory and video features.

- *Knowledge-intensive tasks*—digital technologies have also impacted skilled tasks that involve knowledge, cognitive and learning elements. Some employee knowledge can now be programmed into an algorithm, stored in an app and then accessed by anyone in the firm who needs it. For example, policies around insurance underwriting and the knowledge of underwriters can now be codified into a set of rules that can be used by both other employees and customers.

Employee augmentation. Digital technologies can augment employees in their tasks and improve performance and productivity. In the marketing field, data analytics have been employed to identify specific market segments, deliver more targeted messaging and identify new customers [11]. For example, Harley-Davidson has used machine learning to develop profiles of the riders who purchased their motorcycles and then matched these profiles with data from non-customers. It then ran hundreds of A/B tests to identify the most effective ways to message these potential customers, which led to a significant increase in sales at some dealerships.

Flexible working. Digital technologies have also had an impact on the adoption of flexible working arrangements for employees. Flexible working often includes job sharing, contract work, part-time work and hybrid working. Digital technologies have driven flexible working in the following areas:

- *Increasing prevalence of gig workers*—digital platforms provide firms with access to gig workers who can perform food delivery services, courier services, home repairs and care work. Although these platforms offer flexible working hours and autonomy, gig workers assume responsibility for costs and risks, and forego protections enjoyed by full-time employees. Also, they often have to work at the whim of the employer, and this can reduce their autonomy substantially [12].
- *Hybrid working*—the trend towards hybrid working has been driven by digital technologies and has transformed the role of employees by allowing them to split their time between working remotely and in the office. It tends to be more prevalent in professional service jobs than in manufacturing jobs, where there is a need for physical presence in the job. Firms must strike a balance between the flexibility and cost benefits of hybrid working and the need for building a collaborative culture, which can involve ensuring employees spend sufficient time in the office to develop social relationships with their colleagues.

Illustration 1.2 Is Your Service Job at Risk from Digital Automation?

There is much debate in the popular media on the types of jobs being impacted by digital technologies such as AI. AI has been impacting service jobs that require cognitive abilities, such as in the management consulting field, whilst its impact has not been as significant in service-type jobs that require social interaction and empathy. Factors such as labour costs and low-skilled versus high-skilled jobs are often introduced to explain the types of jobs at risk from digital technologies. However, much of the debate in this area fails to explain fully how jobs are being impacted and often makes sweeping, simple generalisations. The threat level from digital technologies to service jobs is likely to be influenced by the following factors:

- *Customisation* refers to the level of customisation involved in creating and delivering the service. Processes that are highly customised and need to be adapted as circumstances change are more difficult to automate. In the medical field, surgeons undertake medical procedures where changes need to be made during the surgical process. This contrasts with standardised processes such as data entry, accounting and customer ordering, where automation via digital technologies has been widespread.
- *Customer contact* refers to the level of interaction between the customer and the firm in the service delivery process. Many service jobs, such as childcare and nursing, require physical contact, thus making them less vulnerable to automation by digital technologies. These jobs also require a significant amount of social interaction and apply to many service sector roles in the leisure and hospitality industries, where the customer must be physically present when the service is delivered. Alternatively, many other service jobs, such as applying for a bank loan and customer helpdesk services, have been displaced as digital technologies can substitute the role of humans.
- *Knowledge intensity* refers to the level of judgement, professional expertise and experience required to perform a job. A research and development engineer's job can involve extensive specialised knowledge and experience, which can be extremely difficult to automate. Alternatively, the job of a loan administrator in a bank can be codified and structured with clearly defined outcomes, making it more vulnerable to automation.
- *Regulatory issues* refer to the level of regulatory approval required to automate the process. For example, regulation is prominent in the application of AI in the medical field, where medical bodies have to approve the use of AI tools, which can act as an impediment to digital automation. In contrast, few other sectors offer such protections, where regulation plays little or no role in process automation.

These factors can be mapped onto a spectrum, showing how the impact of each factor influences the potential for automating service jobs, as shown in Fig. 1.2.

Consider the following example jobs to illustrate the factors in practice. Many highly standardised jobs with no customer contact, such as financial trading and travel-booking tasks, are on the right-hand side of the spectrum and are straightforward to automate via digital technologies. Alternatively,

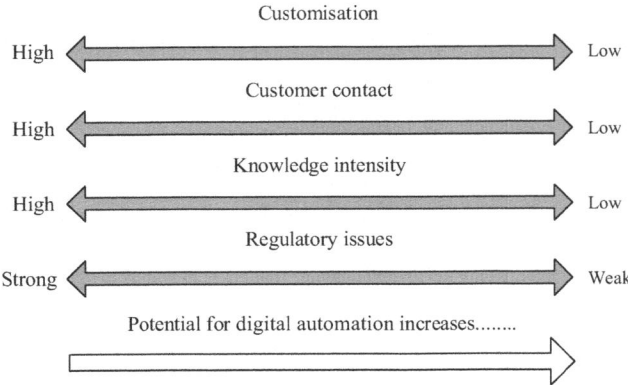

Fig. 1.2 How digital technologies influence service job automation

> jobs with significant regulatory pressures, high knowledge intensity, and high customer contact would include medical consultant jobs, and these fit on the left of the spectrum.
>
> A single factor, such as the need for customer contact, can act as an absolute impediment to digital automation. For example, jobs such as hairdressing and physiotherapy are difficult to automate, as they are less susceptible to the threat of automation because of the need for a high level of customer contact. Moreover, the need for a high level of customisation can outweigh the knowledge intensity factor. For example, lower-skilled jobs, such as that of a plumber or electrician, are difficult to automate, as the needs of customers are often different and customised for each job and require being onsite to deliver the service.
>
> The influence of some of these factors is likely to evolve as rapid advances in digital technologies, such as AI and robotics, continue to automate more service-oriented jobs. Moreover, regulatory and political pressures will also shift as technologies and governments change, and in response to constraints on public sector spending.

1.6 The Digital Transformation Phenomenon

The transformational impact of digital technologies on customer experience, competition, operations and employees has led many firms to embrace digital transformation. Digital transformation involves employing digital technologies to transform processes, products and business models, and it leads to a holistic change in the operations and structure of the firm. Digital transformation has the following features:

Broad in scope—rather than a narrow focus on business process change, it is firm-wide and impacts a range of business functions, including marketing, operations, finance and human resources. Digital transformation involves transforming established organisational structures and work practices to allow firms to react more quickly to digital disruption. For example, digital transformation in some manufacturing firms has radically changed the role of the IT function from providing IT support services to working with research and development in adding digital services to the product during the design process.

Change at the strategic level—change is driven from the strategic level, and a firm often has to redefine its current value proposition and existing relationships with customers and suppliers. Firms need to commit considerable resources to transitioning toward a more digitised business and fusing emerging digital technologies into their existing business models.

Use of digital technologies—although part of the digital transformation effort will often involve improving existing back-end processes and legacy systems, the trigger for digital transformation is often due to developments in digital technologies such as AI, cloud computing, social media and the IoT [13]. These digital technologies can act as a catalyst for transforming the processes, products and business model of the firm.

Transition to a transformed state—the completion of the digital transformation journey will bring the firm to a state where it can readily expand its digital capabilities and exploit the emergence of new digital technologies to create new business opportunities. Many born-digital firms may not have to embark on a digital transformation journey, as they are already architected as digital at inception [14].

Illustration 1.3 How Digital Transformation Can Drive Profit for Smaller Firms

Increasing market share has long been considered a top priority for many firms, as it has a significant positive impact on profit. However, research has found that the digital transformation of firms has altered this relationship and the underlying drivers, particularly for smaller firms. This research challenges the view that 'bigger is always better' in a digital business context. In some cases, digital transformation reduces the importance of market share by, for example, decreasing online distribution costs, which allows firms with smaller market shares to operate more profitably and reduces the scale advantage of larger firms.

Smaller firms that effectively embrace digital transformation can become more profitable in the following ways. Smaller firms can increase their market presence by selling their products in wider geographic markets through digital channels. Digital technologies have lowered barriers to entry across many markets, and the flexible nature of smaller firms has allowed them to reduce the scale advantage of larger firms. The cost of advertising can be reduced through digital advertising, where firms can directly target very specific, niche customer groups. Effectively employing digital technologies means the marginal cost of serving a new customer is almost zero, which allows smaller firms to scale up more efficiently than in a pre-digital context. Digital transformation helps smaller firms employ digital-related outsourcing, where they can access cloud-based services such as servers, networks and databases.

Firms can differ in their focus on digital transformation through either an *external* or *internal emphasis* approach. *External emphasis* refers to the firm's responsiveness and engagement with consumers and extending market reach using digital technologies such as social media, whilst *internal emphasis* refers to employing digital technologies to increase productivity through automating internal processes or outsourcing to increase capacity. Research has found that smaller firms should first concentrate their digital transformation efforts on an *internal emphasis* approach, as this is likely to be more profitable, before moving on to an *external emphasis* approach. The research also highlighted that investors should consider alternative performance criteria to market share when assessing factors that influence the profitability of digital businesses.

Source: Sklenarz, F.A., Edeling, A., Himme, A., and Wichmann, J.R., 2024. Does bigger still mean better? How digital transformation affects the market share–profitability relationship. *International Journal of Research in Marketing*, *41*(4), pp. 648–670.

1.7 Why Digital Transformation Is Challenging

Digital transformation is far from straightforward, as it involves disrupting existing processes, capabilities and business models. Many firms have failed to achieve the anticipated benefits of digital transformation, often due to lacking the capabilities required to address the associated challenges. These challenges are now outlined.

1.7.1 Resistance to Change

Digital transformation can lead to significant disruption in the form of new work practices and changes to business processes, which can result in employee resistance. Resistance to change is likely to be higher in a firm with a rigid culture and where employees are not accustomed to change. Resistance to change can arise for the following reasons:

- *Maintaining the status quo*—firms are often comfortable with existing systems and processes and, therefore, may be hesitant to adopt new technologies or ways of working, which can result in a negative work environment, frustration, low productivity and overwhelmed employees.
- *Failure to experiment with new business models*—digital transformation can involve experimenting with new revenue models, such as subscription and licensing, which can threaten the profitability of existing business models. Many firms have struggled to adapt their existing business models and balance the tension between existing analog capabilities and the new learning required to compete in a digital context.
- *Conflicting demands*—managing conflicting demands is a major barrier to the transformation of complex business models [15]. Contradictions and tensions can exert significant pressure on senior leaders and their teams when they need to integrate established and new digital capabilities into their organisational structures in a complementary way. Senior management in established firms is often dominated by individuals who possess skills and experience that become largely redundant when confronted with changes in the internal and external environment brought about by digital technologies.

1.7.2 Resource Constraints

Digital transformation often requires significant financial investment, and a lack of internal resources in the following areas can be a significant barrier to digital transformation:

- *Skills deficit*—digital transformation requires employees with the appropriate mix of skills and expertise. Firms often lack the required resources to invest in training and development programmes to upskill existing employees in digital technologies. Many senior executives have focused on their current business model and core business and lack the technical expertise required to drive digital transformation.
- *Financial resource*—digital transformation involves investing in new technical infrastructure, new tools and business processes. This issue can be further exacerbated when a firm's business has been disrupted as a result of digital technologies. For example, many high-street retail failures, such as Topshop in the UK and RadioShack in the United States, did not have the finances available to implement turnaround strategies to effectively react to digital competitors due to already-declining profit margins.

1.7.3 Ineffective Technology Infrastructures

Firms often have technology infrastructures that are highly inflexible, developed through a series of disparate projects with little effort to standardise and integrate different systems. Poor coordination and flawed technology implementation have been found to be a leading cause of digital transformation failure [16]. These issues create challenges for digital transformation in the following areas:

- *Cybersecurity*—firms are at risk of cyber threats that can compromise their systems and networks. In some cases, these threats can increase the risks of data breaches and the loss of financial and personal information. A lack of confidence in the ability of firms to protect their data can be a significant impediment to customers embracing digital channels for product and service access.
- *Systems integration*—integrating new digital technologies, such as data analytics tools, with existing legacy systems can be challenging. Firms may have technical infrastructures with current systems that do not work effectively, and integrating digital technologies, such as data analytics tools, with these existing systems can further exacerbate performance problems and cause delays and disruptions.
- *Data quality*—poor system integration can also contribute to the problem of poor data quality in a firm. Whilst firms may collect a lot of data from different sources, including customer transactions, sensors and social media, it may not be in the correct format to derive actionable insights from. For example, data can be stored in different formats that are not accessible by data analytics tools and stored in a way that few employees have access to it. Considerable effort may have to be devoted to removing errors, resolving inconsistencies, and converting the data into a consistent format.

1.7.4 Pressures for Localisation

Digital transformation is often associated with the increasing digitisation of channels with customers and extending the global reach of the firm. However, for some firms, there can be pressures for localisation that can inhibit digital transformation along the following dimensions [17]:

- *Differences in regulatory regimes*—these can have an impact on the ability of firms to offer standard products and services across different territories. For example, financial services firms may be limited in expanding their presence globally due to differing regulations around compliance and governance [18]. Data can also be subject to regulatory restrictions. Regulations around data protection in the European Union are regarded as stronger than those in other countries, and firms have had to adapt their digital transformation strategies to reflect this.
- *The need for physical presence*—many firms still require a physical presence to support their online operations. For high-value, branded retail products such as Apple and Gucci, physical outlets can serve as a high-touch point channel and an opportunity to enhance the buying experience for customers. Physical distance can also hinder the geographical presence of platforms that act as intermediaries for the sales of products. Research has shown that transactions by users on platforms such as eBay decline as the distance between them increases.
- *Culture and language differences*—these differences can limit the ability of firms to establish an effective digital presence outside their home location. For example, digital platforms can be very prominent in large and homogenous nations such as China and the United States, which contrasts with Europe, where different cultures and languages have led to fewer digital platforms.

> **Illustration 1.4 The Myths and Realities of Digital Transformation**
>
> Misunderstandings around digital transformation have given rise to myths, which contrast with reality in practice. Some of these myths, along with the reality of digital transformation, are outlined below.
>
> - *Digital transformation involves only employing emerging or disruptive digital technologies*—experience has shown that digital transformation can come from employing established digital technologies. For example, Uber's business model was based on using established networking technologies such as smartphones, apps and websites that enabled the rapid processing of transactions and location tracking.
> - *Successful firms are more likely to digitally transform* - however, this is often not the case, as financially successful firms are often cautious and resistant to changing practices that have been previously successful. In reality, the impetus for digital transformation can be stronger in struggling firms, where there is an urgent need to transform the business to survive.

- *We need to disrupt our industry before someone else does*—disruption from digital transformation rarely comes from established firms with well-defined business models. Disruption tends to come from start-ups, as evidenced by the success of Airbnb in hospitality and Netflix in entertainment.
- *Digital will replace physical* - although digital technologies have eliminated intermediaries and physical channels across a range of markets, there is still a need for physical channels in many markets. Retailers such as Best Buy in the United States have been combining digital and physical channels seamlessly with customers to enhance the customer experience.
- *Digital transformation is about technology*—although technology plays a major role. Digital transformation involves management focusing on issues such as better serving the needs of customers and changing organisational structures to run a more flexible operation.

Sources: Andriole, S.J., 2017. 'Five Myths About Digital Transformation'. *MIT Sloan Management Review*, 58(3), pp. 20–22; and Furr, N. and Shipilov, A., 2019. 'Digital Doesn't Have to Be Disruptive: the Best Results Can Come from Adaptation Rather Than Reinvention'. *Harvard Business Review*, 97(4), pp. 94–104.

1.8 A Framework for Understanding Digital Transformation

Dealing with digital transformation has become a strategic imperative for established firms across a range of business sectors. Digital transformation is not about technology but about having the management capabilities in place to exploit the opportunities that digital technologies can offer. This section presents a framework for understanding the relationship between digital technologies, digital transformation capabilities, outcomes and customer value, as shown in Fig. 1.3. The framework highlights how employing common digital technologies creates value for customers through driving transformation at the process, product and business model levels.

For example, adding IoT sensors and data analytics features to physical products, such as cars and industrial equipment, allows manufacturers to remotely monitor customer usage and anticipate potential faults, thus creating value for the customer at the product level.

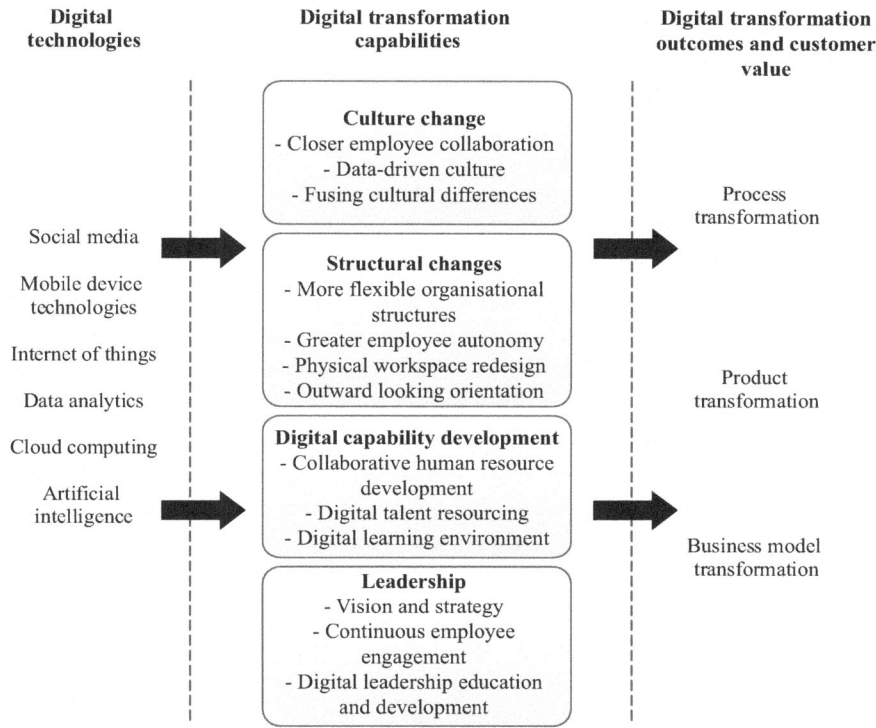

Fig. 1.3 A framework for understanding digital transformation

1.8.1 Capabilities for Digital Transformation

The scale and speed of digital transformation can vary across different sectors, primarily due to the disruptive effect of digital technologies. Despite these differences, there are often common management capabilities required for digital transformation as shown in Figure 1.3. Each of these is now explained.

Culture change. A change in culture is often required to prepare firms for the changes necessary for digital transformation. Driving culture change will involve pursuing the following practices:

- *Closer employee collaboration*—as many business functions rely on digital and analytical skills, functional areas will have to collaborate more closely with IT specialists to ensure they are exploiting the potential benefits that digital technologies offer. For example, as digital features are increasingly integrated into physical products IT specialists will also have to be able to

work with, and be more in tune with, the digital needs of different functions across the firm.
- *Data-driven culture*—this involves creating a culture where data are shared across the firm and not held in silos. Data need to be recognised as a valuable resource and a key driver of digital transformation. This will involve ensuring that employees understand the value of data and its impact on making more effective business decisions around customers, employees, suppliers and competitors [19].
- *Fusing cultural differences*—digital transformation can lead to cultural conflict between groups of employees who have varying levels of understanding of digital technologies. For example, younger 'born digital' employees are likely to have different attitudes and experiences in relation to digital technologies, which contrast with those of older employees. Firms must manage this tension and, where appropriate, fuse these two different cultures to achieve the benefits of digital transformation. Whilst using digital technologies to transform processes, firms must ensure that longer-established employees are involved in the process and do not feel they are being left behind [20].

Structural changes. The increasing use of digital technologies involves corresponding changes in organisational structures to drive the required culture change.

- *More flexible organisational structures*—many established firms have organisational structures that operate on a command-and-control basis, with clearly defined management hierarchies, controls and rules. However, these command-and-control structures are not suited to digital transformation, where firms have to respond more quickly to changing technologies, customer needs and competitor actions.
- *Greater employee autonomy*—where there is information flow and data-driven decision-making, there is a need for more employee autonomy [21]. The shift toward greater employee autonomy amongst employees will be driven by a move away from a command-and-control structure. This will help trigger a cultural shift where the emphasis on data-driven decision-making fosters a more collaborative and flexible organisational structure.
- *Physical workspace redesign*—the design of the physical workplace can also assist in allowing employees to work faster and more collaboratively. Firms must ensure that employees are not encumbered by working

environments characterised by siloed technologies, segregated physical spaces and email communications [22].
- *Outward-looking orientation*—in a digital environment, firms need to look outside the firm to identify any digital technologies or external partners that can help drive business growth. Working with external partners, such as universities and technology specialists, often involves forming alliances that entail less formal, controlled relationships and rely more on personal relationships and trust.

Digital capability development. Organisational structure and culture changes require different skills for those impacted by digital transformation in the following areas:

- *Collaborative human resource development*—Firms need to invest in training and development programmes to enhance the digital skills of existing employees. Increasingly, specialists in marketing, operations and human resources must work together on technology-related projects that require additional skills in technology management.
- *Digital talent resourcing*— new talent may need to be recruited to address any gaps in digital skills. New recruits can bring fresh perspectives and ideas regarding the use of digital technologies to drive digital growth. Digital transformation means firms must attract employees with digital and analytical skills to either augment or replace current employees. For example, in marketing, traditional brand and product marketers are being replaced by digital marketing experts, whilst data analysts are increasingly taking on tasks normally performed by marketing researchers.
- *Digital learning environment*—firms should create an environment that encourages employees to refresh their digital skills on a continuous basis. This could include adopting practices such as mentoring, knowledge-sharing and attending conferences focused on the development of digital technologies. These practices will also help a firm attract new recruits and enhance job satisfaction amongst existing employees.

Leadership. Leadership from senior management is required to ensure there is buy-in, commitment and support from those in the firm impacted by digital transformation. Effective leadership involves outlining a clear rationale for digital transformation, defining the anticipated outcomes, and actively championing it throughout the firm.

- *Vision and strategy*—firms need to establish a clear vision and strategy to understand how digital transformation aligns with the overall goals of the firm. A proper strategy will provide a clear road map to allow a firm to prioritise and allocate resources effectively, as well as make decisions around which digital technologies to invest in and which areas of the business to focus on. Senior management then needs to communicate the strategy, set clear goals, and allocate resources to support the vision.
- *Continuous employee engagement*—active engagement by leaders with employees in the digital transformation process should involve fostering a collaborative environment where ideas and feedback are encouraged and valued. Employee involvement in the process will allow leaders to tap into their expertise, gain valuable insights into how digital technologies can deliver positive outcomes and create a sense of ownership amongst employees of the digital transformation process.
- *Digital leadership education and development*—senior management also requires digital skills development to navigate the digital transformation journey. This will involve pursuing leadership education that allows senior managers to become 'tech visionaries' and develop a digital mindset [23]. This could involve creating new leadership roles, such as a chief digital officer, to ensure that digital technologies are deployed appropriately and aligned with the strategic vision of the firm. Part of this role will also involve ensuring that there is close collaboration between the IT function and other business functions.

1.8.2 Digital Transformation Outcomes and Customer Value

Employing digital technologies can lead to digital transformation at the *process*, *product* or *business model* levels, and digital transformation at these levels should create value for customers, as shown in Fig. 1.3. The logic of the analysis is that firms can manage this process to achieve digital transformation at some or all of these levels.

Process Transformation. Process transformation involves employing digital technologies to transform business processes to create customer value by improving how transactions are processed, how decisions are made, how existing customers are dealt with and how new customers are attracted. For example, in the new product development process, firms can employ social media technologies to acquire new product ideas from customers to improve product design. Moreover, in the marketing process, AI and data analytics tools can be used to analyse social media channels to add more value for customers in the form of a more customised product or service.

Product Transformation. Product transformation involves employing digital technologies to transform products by embedding digital functions that provide additional services and create value for the customer. For example, data gathered from sensors via the IoT on temperature, pressure and energy consumption of heating systems can provide real-time insights on performance during operation, and these data can allow firms to detect signs of potential problems, enable predictive maintenance and reduce downtime. Digital technologies are allowing products such as cars and domestic appliances to be changed and updated during use. These products share some of the features of digital products, such as smartphones, where the operating system of the device and apps can be adapted and improved through software updates.

Business Model Transformation. Business model transformation involves employing digital technologies to re-define current business models and create new value for customers. Advances in digital technologies have been a key driver of business model transformation and have allowed firms to disrupt established business models and challenge the positions of established firms across a range of markets. Examples include manufacturers selling directly to consumers, subscription, commission or franchising revenue models, and consumer-to-consumer transactions facilitated on electronic marketplaces. For example, digital technologies have driven e-commerce by allowing manufacturers to bypass powerful retailers and other intermediaries to sell directly to consumers and reach global markets. Moreover, Airbnb created an online marketplace to allow people to rent out their properties or spare rooms to guests on a commission basis, which has disrupted the established business models of incumbents in the hotel and accommodation industry globally.

Although digital transformation at the process, product and business model transformation levels are distinct concepts, they are often linked and can complement one another. For example, when a manufacturing firm pursues *product transformation* through integrating IoT-enabled services into its products, this can lead to *business model transformation,* as it often has to move towards a subscription-based business model to charge customers for the additional IoT-enabled services offered. Moreover, the data gathered from the product via the IoT can lead to *process transformation* by allowing the firm to generate insights into how the product can be redesigned to improve the customer experience.

Illustration 1.5 Digital Transformation at the Process, Product and Business Model Levels in the Automotive Sector

The automotive industry has been significantly impacted by digital technologies, with software in cars now powering safety systems, remote diagnostics, maintenance reminders, digital security services and navigation. Previously, automakers focused primarily on optimising the hardware product by developing more powerful engines and improving the driver experience in successive new vehicle generations. However, the car has now become increasingly digitised and connected, particularly with the transition towards battery technology, and this has led to digital transformation at the process, product and business model levels, as outlined below.

- *Process transformation*—digital technologies such as AI and the IoT have allowed automakers to improve the manufacturing process through, for example, automated quality inspections and design simulations using digital twins of physical assets. Through employing the IoT and sensor technologies, automakers can track components across the entire supply chain.
- *Product transformation*—by integrating digital technologies into the car, automakers can provide digital services such as personalised entertainment for the customer. These services can be added or removed based on software capabilities rather than altering the hardware of the vehicle, thus allowing the automaker to personalise the vehicle based on individual customer needs during product use. This increasing connectivity and more personalised customer experience allow automakers to generate subscription revenue for these services over the life cycle of the car. Automakers can also access data to better understand assumptions on whether the specifications of the components are correct and avoid costly under- or over-specification of components in the design process.
- *Business model transformation*—the emergence of ride-sharing and pay-as-you-go car services firms has challenged the traditional business models of automakers, which have been based on customer ownership. Services-oriented firms have been providing a substitute for car ownership at a lower cost. These developments are often considered in the context of transportation-as-a-service, which is viewed as a more flexible and lower-cost alternative to car ownership and a means of reducing traffic congestion and emissions in cities. Increasingly, automakers are bypassing their dealer networks and selling directly to customers.

These developments have led automakers to redefine their vision and strategy to include new digitally driven products and services, experiment with new sharing business models and invest in digital capabilities to align their investments with their vision and strategy.

Discussion Questions

1. Referring to Fig. 1.1, outline how digital technologies drive productivity in the entertainment, transportation and construction sectors. Provide examples from each sector at both the input and output levels.
2. Referring to Sect. 1.5.4, outline examples of how digital technologies can be employed for both employee substitution and employee augmentation roles from a firm of your choice. Highlight some of the challenges involved in using digital technologies in these roles.
3. Referring to Sect. 1.7.4, research three firms that have embraced digital technologies and outline how pressures for localisation have impacted the global reach of these firms. Provide examples to illustrate your answer.
4. Referring to the structural change capability of digital transformation in Sect. 1.8.1, research a firm of your choice and critically assess how it drives changes in its organisational structure.
5. Referring to Sect. 1.8.2, select a sector such as agriculture, medical devices or financial services, and analyse how a firm of your choice has embraced digital transformation at the process, product and business model levels. Highlight examples of how digital transformation has created value for customers.

References

1. Porter, M. E., & Heppelmann, J. E. (2014). How smart, connected products are transforming competition. *Harvard Business Review*, *92*(11), 64–88.
2. Furr, N., Ozcan, P., & Eisenhardt, K. M. (2022). What is digital transformation? Core tensions facing established companies on the global stage. *Global Strategy Journal*, *12*(4), 595–618.
3. Iansiti, M., & Lakhani, K. R. (2014). Digital ubiquity: How connections, sensors, and data are revolutionizing business. *Harvard Business Review*, *92*(11), 19.
4. Figure Adapted From Farrell, D. (2003). The real new economy. *Harvard Business Review*, *81*(10), pp.104–112 to include examples from digital technologies.
5. Srai, J. S., Graham, G., Hennelly, P., Phillips, W., Kapletia, D., & Lorentz, H. (2020). Distributed manufacturing: A new form of localised production? *International Journal of Operations and Production Management*, *40*(6), 697–727.
6. Plekhanov, D., Franke, H., & Netland, T. H. (2023). Digital transformation: A review and research agenda. *European Management Journal*, *41*(6), 821–844.
7. Koh, B., Hann, I. H., & Raghunathan, S. (2019). Digitization of music: Consumer adoption amidst piracy, unbundling, and rebundling. *MIS Quarterly*, *43*(1), 23–45.

8. Nadkarni, S., & Prügl, R. (2021). Digital transformation: A review, synthesis and opportunities for future research. *Management Review Quarterly, 71*, 233–341.
9. Bonnet, D., & Westerman, G. (2021). The new elements of digital transformation. *MIT Sloan Management Review, 62*(2), 83–89.
10. See Plekhanov et al. (2023) in reference 6 above.
11. See Furr et al. (2022) in reference 2 above.
12. Vallas, S., & Schor, J. B. (2020). What do platforms do? Understanding the gig economy. *Annual Review of Sociology, 46*(1), 273–294.
13. Piccoli, G., Grover, V., & Rodriguez, J. (2024). Digital transformation requires digital resource primacy: Clarification and future research directions. *The Journal of Strategic Information Systems, 33*(2), 101835.
14. See Piccoli et al. (2024) in reference 13 above.
15. Svahn, F., Mathiassen, L., & Lindgren, R. (2017). Embracing digital innovation in incumbent firms: How Volvo cars managed competing concerns. *MIS Quarterly, 41*(1), 239–254.
16. Oludapo, S., Carroll, N., & Helfert, M. (2024). Why do so many digital transformations fail? A bibliometric analysis and future research agenda. *Journal of Business Research, 174*, 114528.
17. See Furr et al. (2022) in reference 2 above.
18. Ozcan, P., & Zachariadis, M. (2021). Open banking as a catalyst for industry transformation: Lessons learned from implementing PSD2 in Europe. Swift Institute Report. Oxford University Press.
19. See Nadkarni and Prügl, (2021) in reference 8 above.
20. Kohli, R., & Melville, N. P. (2019). Digital innovation: A review and synthesis. *Information Systems Journal, 29*(1), 200–223.
21. Gillani, F., Chatha, K. A., Jajja, S. S., Cao, D., & Ma, X. (2024). Unpacking Digital Transformation: Identifying key enablers, transition stages and digital archetypes. *Technological Forecasting and Social Change, 203*, 123335.
22. Dery, K., Sebastian, I. M. & van der Meulen, N. (2017). The Digital Workplace is Key to Digital Innovation. *MIS Quarterly Executive, 16*(2), 135–152.
23. See Nadkarni and Prügl, (2021) in reference 8 above.

2

Digital Platforms

2.1 Introduction

Digital platforms are increasingly prevalent in the global economy, with many individuals interacting with them on a frequent basis. Familiar examples include eBay, Facebook, Instagram and LinkedIn, where users interact with each other, and in some cases, third parties sell products and services on these platforms. Platform businesses have been around for many years in the physical world. Real-estate agents have connected house buyers with sellers, and newspapers have connected readers with advertisers.

Digital technologies have reduced the need for physical assets and allowed digital platforms to scale up both rapidly and globally, thus posing a threat to a whole range of businesses. Digital platform firms such as Google, Amazon and Apple have become some of the most valuable firms in the world. By exploiting the value created by digital interactions and network effects, successful platform firms have been able to disrupt markets and industries. For example, Airbnb's platform allows it to coordinate transactions between homeowners and travellers, thus disrupting the nature of competition in the hotel industry.

In response to the increasing prevalence of digital platforms, many established firms, such as Nike and Procter and Gamble, have been developing their own digital platforms as part of their digital transformation journey. These firms have watched digital platforms, such as Amazon and Google, enter a range of product and service markets and grow to achieve market dominance at a pace that is not possible with traditional management approaches. At the same time, some firms have established digital platforms and experienced failure as a result of being unable to acquire and retain a sustainable community of participants on the platform. Therefore, firms need to understand the benefits and challenges of establishing a digital platform. This chapter presents an overview of digital platforms and highlights the key issues firms should consider when establishing digital platforms.

> **Learning Outcomes**
> - Define the types of digital platform firms.
> - Outline the key elements of digital platforms.
> - Contrast the value chain with digital platform firms.
> - Understand why managers struggle with digital platform strategy.
> - Understand how digital platforms create value.
> - Understand how to measure value on digital platforms.
> - Highlight the risks for firms dependent on digital platforms.
> - Understand why digital platforms fail.
> - Highlight potential strategies for reducing the threats to digital platforms.

2.2 Types of Digital Platforms

Digital platforms can be categorised into innovation, transaction and hybrid. Examples of each of these categories are shown in Fig. 2.1.

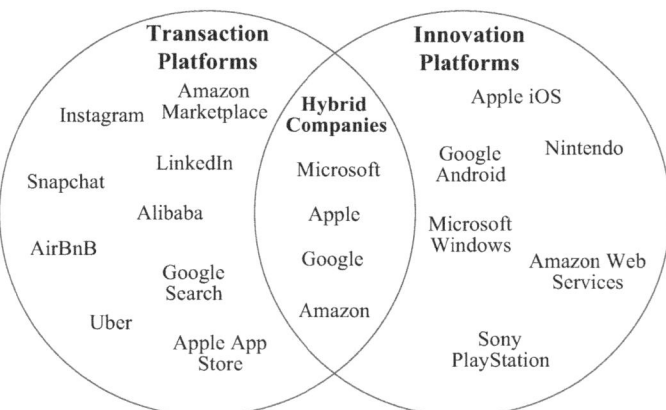

Fig. 2.1 Types of digital platforms [1]

2.2.1 Innovation Platforms

These platforms allow firms to develop complementary products, services or technologies, and these can include smartphone apps developed mainly by third-party companies without conventional supplier contracts. Apple iOS, Google Android and Microsoft Windows are common digital innovation platforms.

The technical architecture of the innovation platform should have modules or building blocks that can be accessed and complemented by software developers to build apps [2]. This complementary aspect of the technical architecture allows the continual addition of functionality or assets to the platform, which can be a source of network effects. The platform will become more attractive to users and other potential market players as the number of complements increases and/or their quality improves.

Innovation platforms create value by directly selling or renting a product, as in the case of traditional businesses. Where the platform is free, platforms generate value by selling advertising or other supplementary services.

2.2.2 Transaction Platforms

These are sometimes referred to as multi-sided markets or exchange platforms. They facilitate transactions between different organisations, players and individuals, which can involve connecting buyers with sellers, recruitment companies with job seekers and taxi drivers with passengers. Google Search, Instagram and Airbnb are examples of transaction platforms. Transaction platforms can be segmented into the following categories based on the nature of the exchange being facilitated [3]:

- *Digital marketplace*—where buyers and suppliers are matched, and examples include Uber, eBay and Amazon Marketplace. Amazon Marketplace allows third-party sellers to establish shops, collaborate with other merchants and technology providers, and facilitates consumer interactions by offering features such as online reviews, peer validation of reviews and question-and-answer lists.
- *Digital search*—which helps users find information stored on the internet or other databases based on search terms; examples include Google Search, Bing and Yahoo!
- *Digital repository*—which allows users to deposit items into a digital library that can be retrieved later by other users. Examples include videos uploaded to YouTube or users contributing to or editing articles on Wikipedia.

- *Digital communication*—which allows multiple individuals to exchange messages or documents with other individuals and interact via video or voice in real time. Examples include Snapchat, Instagram and WhatsApp.
- *Digital community*—which allows individuals to connect and exchange information with each other over a longer time period. Examples include Facebook and LinkedIn, which allow friends and users with similar interests to network with others.
- *Digital payment*—which allows individuals to pay for products and services using methods such as digital wallets, mobile payments and credit or debit cards. Examples include PayPal and Apple Pay.

Network effects are important, as the platform becomes stronger as more participants and functions become available. Value is created on the platform through enabling transactions that would not occur without the platform, and value can be captured through collecting transaction fees or charging for advertising. Table 2.1 summarises some of the key characteristics of transaction and innovation platforms.

> **Illustration 2.1 Kaggle as a Transaction Platform**
>
> Kaggle is an example of a digital community transaction platform with a large community of data scientists, engineers, AI experts, students and firms. It allows users to find datasets for use in AI model development, publish datasets and collaborate with data scientists and machine-learning engineers. It also brings together firms with data science problems and matches them with individuals who solve these problems via competitions. Firms can share a range of data science tasks and offer generous rewards to data scientists for solving these tasks.
>
> Kaggle has facilitated collaboration and peer learning between competition participants, whilst at the same time nurturing learning on the challenges and experiences amongst the participating firms. Individuals can learn by competing and collaborating with some of the experts in the field through the exchange of valuable insights in discussions and public notebooks. More experienced users can enhance their rankings on the platform by making comments and suggestions on code shared by other less-experienced users. In this way, the platform can work as a mentoring system by recognising and rewarding users based on their contributions.
>
> As Kaggle is one of the most popular platforms for data science and AI specialists, it attracts recruiters from the technology industry, and data scientists can use the platform to enhance their profiles amongst prospective employers. For example, individuals can compete in competitions to achieve a higher position on the competition leader board and thus enhance their profile. Kaggle also runs a progression system to recognise and reward users based on their contributions and achievements on the platform.

Table 2.1 Characteristics of innovation and transaction digital platforms [4]

Type	Transaction	Innovation
Purpose	Matches users or groups with the value for a user increasing with the number of users on the platform	Enables the creation of applications and services by third-party developers based on combining and recombining functionality sourced from the core of the platform
Digital features	Increasing digital information increases scope and scale of platform	Potential for innovation driven by generativity
	Digital processing power enables search and exchange of information, thus reducing the friction and costs associated with these operations	Driver by recombining digital information and functionality Easy access to digital tools to facilitate software development at scale
Basis of value creation	Enabling the exchange of information and services between third parties	Enabling innovation of new services by third parties
	• Matchmaking—value from increasing the size of the network, thus increasing the potential for a better match	• Platform opens up functional capabilities for third parties to innovate with
	• Reducing friction and making interactions and transactions as easy as possible	• Provides resource for developers to innovate with
Source of value capture	Charge for access to the platform or commission on sales through the platform. Advertising a further source of revenue	Charge access to the platform via licensing agreements or charging sales commissions on complementary services. Advertising a further source of revenue
Examples	Alibaba, WhatsApp, Uber and eBay	Android, iOS and SAP

2.2.3 Hybrid Firms

Hybrid firms have evolved to include both innovation and transaction platforms [5]. Previously, innovation and transaction platforms were focused on distinct business areas. Platforms such as eBay, which connected buyers and sellers, advertisers and consumers, were different from platforms such as Apple iOS that encouraged external players to develop complementary innovations, such as software developers creating apps. Increasingly, successful innovation platforms have begun to integrate aspects of transaction platforms into their businesses.

Some transaction platforms, such as Facebook, have opened their application programming interfaces to attract other players to develop complementary apps and services. Also, Airbnb and Uber have allowed third parties to offer complementary services on their platforms. The logic of this strategy is the recognition that not all innovation can come from inside the digital platform, and there are benefits to sourcing external innovation from other players on the platforms.

Illustration 2.2 How Network Effects Can Diminish

Network effects are regarded as a key driver of the dominant position of many digital platforms. However, network effects alone cannot deliver a sustainable competitive advantage for digital platforms and, in some cases, can be a fragile barrier to entry, diminishing over time. The strength of network effects should be considered when assessing the sustainability of digital platforms. The strength of network effects will be influenced by the level of switching costs for participants on the platform. Switching costs refer to the costs incurred by participants when moving from one platform to another. Network effects, along with switching costs, create lock-in, which influences the ease with which participants can migrate to another platform. Switching costs can be either:

- *Formal*—which includes technical or legal barriers to switching content to other platforms. For example, Google Play Music does not allow users to technically or contractually transfer music saved in their user library to another platform.
- *Informal*—which includes implicit costs of migrating to another platform. For example, migrating from a platform such as Facebook means a user will have to transfer all their contacts, media and memories to another platform, which can be a significant barrier to switching.

The strength of network effects can change over time, which diminishes the competitive position of the platform. For example, in the 1990s, Microsoft Windows had strong network effects, which, in turn, allowed it to dominate the personal computer (PC) industry. This was due to most PC applications being written specifically for the Windows platform, which meant that the value of Windows increased as more and more software companies wrote applications for the platform. However, these network effects started to weaken as internet-based apps, which worked on a range of operating systems, began to proliferate. Entry barriers to the PC industry started to fall, and this led to Android, Chrome and iOS gaining a foothold on PCs, smartphones and tablets.

Sources: Zhu, F. and Iansiti, M., 2019. "Why Some Platforms Thrive … and Others Don't: What Alibaba, Tencent, and Uber Teach Us About Networks That Flourish." *Harvard Business Review*, 97(1), pp. 118–125; and Knee, J.A., 2018. "Why Some Platforms Are Better Than Others." *MIT Sloan Management Review*, 59(2), pp. 18–20.

2.3 Key Elements of Digital Platforms

Platforms in a business context exist in an ecosystem. An ecosystem refers to a network of relationships between firms, customers, suppliers, government agencies, academic institutions, new start-ups, and even competitors who are involved in creating specific products or services. Ecosystems are dynamic and evolve in response to new technologies and changes in the business environment, where parties in the ecosystem can work both in collaboration and in competition to meet the needs of customers.

Digital platforms such as Apple and Facebook often have an ecosystem with a similar structure, including four players, as shown in Fig. 2.2. The *owners* of platforms control their intellectual property and governance. The owner decides who can participate in the ecosystem, the technology architecture and the rules for connecting to the platform. The platform coordinator also establishes the rules for participation and enforcement.

The platform owner must determine how the value that the platform creates is captured and shared with other participants on the platform [7]. This will involve employing data analytics tools to facilitate searching, filtering and matching mechanisms. The platform should have mechanisms based on data and algorithms that allow participants to find each other, interact, collaborate and transact more easily on the platform than outside it. *Providers* serve as the interface of the platform with users. *Producers*, such as app developers, create offerings for the platform. *Consumers* use those offerings on the platform.

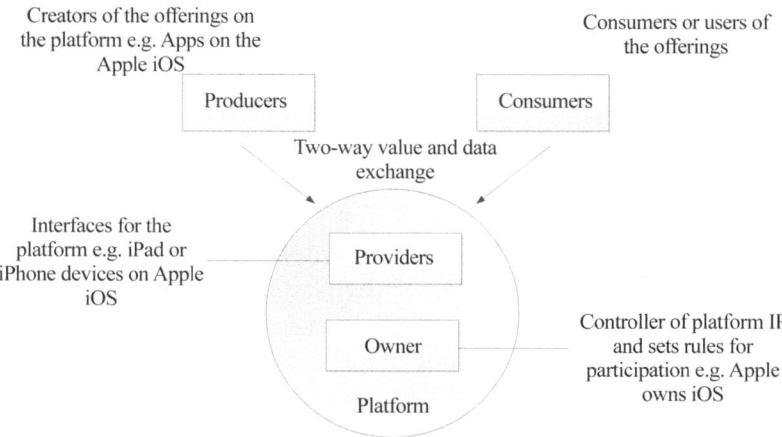

Fig. 2.2 Platform players [6]

2.4 Why Some Digital Platforms Dominate Markets

Digital platform firms such as Google, Facebook and Alibaba have achieved significant success through dominating their respective markets, which has led to huge profits. These platforms have achieved dominant market shares relative to other businesses, and in some instances, platforms have adopted a winner-takes-all strategy to achieve a near-monopoly position. There are a number of reasons why some digital platforms can achieve such dominant financial and market positions:

- *External value creation*—more value is created outside the firm through relationships with external players on the digital platform, sometimes referred to as the inverted firm [8]. The platform is responsible for co-ordinating external value creation. For example, Facebook does not create many of the web pages or posts it delivers, whilst Apple does not develop many of the apps that appear on its platform.
- *Fewer assets to own and manage*—the focus on external value creation means that the platform has fewer human and physical assets to own and manage. For example, Airbnb is the largest accommodation firm in the world but does not own any physical property for fee-paying travellers, whilst Alibaba is one of the largest global retailers but carries little inventory. These companies have fewer employees and physical buildings to own and manage, which reduces their cost base and increases their profit margins.
- *Rapid consumer and producer acquisition*—it is normally straightforward for consumers and producers to quickly sign up to a platform with no need to negotiate terms. Many platforms, such as Google, do not charge for any of the consumer services involved. Moreover, advertisers can easily use the Google AdWords website by inputting credit card details and then gaining instant access to tools that allow them to test and launch an advertising campaign.
- *Network effects*—a digital platform can employ network effects to create a virtuous cycle where the value of the platform increases as more users join. This can lead to strong user engagement and retention on the platform, with users being more likely to remain and connect with a larger community. For example, the more friends a person has on Facebook, the more likely they are to attract additional friends through the connections of their friends, thus strengthening Facebook's network.

Digital platforms can have a positive impact in a range of areas, including allowing small firms to connect to customers globally and enabling third-party firms, such as software companies, to find markets for large numbers of complementary apps on these platforms. However, these platforms also have negative impacts in the form of market monopolisation, a lack of innovation and data privacy concerns. These contradictory impacts of digital platforms are summarised in Table 2.2.

Illustration 2.3 The Potential Threat of Digital Platforms to Germany's Industrial Supremacy

Germany has long been regarded as the economic powerhouse of Europe, home to leading industrial companies such as Volkswagen, Daimler, Bayer, BMW, BASF and Siemens. Germany's economic strength has been built largely on engineering and manufacturing excellence, which has given it leadership in cars and a range of other products. Recently, some German firms, such as BMW and Volkswagen, have experienced declines in their market positions and have had

---

Table 2.2 Contradictory impacts of digital platforms [9]

Contradictory impact
Rapid user base growth versus monopoly risk
• Digital platforms can rapidly attract and expand their user base due to network effects, thus generating revenue
• However, rapid growth can lead to market monopoly, reduced competition and hinder innovation
Data network effects versus privacy concerns
• Significant amounts of data provide digital platforms with significant user insights and competitive advantage
• However, this leads to concerns around user privacy. Some platforms encourage users to trade personal data for convenience and personalised experiences
Economies of scale versus market saturation
• Digital platforms benefit from economies of scale, thus allowing them to offer services more efficiently
• However, efficiency and market dominance can lead to market saturation where new entrants find it difficult to compete, thus limiting customer choice
Platform stickiness versus high user switching costs
• The more users a platform has, the more 'sticky' it becomes, thus enhancing user loyalty
• However, users can be locked onto a platform, thus facing high switching costs, even where there is a better platform available
Innovation incentives versus disincentives to innovate
• Network effects provide the resources and user base required for innovation and service improvements
• However, where a digital firm becomes dominant, it can lose the incentive to innovate by relying on its established user base and market dominance

to lay off workers and close factories. This situation has been further compounded by uncertainty around tariffs introduced by the Trump administration in the United States.

The fear amongst German industrialists is that some of the difficulties faced by German firms are due to being slow to react to the new era of software and data in manufactured products, as well as the emergence of digital platforms. This fear is given credence by the fact that, in 2024, Apple, Google and Microsoft each achieved market capitalisations that surpassed the values of all the firms on the German DAX stock exchange. Leading-edge sectors such as machine building and chemicals could be disrupted in the same way as music and media, with digital technologies starting to take over the hardware- and engineering-oriented manufacturing models.

Digital platform firms such as Amazon, Apple and Google, with their strong cash positions, could potentially enter and compete in sectors of the German economy. Although Apple makes smartphones and computers, it has already entered a range of diverse sectors such as media and finance and has ambitions in the healthcare field. These digital platform firms have used their cash-rich positions to enter markets and buy market share by offering free services to customers, making it difficult for existing players to compete. Merck Group, the German life sciences company, is concerned about the potential 'Uberisation' of healthcare, where digital intermediaries become more powerful than the firms that manufacture and administer medication as digital intermediaries possess the data that can create specific medications for patients. Digital platforms also have the potential to become powerful intermediaries between customers and German manufacturers, who only sell physical products and do not build customer relationships around data over the life cycle of the product.

This fear is particularly acute in the German car industry, where its century's worth of combustion engine knowledge might be rendered redundant with the entry of battery car makers into the market. Firms such as Tesla are pursuing a platform strategy by selling directly to customers rather than through a dealer network, and this allows them to perform over-the-air software updates and build a relationship with the customer over the life cycle of the car. This has led some to predict that the car is likely to become an iPhone on wheels, where the car is no longer only a means of transport but a platform for other services.

Sources: Richter, K., 'Germany's car industry is losing its famous Vorsprung, and it can't all be blamed on Trump and tariffs', *The Guardian*, 14th November 2024; and McGee, P., and Chazan, G., 'The fear of being bitten by big tech: Apple is now worth more than the combined value of the 30 leading companies in Germany. Industry executives fear the country is being left behind by a new technology boom based on software and data', *Financial Times*, 30 January 2020.

2.5 Digital Platforms Versus Value Chain Firms

Value chain firms focus on a sequence of value-adding activities that have to be performed to create and deliver a product or service to a customer. Digital platform firms differ from value chain firms in the following dimensions:

- Value chain firms create value for customers by controlling a set of linear activities in a value chain, which involves transforming a series of inputs in a supply chain—right from raw material suppliers—into delivering a final product to end-consumers [10].
- In contrast, digital platform firms function as intermediaries, where value is created through facilitating interactions between producers and consumers.
- The focus in value chain firms is on creating value for customers, whilst online platforms create value for the overall ecosystem [11].
- Value chain firms develop and deploy resources to create customer value, whereas online platforms configure information and coordinate interactions to create value for the entire ecosystem.
- Finally, value chain firms pursue a competitive strategy of increasing the scale of their own operations, and at the same time, the online platform focuses on scaling the platform to create differentiation.

2.6 Why Managers Struggle With Digital Platform Strategy

When establishing digital platforms, managers often struggle to understand how strategy and competition are different in a digital platform context. Managers of value chain firms are accustomed to a strategy of competing on product features such as price, variety and functionality. Normally, these managers pursue either a capability-based approach to strategy or an industry-positioning approach. However, neither of these approaches can fully explain the dynamics of digital platform strategy, as outlined below.

2.6.1 The Capability-Based View

The logic of this view is that the real sources of competitive success lie in the ability of managers to consolidate firm-wide technologies and production skills into core competencies [12]. Firms can gain a competitive advantage by owning and controlling scarce and valuable resources that are difficult to replicate. For example, value chain businesses such as Tesco in the UK and Wal-Mart in the US pursue this approach by having a large network of store locations and logistics infrastructure, a resource that is difficult for other firms to replicate.

2.6.2 Why the Capability-Based View Cannot Fully Explain Digital Platform Strategy

In the case of a digital platform, the network of external producers and consumers, such as buyers and sellers on eBay, is the core resource [13]. In other words, the resources that are difficult to replicate are the community of producers and consumers on the platform, as well as the resources the members own and contribute. Facilitating interactions between the network of producers and consumers is an important aspect of the value creation process for managers of the platform. Ecosystem governance is another key resource that involves encouraging consumers and producers to join and stay on the platform.

2.6.3 The Industry-Positioning Approach

In the industry-positioning approach, managers assess the attractiveness or profit potential of an industry by analysing the relative impact of the five competitive forces, including the threat of new entrants, the threat of substitutes, the power of buyers, the power of suppliers and rivalry between competitors in the industry [14]. With this approach, managers seek competitive advantage by understanding the drivers of industry structure and developing a competitive strategy that defends or strengthens their position in relation to the industry forces. For example, a key aspect of the competitive strategy of Tesco is based on having a large store network, economies of scale and significant buyer power, which, in turn, reduce their fixed costs and act as a barrier to new entrants. Therefore, competitive strategy is about controlling resources, reducing costs and resisting challenges from the five forces.

2.6.4 Why the Industry-Positioning Approach Cannot Fully Explain Digital Platform Strategy

Although the five forces still must be considered by managers of digital platforms, the forces can behave differently, and new factors can emerge [15]. Strategy in platform businesses is about optimising the total value of an expanding ecosystem in a circular and iterative process rather than erecting barriers to new entrants. Managers must carefully analyse the interactions of producers and consumers on the platform and ensure that the platform continues to attract new players. The success of a digital platform depends on matching a large base of consumers and producers and providing consumers with a wide range of products and services. Moreover, the platforms need to make the entry costs for producers and advertisers as straightforward as possible.

Table 2.3 summarises how the principles of strategy differ across value chain and digital platform firms.

2.7 How to Create Value on Digital platforms

When establishing a platform, a firm must decide how the platform will create and capture value through interactions on the platform, and then how value is shared amongst platform users. The owner should provide value on the platform by including searching, filtering and matching mechanisms.

Table 2.3 How the principles of strategy differ between digital platforms and value chain firms

Value chain firm	Principles	Digital platform firm
Controlling a linear set of activities in a value chain	Value creation	Orchestrating interaction between consumers and producers
Core competencies	Focus	Core interactions
Control of difficult to replicate resources and capabilities	Resources	The community is the core resource
Inside the firm	Innovation	By the firm and the ecosystem
Distinct buyers, suppliers, substitutes, entrants and competitors	Industry forces	Overlap between consumers and producers, competitors and complementors
Cost leadership and/or product differentiation	Metrics	Engagement and fair governance
Entry barriers	Access	Permissionless entry, open around key control points

Moreover, the platform should attract external players as members of the ecosystem to participate on the platform and add value. For example, innovation and transaction platforms can create value in the following ways [16]:

- *Innovation platforms* create value through the following sources: the provision of applications and services, payment handling from the marketplace sales function, user reviews and evaluations, the platform application review process, the availability of development resources, and the availability and reliability of applications.
- *Transaction platforms* create value through the following sources: transaction processing, review and rating systems, publicity, technology reliability, safety, membership and affiliations, work flexibility, and rewards and support.

There are four drivers of value creation in a digital context that provide a useful basis for assessing how a digital platform can create value, and each of these is explained below [17].

2.7.1 Complementarities

This involves bringing a bundle of products and services together that provide more value than offering them separately on a digital platform. For example, digital platforms such as Alibaba can offer a wide variety of complementary products and services together in one marketplace.

2.7.2 Efficiency

Transaction efficiency increases when the costs per transaction decrease. Digital technologies reduce the costs of conducting transactions on digital platforms. For example, digital platforms such as Amazon can reduce product search costs by making it easy to find and use the products needed on the platform. Moreover, digital platforms can simplify the transaction process through ease-of-access mechanisms.

2.7.3 Novelty

This involves the potential for first-mover advantage through creating new transaction mechanisms and content, as well as new types of business. For example, a platform can offer new features or processes to existing products and services on the platform.

Table 2.4 Value drivers in digital platforms [18]

Complementarities	Efficiency	Novelty	Lock-in
Variety—including competing products and services	Channels search cost—accessible on multiple types of devices or channels	New content—new products, services or information	Reward repeat use or purchase from the platform
Related services—ensuring access to related products and services	Search cost—easy to locate and use the products needed on the platform	New features: introduce new features or processes in existing products, services of information	Ensure data protection, safety and security
Linking services—automatic access to features of product X while using another product Y	Peer reviews—system for rating and reviewing suppliers and service providers	Restructure existing processes or transactions offered previously in the marketplace	Customisability of products allow users to customise products on the platform
Combining online and offline capabilities	Selection range—offer a range of products to serve specific needs of different customers	Onboard new services—provide existing products or services through the platform the first time	Virtual Community—create and moderate a virtual community for users to interact
Combining multiple technology capabilities	Information symmetry—provide up–to-date and complete information on each product offered on the platform		Increase user base actively
	Transaction simplicity—ensure that performing transactions across the platform is simple to users		Guarantee quality and reliability

2.7.4 Lock-In

This involves creating value that encourages consumers and producers to stay with the platform and not migrate to competing platforms. Platforms can reward consumers for repeat use and purchases from the platform. Building trust through data protection, safety and security features is a further source of value that can lock consumers into the platform. Examples of digital platforms facing trust issues include Facebook's lack of attention to controlling fake news from malicious users and Amazon Marketplace's difficulties with counterfeit products influenced by fake reviews and transactions.

Table 2.4 summarises how digital platforms can create value along each of the dimensions of complementarities, efficiency, lock-in and novelty.

2.8 How to Measure Value on Digital Platforms

Firms must have performance metrics to measure value creation on their platforms. It is not possible to measure platform value or success by sales revenue and market share alone. The platform has to measure and analyse sources of value such as commissions, subscription fees, advertising revenues, non-monetary benefits from consumer insights and direct feedback [19]. This involves considering metrics such as customer growth, their usage and ratings of third-party offerings, user satisfaction, and the willingness of users to recommend the platform, along with the analysis of search results. There are a number of potential metrics that can be employed to assist with this analysis [20]:

- *Interaction failure* refers to the failure to match a consumer with a product or service. For example, when Uber fails to have cars available consistently on its platform, passengers will not use the Uber platform. Passengers who experience this issue will stop using the platform, leading to more driver downtime, which will result in drivers leaving the platform.
- *Level of engagement*—the platform should monitor the level of participation of members on the platform. This will involve tracking usage patterns and user recommendations.
- *Match quality* refers to the platform not meeting the needs of consumers and producers on the platform. For example, Google monitors the search

activities of its' users to allow it to refine its search results to meet more closely the needs of users.
- *Negative network effects*—negative feedback loops in the form of, for example, not meeting the needs of consumers or poor consumer ratings—can harm the platform. The platform has to monitor negative network effects and implement mechanisms to limit the potential harm.

2.9 Risks for Firms Dependent on Digital Platforms

The analysis so far has highlighted the need for some digital platforms to pursue strategies that attract both consumers and producers. However, it is increasingly recognised that there are significant risks for producers who are dependent on platforms for selling their products and services. Platforms can pose risks to the competitive strategy of platform-dependent businesses along the following dimensions [21].

2.9.1 Loss of Control of Differentiation

It can be difficult for a firm to differentiate its offerings from competitors, as platforms tend to standardise the presentation of products, which limits the ability of the firm to highlight a basis of differentiation to customers. For example, in the case of Amazon, the unique features of products on its site—including search terms, product descriptions, images and product reviews—are dictated by Amazon to allow consumers to compare products. Amazon bundles products from as many sellers as it likes, who then have to compete within market segments that they cannot define [22]. Similarly, Apple creates playlists of different artists along themes and listener preferences, which can hinder the ability of artists to differentiate themselves.

Web page design by the digital platform encourages consumers to compare products based on a limited number of features, such as pricing or consumer ratings. Product competition occurs not only between brands but also within them, as different retailers on the platform may offer the same product at different prices. Platforms often encourage consumers to search for types of products rather than specific brands. This allows platforms such as Amazon to position their own featured products more prominently, thus moving branded products to commodity status.

2.9.2 Risk of Competitor Imitation

As sellers lose their basis of differentiation on the platform, it becomes more straightforward for competitors to copy their offerings. It is more difficult for the seller to develop a unique value proposition for customers and continue to refine and improve it. Selling on platforms allows competitors to replicate key elements of a seller's offering, including product descriptions, pricing and targeted search terms.

2.9.3 The Platform Controls the Relationship

The platform controls the flow of information in the relationship and only lets the seller know what it wants them to know. The platform enforces a fundamental asymmetry in information about the customer in the platform's favour. Furthermore, many trading platforms will attempt to prevent any off-platform contact between buyers and sellers due to the risk of the buyer and seller dealing directly off the platform.

2.9.4 When Platforms Become Competitors

Platforms can also offer products or services that compete directly with the seller's offerings, thus becoming competitors. Weather apps, password apps and flashlight apps have struggled since Apple made these functions standard features on its platform. Platforms can feature their own competing products more prominently over the products of other sellers. Platforms can monitor products or services offered by sellers that have strong sales performance and then increase the commission they charge to the seller or introduce a product that directly competes with it. Some platforms have been accused of running their platform as a test bed for letting sellers compete against each other and then selecting the best products under their own brand name. Moreover, products sold directly by the platform can often become more prominent in search results.

Illustration 2.4 Digital Platforms and Anti-Competitive Practices

The market capitalisation of digital platforms, including Amazon, Apple, Google, Meta and Microsoft, means that these firms are wealthier and more influential than many countries. However, analysis by a US government committee found that the power of these firms has had harmful impacts on the US economy and democracy in the following ways:

- These digital platforms acted as gatekeepers over key distribution channels and controlled access to markets, thus allowing them to pick winners and losers in the US economy. They abused their power by charging exorbitant fees, imposing unfair contractual terms and extracting valuable data from firms and individuals that depend on them.
- Each platform uses its gatekeeper position to retain and build its power by controlling the rules around access to the digital platform. They surveil other firms to identify potential rivals, and their economic power allows them to acquire, copy or exclude competitive threats from their platforms.
- These platforms have abused their role as intermediaries to further expand their dominance through, for example, self-preferencing and predatory pricing. Many firms that use these platforms claimed they exploited their power to dictate terms and extract concessions that would not have been possible in a competitive market.
- The analysis also asserted that the dominance of platforms reduced consumer choice, eroded innovation and entrepreneurship in the US economy, and weakened a free and diverse press.

An illustration of some of these issues is the case of the online gaming firm Epic Games when it introduced a direct payment option for its Fortnite gaming app. This allowed Epic Games to bypass Apple's 30% commission fee for in-app add-ons when the user decided to pay for the app directly rather than via Apple's App Store. In response, Apple removed Fortnite from its App Store and terminated Epic's developer accounts, which eliminated Epic's primary sales channel. When this issue went to court, Apple won by using the argument that it needed oversight of the approval process for security purposes, and this transcended the rights of individual firms operating on its platform.

Sources: Lv, D.D. and Schotter, A.P., 2024. The dark side of powerful platform owners: Aspiration adaptations of digital firms. *Academy of Management Perspectives*, in press; and Gawer, A., 2022. Digital platforms and ecosystems: remarks on the dominant organisational forms of the digital age. *Innovation*, 24(1), pp. 110–124.

2.10 Why Digital Platforms Fail

Some digital platforms, such as Alibaba, Facebook and Airbnb, have been thriving, whilst others, such as Uber, have suffered from increased competition and threats to their market position. It is often relatively straightforward for a platform to achieve scale, but more difficult to maintain. Therefore, it is important to understand why some digital platforms are performing more strongly than others. There are a number of threats to platform businesses that are highlighted below.

2.10.1 Network Clustering

This is related to the ability of the platform to sustain its scale. Where a platform is fragmented into local clusters, the more likely it is that those clusters are isolated from one another, which makes the platform more vulnerable to competition [23]. Uber is at risk of network clustering as it has to build a similar network in each local location, such as a city, which contrasts with Airbnb, which operates a single global network.

In the case of Uber, it is straightforward for a competing taxi company app to establish a strong position in a local market. Drivers and passengers can easily transfer to other platforms in local markets. However, in the case of Airbnb, travellers are not interested in the number of hosts in their local cities but are concerned about how many hosts there are across a wider number of cities. Therefore, it is more difficult to compete against Airbnb's platform, and a new entrant would have to enter the market on a global scale.

2.10.2 Value of Data

The value of data that platforms can gather from and provide to participants on the platform will influence their sustainability and ability to retain participants. This includes the following [24]:

- *Crowdsourcing* refers to participants drawing value from other participants on the platform. This could include accessing reviews of product and service experiences from previous customers, as in the case of Airbnb travellers rating experiences of previous accommodations. Moreover, this can include advice forums where consumers can get advice on products to purchase and elicit specific advice from third parties on the platform.
- *Crowdsending* refers to participants providing value to the platform and other participants by contributing products, services and other related content. For example, Adidas offers training schedules, shares running

routes and photographs, along with instructional videos of product and service usage on its platform.

Where there is a high level of intensity in crowdsourcing and crowd-sending amongst participants on the platform, there is likely to be strong lock-in to the platform. The high intensity of interactions between the digital platform and participants means there is a deeply embedded relationship, and participants are less likely to migrate to other digital platforms.

2.10.3 Disintermediation

Disintermediation occurs when consumers and producers bypass the platform and deal directly with each other. This is a particular problem for platforms that offer matching or facilitating services, and there is limited potential to lock-in the consumer or producer into returning to the platform. For example, in the case of services such as home cleaning, once the customer has found a cleaner they are satisfied with, they can transact off the platform and there is little incentive for the client to return to the platform to look for another cleaner. Platforms can attempt to reduce the threat of disintermediation by introducing terms of service prohibiting off-platform contact and preventing the exchange of information between the consumer and producer [25]. Furthermore, offering additional services such as insurance and dispute resolution facilities on the platform can help retain consumers and producers.

2.10.4 Multi-Homing

Multi-homing occurs when consumers and producers form relationships with a number of platforms simultaneously. This is likely when it is straightforward for consumers and producers to sign up to multiple platforms with no need to negotiate terms. The presence of multi-homing means it is difficult for the platform to generate revenue and create network effects. Uber has attempted to limit multi-homing on the passenger side of the business by giving bonuses for certain

	Offer new services	Nurture new transactions
Enhanced	For example, offer complementary services to consumers to improve initial value proposition.	For example, establish a multi-channel presence to enhance consumer experience.
	Enhance interactions	**Enhance capabilities**
Initial	For example, employ better transaction data analytics to improve customer experience.	For example, offer incentives to providers to join and stay on the platform.
	Initial	Enhanced

Value proposition on consumer side (rows: Enhanced / Initial)

Value proposition on producer side

Fig. 2.3 Strategies for reducing the threats to digital platforms [26]

numbers of trips. Moreover, subscribers to Amazon Prime are often offered preferential delivery terms to discourage multi-homing to other online retailers.

2.11 Strategies for Reducing the Threats to Digital Platforms

Digital platforms must continually adapt and improve the value offered to participants on their platforms to counteract potential risks and competitive threats. Firms can map the relationship between the value provided on both the producer and consumer sides of the digital platform to highlight potential strategies for reducing the threats to their competitive position, as shown in Fig. 2.3.

2.11.1 Enhance Interactions

This involves improving the matchmaking between the producers and consumers on the platform by better leveraging transactional data. In contrast to offline platforms, digital platforms have access to large volumes of transaction data, which they can analyse to generate meaningful insights and enhance interactions between the two sides of the platform.

The initial value proposition for the producer and seller when joining the platform can be improved further via data analysis. For example, Amazon regularly analyses transaction data to personalise its offerings to different customers on its platform. Therefore, the platform needs to keep users engaged by enhancing their offers and interactions, which helps to strengthen network effects for the platform. Moreover, Google Search provides recommendations as words are input into the search bar, which leads to better matching. This is likely to create stronger lock-in and reduce the likelihood of the user switching to another search engine.

2.11.2 Enhance Capabilities

This strategy involves enhancing the capabilities on the producer side of the platform. Enhancing capabilities can take the form of the platform providing consultancy, financial assistance and other services to producers. For example, some global digital platforms, such as Alibaba, have offered financial loans at reduced interest rates to some of their suppliers. Financial support can lock-in a producer and improve their loyalty to Alibaba. It is worth highlighting that digital platforms often know more about their producers than most financial services organisations. Moreover, some digital platforms have enhanced the capabilities of smaller retailers by applying digital technologies. Udaan, the Indian business-to-business digital trading platform, has employed AI to calculate creditworthiness, optimise routes and provide other data-driven services to sellers [27].

2.11.3 Offer New Services

This involves offering additional related services on the consumer side of the platform. Related services can enhance the initial value proposition for the consumer and strengthen the network effects of the platform. For example, Facebook offers services such as newsfeed, advertising and third-party apps to its existing user base.

2.11.4 Nurture New Transactions

Nurturing new transactions involves expanding the range of channels available to consumers and reaching new customers through alternative channels. Expanding the range of channels can be part of an omni-channel strategy that may involve a digital platform establishing an offline presence, either directly or through a franchised arrangement. Some digital platforms have established experience centres where consumers can experience products offline and then purchase the products online, or vice versa. For example, Apple has opened a global network of offline stores to act as experience centres and build the brand. Such a strategy can also allow the platform to reach new customers.

> **Discussion Questions**
> 1. Referring to Sect. 2.4, select a digital platform with a dominant market position and analyse the reasons for its market dominance. Also, referring to Table 2.2, highlight the positive and negative impacts of the dominance of the digital platform.
> 2. Select a digital platform in a sector such as agriculture, entertainment, healthcare or financial services, and, referring to Sect. 2.7, analyse how the platform creates value along the *efficiency, complementarities, novelty* and *lock-in* value drivers.
> 3. Referring to Sect. 2.9, critically assess how digital platforms such as Amazon Marketplace and eBay build in dependency for participants on these platforms.
> 4. Referring to Sect. 2.10, undertake research on a digital platform failure case. Highlight how the relevant factors in Sect. 2.10 led to its failure.
> 5. Referring to Fig. 2.3, critically assess how digital platforms from different sectors pursue strategies to counteract risks and threats to their viability. Outline some examples of how they *offer new services, nurture new transactions, enhance interactions* and *improve capabilities*.

References

1. Figure adapted from Cusumano, M. A., Yoffie, D. B., & Gawer, A. (2020). The future of platforms. *MIT Sloan Management Review, 61*(3), 46–54.
2. Gawer, A. (2014). Bridging differing perspectives on technological platforms: Toward an integrative framework. *Research Policy, 43*(7), 1239–1249.
3. Meyer, R. (2023). Digital platform map, 1st March, Retrieved from TIAS, School for business and Society, https://www.tias.edu/en/news-and-articles/item/digital-strategy-digital-platform-map.

4. Table adapted and augmented with real-world examples from, Bonina, C., Koskinen, K., Eaton, B., & Gawer, A. (2021). Digital platforms for development: Foundations and research agenda. *Information Systems Journal*, 31, 869–902.
5. See Cusumano et al. (2020) in reference 1 above.
6. Figure adapted from Van Alstyne, M. W., Parker, G. G., & Choudary, S. P. (2016). Pipelines, platforms, and the new rules of strategy. *Harvard Business Review*, *94*(4), 54–62.
7. Anderson, E. G., Bhargava, H. K., Boehm, J., & Parker, G. (2022). Electric vehicles are a platform business: What firms need to know. *California Management Review*, *64*(4), 135–154.
8. Van Alstyne, M. W., & Parker, G. G. (2021). Digital transformation changes how companies create value. *Harvard Business Review Digital Article*, December 17, 2021.
9. Adapted from Lv, D. D., & Schotter, A. P., (2024). The dark side of powerful platform owners: Aspiration adaptations of digital firms. *Academy of Management Perspectives*, In press.
10. Sanchita, K., & Gupta, S. (2023). Strategies for Value Reconfiguration in Online Platforms. *California Management Review*, *66*(1), 72–95.
11. See van Alstyne et al. (2016) in reference 6 above.
12. Prahalad, C. K., & Hamel, G. (1990). The core competence of the corporation, *Harvard Business Review*, 68, 4, 79–91 and Barney, J. B. (1991). Firm resources and sustained competitive advantage. *Journal of Management*, *17*(1), 99–120.
13. See van Alstyne et al. (2016) in reference 6 above.
14. Porter, M. E. (1985). *Competitive advantage: Creating and sustaining superior performance*. Free Press.
15. See van Alstyne et al. (2016) in reference 6 above.
16. Ghazawneh, A., & Mansour, O. (2015). Value creation in digital application marketplaces: A developers' perspective. In Thirty Sixth International Conference on Information Systems. Fort Worth, Texas (pp. 2015).
17. Amit, R., & Zott, C. (2001). Value creation in e-business. *Strategic Management Journal*, *22*(6-7), 493–520.
18. Kieti, J., Waema, T. M., Ndemo, E. B., Omwansa, T. K., & Baumüller, H. (2021). Sources of value creation in aggregator platforms for digital services in agriculture-insights from likely users in Kenya. *Digital Business*, *1*(2), 100007.
19. Wichmann, J. R., Wiegand, N., & Reinartz, W. J. (2022). Building your own brand platform. *Harvard Business Review*, *100*(5), 47–53.
20. See van Alstyne et al. (2016) in reference 6 above.
21. Cutolo, D., Hargadon, A., & Kenney, (2021). Competing on platforms, *Sloan Management Review*, Spring, pp.22-30 and see Wichmann et al. (2022) in reference 15 above.
22. See Cutolo et al. (2021) in reference 20 above.

23. Zhu, F., & Iansiti, M. (2019). Why some platforms thrives ... and others don't what alibaba, tencent, and uber teach us about networks that flourish. The five characteristics that make the difference. *Harvard Business Review*, *97*(1), 118–125.
24. See Wichmann et al. (2022) in reference 19 above.
25. See Zhu and Iansiti (2019) in reference 23 above.
26. This figure had been adapted with examples from Sanchita and Gupta (2023) in reference 10 above.
27. See Sanchita and Gupta (2023) in reference 10 above.

3

The Internet of Things and Digital Transformation

3.1 Introduction

Many established firms have been using digital technologies, such as web channels, to allow customers to purchase their products and services, and this has enabled them to analyse purchase data to generate important insights into buyer behaviour. At the same time, these firms have looked on with envy at companies such as Amazon and Apple, which have been collecting and analysing data across a whole range of customer touch points that go well beyond simple purchasing transactions. Much of this phenomenon has been driven by developments in the internet of things (IoT), which is a network of devices that communicate with each other and other digitally enabled devices and systems via an internet connection. The IoT has enabled a range of devices to connect and interact with one another to analyse data in real time, allowing the functions of the product to be monitored and optimised remotely.

3.1.1 The IoT and the Smart Inhaler

A smart asthma inhaler provides an illustration of the IoT in action in a healthcare context [1]. A standard asthma inhaler has a canister that holds the medication and a plastic actuator that releases the proper medication dose when pressed. However, a smart inhaler has a sensor on the plastic actuator that collects data and transmits it via Bluetooth connectivity to a smart phone or wearable device, as well as to the inhaler manufacturer and other partners.

The smart inhaler generates data such as the time and date, the location of the user and the dose inhaled, and it can collect and use environmental data from other IoT devices within homes, such as those that detect mould or dust mites. It can also access other real-time environmental data on pollen, humidity, pollution and other irritants that can cause an asthma attack.

These data allow the smart inhaler manufacturer to offer customer features such as reminders of when to take preventive doses and to carry inhalers when leaving home. Moreover, a key benefit of smart inhalers is improved adherence to medication doses, better control of asthma and fewer acute attacks. Access to these data can allow the manufacturer to customise predictions via better insights into which irritants are more likely to trigger attacks in an individual user, and also help physicians adapt dosages for individual patients.

3.2 The Power of the IoT

The case of the smart inhaler provides a useful context for understanding the power of the IoT through the following attributes:

- *Multi-dimensional connectivity*—where the internet allowed people to connect with firms and people to connect with people via, for example, social media, the IoT has enabled people to connect with devices, and devices to connect with devices. In the case of the smart inhaler, the wearable technology and the smart phone are the devices that are connected to each other, and these are also connected to the user of the inhaler. This multi-dimensional connectivity can happen without human intervention and allows data to be collected in real time from a range of sources, including the user, the environment and IoT devices.
- *Data as a strategic resource*—the IoT significantly improves the diversity, granularity and timeliness of data, thus enhancing the strategic value of data to many firms [2]. Firms can use data to both reduce internal costs and create new value for customers. In the case of the smart inhaler, the data collected on the usage patterns of the inhaler user and the general environmental conditions can be analysed to inform the design of the inhaler and generate insights into how the inhaler can be redesigned and improved.

- *A multi-dimensional and dynamic understanding of the customer*—in the internet era, firms could collect customer data through limited channels such as PCs and smartphones, with this data tending to be fragmented. However, in an IoT environment, there are a range of access points through which data can both flow and be analysed, allowing firms to develop a multi-dimensional and dynamic understanding of the needs of the customer. In the case of the smart inhaler, the IoT allows the manufacturer of the inhaler to collect highly detailed and varied data from the user of the inhaler and devices in real time to offer more personalised medication doses and identify specific irritants likely to cause an asthma attack in certain locations.

> **Learning Outcomes**
> - An overview of the key building blocks of the IoT.
> - Understand the capabilities of the IoT.
> - Understand how the IoT impacts business functions.
> - Understand how the IoT transforms customer relationships.
> - Understand how the IoT transforms supply chains.
> - Understand the relationship between the IoT and servitised business models.
> - Understand the privacy and security implications of the IoT.
> - Understand the key issues involved in implementing the IoT in digital transformation.

3.3 The Key Building Blocks of the IoT

The idea of smart, connected products provides a useful analogy for the key building blocks of the IoT, as outlined below [3]:

- *Physical components* include the mechanical and electrical parts of the product. In the case of a car, this includes the engine block, tires and batteries.
- *Smart* components include sensors, microprocessors, data storage, software and typically an embedded operating system along with an enhanced user interface. In the case of a car, this includes the engine control unit, anti-lock braking system and rain-sensing windscreen wipers.
- *Connectivity components* include the ports, antennas and protocols that enable wired or wireless communication with the product. Connectivity can take three forms:

- *One-to-one*—where the product connects to the user, the manufacturer or another product through a port or other interface. In the case of a car, this involves linking it to diagnostic equipment.
- *One-to-many*—which includes a central system connected to many products simultaneously. For example, many cars are now connected to the systems of the manufacturer to allow performance monitoring, remote service and upgrades.
- *Many-to-many*—multiple products can be connected to many other types of products and often to external data sources. For example, farm machinery can be connected to one another and to geo-location data, which can help to manage and optimise the farm system.

Connectivity allows information to be exchanged between the product and its operating environment, its maker, its users, and other products and systems. It also enables some functions of the product to exist outside the physical device, which can include the product cloud.

3.4 The Capabilities of the IoT

3.4.1 Connecting

The IoT allows firms to connect and integrate devices and people from the physical and digital world. This allows data to be shared to improve situational awareness and avoid information delay and distortion. For example, apartment blocks can have smart connected meters that allow apartments to be heated or cooled automatically based on occupancy levels. Where sensors are positioned in a retailer with refrigeration units, alerts can be sent to the store manager when the refrigerators break down [4]. Managers can then communicate with the relevant employee who is responsible for dealing with equipment breakdowns via the IoT-enabled mobile device.

3.4.2 Collecting

IoT devices with sensors can collect enormous amounts of data that can be analysed by analytics tools to assist managers in making business decisions. For example, advances in the IoT and data analytics can allow individual health data to be analysed to personalise patient care and pre-empt health issues. In a care home setting, remote monitoring of patients' normal patterns of movement and activity via sensors and data analytics tools can help prevent adverse events, such as patient falls, from escalating into accident and emergency visits.

3.4.3 Monitoring

Remote monitoring of connected devices and people can provide a rich, detailed source of data in real time. The IoT can provide monitoring data on equipment performance, energy use and environmental conditions, allowing managers to track performance in real time. Remote monitoring can also highlight patterns and potential improvement areas, and predict future outcomes. For example, logistics companies have developed sensors for inside containers to track conditions, including temperature, humidity, pressure and movement.

3.4.4 Optimising

The IoT can deliver new levels of efficiency, thus providing significant opportunities for potential cost, energy and time savings. The IoT, along with data analytics tools, can be applied to in-use or historical data to improve productivity. For example, in wind turbines, a microcontroller can alter each blade on every revolution to capture the maximum level of wind energy [5]. Monitoring the condition of a product in real time allows a firm to optimise service by undertaking preventative maintenance when failure is likely, which reduces product downtime and the need to deploy repair personnel on-site.

3.4.5 Autonomising

Autonomy refers to the IoT that enables autonomous operations, automated decision-making and self-diagnosis [6]. Products can learn about their environment, self-diagnose their own service needs and adapt to the needs of customers. For example, some industrial equipment with IoT has the capability to decide whether to perform actions such as preventative maintenance without human involvement. Autonomy can, therefore, reduce the need for operators in dangerous environments and facilitate operation in remote locations. The IoT in products can report information remotely in real time to monitor elements of the product's operation, including location or usage data, and then report this information back to managers as required.

> **Illustration 3.1 The Capabilities of the IoT in Action: The Nest Thermostat**
>
> In many ways, the Nest thermostat functions like an ordinary smart thermostat by monitoring temperature and turning heating and cooling systems on and off to maintain the target temperature. However, the Nest can also sense humidity, activity and light, and its built-in intelligence, learned during its first few days of operation, allows it to understand the temperatures that the individual prefers and when they prefer them. A Nest can then programme itself and create a weekly temperature schedule. A Nest also learns how quickly a home heats and cools, as no two homes are exactly the same, and it considers weather conditions so that it can assess how early or late in the day it needs to turn on the heating system. The value of the Nest is further enhanced when it is connected to a utility firm or another Nest account via a home WiFi network, as it allows people to monitor and change the temperature remotely, adjust the heating schedule and analyse their heating activity. It also enables utility firms to offer incentives for using less power during peak times or to provide additional related services.

3.5 How the IoT Impacts Business Functions

The IoT has been impacting various business functions, as summarised in Table 3.1. Each of these is now outlined with practical examples below.

3.5.1 Design and Development

Bosch, the German automotive supplier, has used IoT field data, such as device state, usage and failure information, to define technical specifications for its connected brake systems. Prior to this development, Bosch was collecting data through a diagnostic tool on vehicle fleet data and customer data from repair centres. The firm has now moved from a position of collecting data manually to collecting highly frequent, detailed and automated data. This has allowed the firm to gain insights into the usage behaviour of drivers, as well as stresses on the brakes in the field. Crucially, this allows Bosch to better understand its assumptions on whether the specifications of the brakes are correct and avoid costly under- and over-specification in the design of its braking systems.

Table 3.1 Examples of IoT applications in business functions [7]

Business area	Description	Case firm
Design and development	Operational IoT data such as device usage or failure information are used to define technical specifications	Bosch chassis control: specification of connected brakes
	The IoT field data and remote software updates in prototypes and field devices are used to accelerate and improve product validation	Konecranes: virtual validation of smart cranes
Manufacturing	Data transmitted from the IoT devices are used to highlight challenges in the production process of products	Toyota: car field data for production optimisation
	The IoT data support the optimisation and customisation of production processes and end products	Bosch Heating Systems: customised production processes
Marketing and sales	The IoT field data allow manufacturers to conduct complementary market research and learn about customer preferences	Heidelberger Druck: sales lead generation
	Identification of customer segments that use solutions for different purposes and have differing expectations and preferences	Procter and Gamble: the IoT field data for market segmentation
After-sales service and support	The IoT field data enable manufacturers to reduce inefficiencies related to analyses of physical shipment of warranty cases	Bosch Heating Systems: improving the warranty claims process
	The IoT data transfer improves service efficiency through, for example, increasing communication quality and minimising downtime	Heidelberger Druck: predictive monitoring to identify equipment faults

3.5.2 Manufacturing

The IoT sensors can collect data on problems during the manufacturing process, which allows firms to react quickly and identify the causes of the problems. For example, Toyota has been using IoT data to identify and rectify problems in areas such as product throughput and quality. It has extended this analysis into the supply chain to identify poorly performing suppliers and has put in place measures to reduce the risk of supplier failure.

3.5.3 Marketing

In the past, manufacturing firms depended on historical customer data, market surveys and research to understand their markets. The IoT now provides real-time data to allow these firms to segment their markets and target specific customers. For example, Heidelberger Druck has employed the IoT data to identify potential customers for offering add-on solutions. This allows the firm to improve sales and enhances the ability of marketing people to address the needs and concerns of customers. Moreover, the IoT allows firms to segment the market based on the actual usage behaviour of customers rather than relying on assumptions, hunches or surveys. Therefore, these data allow firms to obtain a better understanding of what kinds of market segments exist in practice.

3.5.4 After-Sales Service and Support

Warranty processes, often required by regulators or as a basis for competing in the marketplace, are an area where IoT has had an impact. For example, Bosch Heating Systems has deployed the IoT to gain a deeper understanding of the reasons for components breaking down, something which was difficult to do previously. The IoT provides data on the usage of heating systems when in the field, including the average heating temperature and customer heating behaviour, and this has been used to determine patterns for fault detection and, in turn, provide a better understanding of the conditions under which certain warranty issues may arise.

3.6 How the IoT Transforms Customer Relationships

The IoT can allow firms to establish deeper relationships with customers and transform the customer experience. The availability of product usage data can provide novel insights into how products and services create value for customers, which allows the firm to better adjust and position the functionality of their offerings to customers. This approach will be most effective when products and services can be altered through over-the-air software technologies whilst in use. For example, whereas in the past an engine manufacturer had to produce multiple engines with different levels of horsepower for different markets, it can now adjust the horsepower rating on the same engine using software alone. There are a number of ways in which IoT transforms customer relationships, as outlined below.

3.6.1 Offer Ever-Evolving Additional Customer Services

The IoT has led to a shift in firms providing continual value to the customer over the life of the product. Firms now have a means of building a direct and ongoing dialogue with customers as they are connected to customers via the product. Therefore, firms can monitor customer interactions in real time, enabling them to respond quickly to customer needs. Firms are now recognising that the product is a window into the needs and satisfaction of customers, rather than relying on customers to learn about product needs and performance [8].

3.6.2 Greater Personalised and Customised Products and Services

The IoT can gather data on customer preferences and buyer behaviour, thus allowing the firm to customise products and services to the needs of individual customers. The IoT is also situationally aware and can quickly adapt to its environment, which can facilitate personalisation. For example, a personalised temperature service developed for an individual to keep the room temperature at home to meet their preferences means that an air-conditioning unit can interact with wearable sensors and develop a personalised service [9]. In an IoT environment, the completion of the purchase of the product does not mean the end of the relationship with the customer, but the beginning of a new round of continuous interaction. This new relationship should allow the firm to continuously analyse the needs of customers and promote the customisation of product and service solutions for them [10].

3.6.3 Build Longer-Term Relationships with Customers

The IoT allows firms to establish relationships with customers who are willing to become life-long users of the product and service offering. The

IoT can enable continuous customer engagement through better communication in areas such as, for example, connected appliances, where firms can send alerts or notifications to keep customers engaged. Product-based services, such as maintenance contracts, are a long-established way for firms to provide added value to customers during the life of the product [11]. The IoT allows firms to go even further and provide a dynamic product and service environment where maintenance can be performed based on actual need rather than when it is assumed that it should be done. Therefore, the IoT provides a basis for longer-term relationships between the firm and customers, as the relationship is based on real-time data and proactive service.

> **Illustration 3.2 IoT Applications in Healthcare**
>
> The IoT has had a significant impact on healthcare by allowing medical devices to communicate autonomously and collect and transmit data on personal health to medical service providers. The potential of IoT technologies can improve patient health outcomes, optimise the use of resources and transform healthcare delivery into a more personalised approach, as evidenced by the following applications:
>
> - *Onsite monitoring systems*—the IoT can track patients and healthcare staff through wearable devices, radio-frequency identification (RFID) tags or smartphone apps, allowing the real-time monitoring of patient conditions and movements, and thus improving emergency response times. Medical assets and equipment can be tracked, which allows medical providers to monitor device location, usage and maintenance requirements. IoT devices can monitor the environment in healthcare facilities by using sensors to track temperature, humidity, air quality and occupancy, ensuring that patients are in a comfortable and safe environment.
> - *Remote patient monitoring*—IoT devices such as wearables and sensors can be used to remotely monitor patient health conditions, collect health data and allow virtual consultations with health professionals. This enables healthcare to be delivered in remote areas and allows patients with limited mobility to receive the required healthcare from the comfort of their own homes. Wearable devices can track health parameters such as heart rate, blood pressure and glucose levels, which allow healthcare providers to assess patient conditions, amend treatment plans and provide guidance without the need to visit healthcare facilities.
>
> These applications have the potential to significantly reduce healthcare costs by automating routine tasks and reducing the need for expensive healthcare professional interventions. IoT technologies can also automate many administrative processes, which can further reduce costs. The continuous monitoring capabilities of IoT in healthcare should lead to early detection of health conditions, avert costly medical procedures and thus lower healthcare

> expenses. Patients can also have greater control over their healthcare by being able to track their own health data and communicate directly with healthcare providers. However, there are considerable challenges with the IoT in healthcare, including issues around data privacy and security, the need for standardised protocols and regulations, and integration with existing systems.
>
> Source: Li, C., Wang, J., Wang, S., and Zhang, Y., 2024. A review of IoT applications in healthcare. *Neurocomputing*, 565, p. 127,017.

3.7 How the IoT Transforms Supply Chains

Firms have been investing in the application of digital technologies such as GPS tracking, RFID and cloud technologies to digitise their supply chains to enhance visibility and transparency [12]. These firms have recognised the importance of information sharing in areas such as consumer purchases, inventory levels and warehousing capacity between supply chain members as a source of competitive differentiation.

The IoT has allowed firms to access and analyse a vast array of data from companies and devices across the supply chain to make more informed decisions. For example, typical types of data for a manufacturer in a retail supply chain can include the following [13]:

- *Internal data* include deliveries to retailers, prices, discounts, promotions and various product characteristics.
- *Consumer demand* is accessible via point-of-sale systems in the retailer or provided by consultancy firms such as Nielsen.
- *Macro-economic information* includes data that explain consumer behaviour, seasonality and trends, including GDP levels, Purchasing Managers' Indices, unemployment rates, inflation rates, etc.
- *External data* are on other factors that can influence demand, such as web searches, social media mentions of products, weather conditions, holidays and competitor prices.

The *operational efficiency* and *responsiveness* view of supply chain strategy is a useful framework for highlighting the transformational impact of the IoT in supply chains [14]. The IoT can play an important role in each of these strategies by providing better visibility and transparency in the supply chain, as outlined below.

3.7.1 An Operational Efficiency Supply Chain Strategy

This involves reducing costs across the supply chain, basing manufacturing decisions on long-term forecasts, and locating end products close to customer demand [15]. Functional products, such as basic foodstuffs and household consumables, are often associated with operational efficiency-focused supply chains. These products have long product life cycles and low product variety, and therefore stable and predictable demand. They tend to have stable, long-established supply chains and low complexity in manufacture, resulting in low supply uncertainty. The IoT can positively impact these supply chains in the following ways:

- The IoT can reduce supply chain costs and improve sustainability through tracking and optimising energy use in factories, warehouses and transportation fleets.
- Although in-store inventory and service levels may indicate that the supply chain is running smoothly, shipment tracking data provided by the IoT may highlight that lead times are likely to increase and service levels decline [16].
- Firms are integrating IoT-enabled GPS trackers into their operations to track assets and prevent theft, which allows them to respond more quickly to disruptions in the supply chain.
- Logistics companies such as DHL, Maersk and UPS, and have been using the IoT to optimise distribution routes, monitor driver behaviour and reduce fuel costs across the supply chain.

3.7.2 A Responsiveness Supply Chain Strategy

This strategy involves competing on time-to-market, rapidly meeting customer demand, and eliminating stock-outs. Manufacturing is driven by actual customer demand rather than forecasts; products can be customised and speed is more important than cost in supply chain decisions. Innovative products, such as fashion products and customised products, are often associated with responsiveness-focused supply chains. These supply chains have shorter product life cycles and high variety, and therefore, unstable and unpredictable demand. The IoT can positively impact these supply chains in the following ways:

- Rather than relying on an inaccurate forecast, real-time tracking and monitoring of actual customer purchases in the retailer via the IoT mean these data can be shared with suppliers to give them better visibility of future demand and reduce amplified demand fluctuations, sometimes referred to as the bullwhip effect.
- IoT data from sensors and connected devices can help firms better predict demand, manage inventory and reduce waste. For example, soft drink firms can analyse data from vending machines and refrigerators to monitor performance metrics for inventory levels and predict demand for specific product options over different time periods.

3.8 The IoT and Servitised Business Models

Servitisation refers to the process of creating value by adding services to products and developing service-oriented business models in a manufacturing context [17]. The trend towards servitisation has largely been driven by the view that offering services with products will allow firms to avoid competing on price, develop customer relationships based on differentiation and, in some cases, create new revenue streams for the services provided [18].

A commonly cited exemplar of servitisation is the case of Rolls-Royce, which altered its business model from selling aircraft engines to power-by-hour service contracts. Customers purchase hours of flying capabilities instead of engines, whilst Rolls-Royce provides support services such as maintenance and spare parts provision to ensure the engines continuously run smoothly.

Proponents of the servitisation concept have increasingly embraced the capabilities of the IoT to further extend the services bundled as part of the customer value proposition. The IoT provides valuable product usage and process data that can be used to differentiate manufacturers from their competitors. Analysis of product usage and process data is a critical element of the capabilities required by manufacturers for servitisation. The IoT can improve a manufacturer's knowledge of customer behaviour in specific contexts and thus lead to a more informed understanding of customer needs. Linking servitisation with the IoT has led to changes in business models, such as the trend away from ownership to non-ownership business models. IoT-enabled servitised business models can be categorised as follows [19].

3.8.1 The Add-On Business Model

The add-on business model involves employing the IoT to enable additional product functions or adding personalised services to the physical product or service. One example is the development of wearable technologies, such as the Apple Watch, which monitors the health and fitness activity of individuals. These technologies can transmit health and fitness data to a smartphone, which in turn allows the individual to monitor their training activity and perform health analysis in a way that was not accessible prior to the development of these devices. A further example is when firms analyse customer data to offer more customised services or provide integrated product and service offerings to the customer.

3.8.2 The Sharing Business Model

The sharing business model involves customers paying to use or access a product for a limited time period, and this allows other customers to use the product when it becomes available. This business model enables the provider to increase asset utilisation, whilst at the same time being responsible for ensuring that sufficient products are available for customer use. Although the sharing business model is similar to renting, there tend to be shorter periods of use and frequent changes of ownership, as illustrated by comparing car rental and car sharing schemes. For example, car sharing schemes allow the car to be recycled amongst customers without needing to be returned to the provider after use. Digital technologies eliminate the need for booking, enable more accurate usage and payment mechanisms, and facilitate the tracing of product use.

3.8.3 The Usage-Based Business Model

The usage-based model is based on the amount of product usage and allows customers to either pay for or subscribe based on their actual usage and needs. Under a pay-per-use arrangement, the customer is charged for actual usage of the product or service, with the provider employing IoT to monitor and measure product usage. Under a subscription arrangement, the customer is charged for unlimited access to the product or service, which is restricted by the subscription time period. Therefore, the customer will have to pay a fee for access to the product or service.

3.8.4 The Solution-Oriented Business Model

This business model employs the IoT to provide solutions to customer needs and can be categorised into the following:

- *Availability*—in this business model, providers offer customers continuous, uninterrupted usage of products that provide a specified function. The provider is responsible for maintenance and support to ensure that the product delivers the promised level of service without interruption during the contract.
- *Optimisation*—in this business model, the provider employs the IoT to monitor the current usage of the product and analyse usage patterns to offer solutions such as optimising equipment usage. The provider is not only ensuring the availability of the product but also improving the customer's operations.

3.9 Privacy and Security Implications Around the IoT

There are significant concerns for firms and consumers regarding the implications of the IoT for data privacy and security. In many instances, there is a vast array of data flowing around IoT devices and applications, with individuals sharing data with firms both directly and indirectly. The IoT is increasingly generating enormous amounts of personal data on households, health and financial status. These developments have highlighted the importance of firms considering privacy as a key concern.

There is an onus on firms to put in place security mechanisms to protect data privacy, something which has been lacking in many IoT-based services. The potential cybersecurity threat is likely to increase as a growing number of connected devices are added to IoT networks. The IoT is vulnerable to malicious cyber threats for the following reasons [20]:

- The IoT does not have well-defined perimeters.
- The IoT is highly dynamic and diverse.
- The IoT is continuously changing because of mobility and therefore cannot be given the same protection put in place for an internal digital infrastructure within the firm.

- The proliferation of IoT services means that traditional human-driven security solutions cannot meet the security demands, as security analysts or service users are unable to carry out the required security activities quickly enough. These activities include approving the granting of permissions to IoT devices and establishing access control policies.

Many firms recognise the importance of dealing with cybersecurity threats in the context of the IoT, as privacy and security concerns are creating resistance to the adoption of IoT by firms and individuals. Some firms have been putting in place training for application developers to integrate security mechanisms, such as firewalls, into products and encouraging individuals to use security features built into devices. Governments have also been addressing privacy and security concerns through enacting legislation, as highlighted in the case below.

> **Illustration 3.3 The IoT and Regulation in the UK and EU**
>
> Legislators in the UK and EU have enacted legislation to ensure makers of IoT devices prevent cyberattacks on individuals. This legislation has been prompted by concerns that customers are vulnerable to eavesdroppers and hackers as a result of firms not doing enough to protect customer data. In the case of the UK, the law forces firms to explicitly state how they will provide security updates for customers when they purchase the product. Whilst firms such as Amazon, Apple and Google often provide years of software updates for their smart phones or other devices, many manufacturers do not give a commitment at the time of purchase regarding how long they will provide support to customers. Under the law, manufacturers are also required to deliver devices to customers with unique passwords so hackers cannot take advantage of customers who fail to change default login details.
>
> The EU has enacted legislation that imposes heavy fines if firms do not meet rules regarding the prevention of cyberattacks. For example, firms are required to obtain mandatory certificates that demonstrate they are meeting the basic requirements of cyber safety, which minimise the risk of attacks. Failure to comply could lead to a fine of up to 2.5% of the previous year's annual turnover, as well as the recall or banning of products that are not compliant. IoT firms are also required to inform authorities and customers about cyberattacks and ensure they have practices in place for quick fixes. One of the reasons for the legislation was based on research that found previously detected breaches had not been fixed by the firms involved. Where firms fail to comply with the new legislation, they will not be granted access to the EU market.
>
> Sources: Espinoza, J. (2022, Sep 09). EU targets 'internet of things' product makers: Technology. *Financial Times*. Retrieved from https://www.proquest.com/newspapers/eu-targets-internet-things-product-makers/docview/2722746839/se-2; and Bradshaw, T. (2020, Jan 28). UK targets 'internet of things' security: Technology. *Financial Times*. Retrieved from https://www.proquest.com/newspapers/uk-targets-internet-things-security/docview/2365976375/se-2

3.10 Challenges Around Implementing the IoT

Although the IoT offers considerable benefits to firms, there are potential implementation challenges, as outlined below:

- *Privacy and security*—many firms struggle to fully consider the regulatory implications around data storage and sharing with third parties. These risks are further amplified when data on individuals are combined with data generated from other devices and third parties to provide detailed insights into an individual's behaviour. Moreover, data security risks, such as hacking, can increase due to the high number of devices connected across a network.
- *Lack of trust with data sharing*—where a firm is integrating devices from a number of other firms, there may be a lack of willingness to share data. For example, this is a common problem in retail supply chains, where some suppliers may not be willing to share data with retailers due to a lack of trust and concerns about who the data will be shared with.
- *Technical*—connecting devices together securely and efficiently can be challenging, as there may be a lack of interoperability and compatibility of systems across the network. Existing internal systems often have to be adapted to allow for the management and addition of devices across the network.
- *Changes in business models*—firms often must implement new business models to take advantage of the benefits of IoT [21]. For example, the move towards usage-based business models associated with the IoT is a significant challenge for employees in some firms that have been more accustomed to operating in product-based selling environments.
- *Skills development*—firms face the challenge of having to develop and acquire new skills in managing data in an IoT environment [22]. The large amount of data generated by the IoT means firms have to develop new capabilities to analyse these data to provide greater value to customers than before.
- *Initial investment*—the IoT can require a significant initial investment in technical infrastructure, involving a range of sensing and actuating devices and changes to existing systems. This can be a key inhibitor for some firms, particularly when the return on investment spans a long time period and thus involves an increased payback period [23].

3.11 A Framework for Implementing the IoT in Digital Transformation

This section presents a framework outlining the key issues that firms should consider when implementing IoT in digital transformation, as shown in Fig. 3.1.

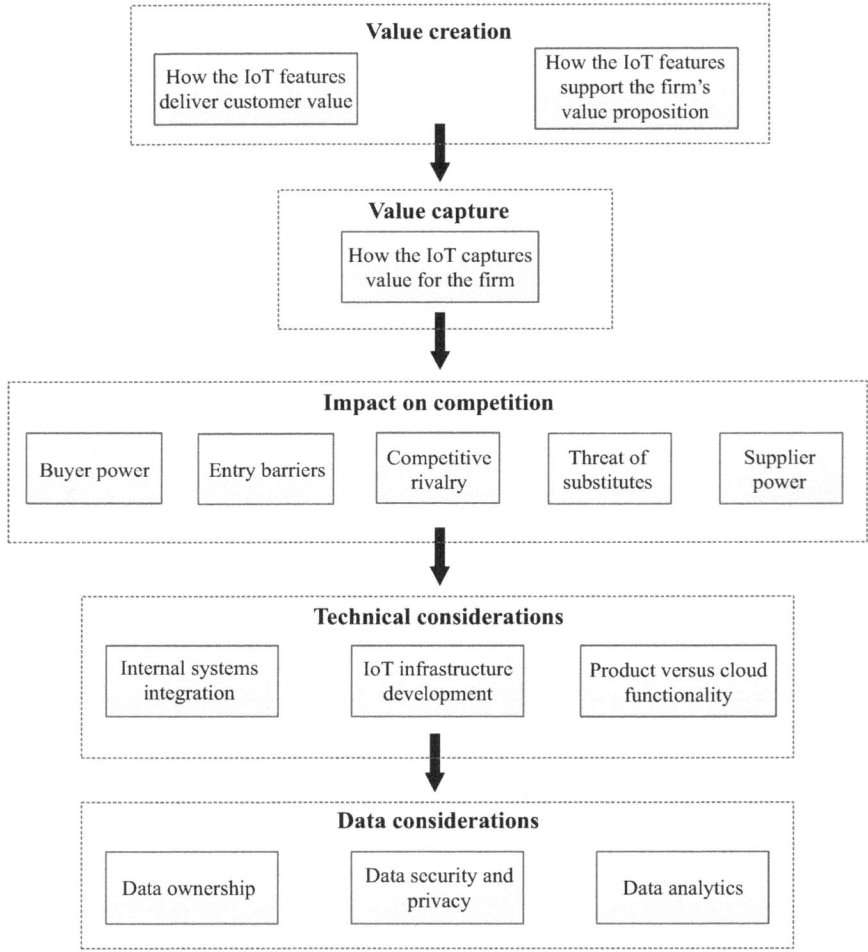

Fig. 3.1 A framework for implementing the IoT in digital transformation

3.11.1 How the IoT Creates Value for Customers

There has been a lot of hype around the potential benefits of the IoT for both firms and consumers alike, yet some firms have not achieved the desired benefits despite the investment involved. Firms have added IoT-enabled features to their products that customers do not value and are unwilling to pay an additional price for. Therefore, firms need to determine how IoT-enabled functions and capabilities create value for customers. The following issues should be considered here:

- *How the IoT features deliver customer value*—the firm has to determine the features that will deliver real value for customers, whether customers view these features as a source of value and whether they are willing to pay a price premium [24]. The integration of software functions into the product means that firms can incorporate more targeted and personalised functions into the product for the customer whilst the product is in use. For example, car makers can update and add functions to the vehicle's software system through over-the-air technology, which can enhance the driving experience for the owner in real time via the IoT. The firm can also consider how it can target customer segments under different scenarios to better meet the needs of customers. Personalisation through software functions allows firms to provide different solutions to different segments of customers. This development can potentially go further by meeting the specific needs of a customer in a particular scenario and offering services customised to their specific needs.
- *How the IoT features support the firm's value proposition*—a firm should integrate features that support its current value proposition for customers. Where a firm is competing at the premium level of the market through differentiation and superior customer service, it may add a range of features that reinforce this position. Alternatively, where a firm is at the lower end of a market, it may add only basic features, as customers do not view them as a source of differentiation and are not willing to pay a price premium. Additionally, these features may be costly to implement.

3.11.2 How the IoT Captures Value for the Firm

This involves considering the likely value that the IoT is going to capture for the firm. Table 3.2 summarises the potential benefits that

Table 3.2 Potential benefits of the IoT for firms [25]

Benefits	Description
Generate additional revenue	Firms offer additional features to their current products or services and generate additional revenue from these services
Generate ongoing income	Generate income more steadily as longer-term contracts replace sales
Reduce operational costs	The IoT allows firms to reduce resources used in creating the services including labour costs. For example, fault diagnosis can be undertaken remotely and, in some cases, can be automated
Maintain longer-term relationship	The IoT technology allows firms to develop long-term solutions and create significant value for customers, which can lead to a deep relationship between customers and firms
Extend current business	The integration of the IoT technology allows firms to extend their portfolio of products and services, and in turn extend their current business
Improve product-service offering	The IoT can be used to improve current services through, for example, what is viewed to be more convenient for the customer
Increase resource utilisation	Firms can improve their resource utilisation as the IoT allows them to obtain insights into product usage behaviour and resource usage rates
Gain competitive advantage	Firms potentially gain competitive advantage from the IoT-enabled services through integrating technology with the product-service offering that competitors find difficult to imitate

the IoT can deliver for firms. Of course, it is unlikely that firms will obtain all these benefits when implementing the IoT, and it is likely to depend on the business model. In the case of a solution-oriented business model, the key benefits are likely to focus on maintaining a longer-term relationship with the customer and improving the product and service offering.

For example, the IoT allows products to be optimised and improved whilst in use and maintains an ongoing relationship with the customer-owner throughout the life of the product. Firms can continually interact with the product and owner and get usage data in real time. Through employing digital technologies such as AI and data analytics, firms can obtain valuable insights from user data that allow them to improve products and services.

3.11.3 How the IoT Impacts competition

A firm needs to consider the implications of the IoT for the five forces that influence competition, including the bargaining power of buyers, the threat of new entrants, rivalry amongst existing competitors, the threat of substitute products and services, and the bargaining power of suppliers. The strength of these forces can affect the profitability of firms and can also be influenced by digital technologies. For example, the introduction of online channels has allowed new entrants to enter many retail markets and adversely affect the profitability of existing players in these markets. The five competitive forces are also useful for a firm when examining the implications of the IoT on competition. Clearly, a firm should consider how it can employ the IoT to strengthen its competitive position along each of the five forces, as outlined below.

- *Buyer power*—the IoT can reduce buyer power by allowing the firm to differentiate its product offering from competitors and potentially shift competition away from price [26]. Through collecting and analysing customer data, the firm can both extend the warranty service offering whilst simultaneously customising the product to better meet the needs of customers. This should enable the firm to develop a closer, longer-term relationship with the customer and lock the customer into the relationship, thereby reducing buyer power.
- *Entry barriers*—firms need to consider the impact of employing the IoT on barriers to entry. In some instances, a firm may have to make a considerable investment to deploy the IoT effectively. It is possible that these required investments in product design and IT infrastructure may prove to be a significant barrier for other firms entering the marketplace, thus limiting the threat to the firm's competitive position. Timing of entry can be particularly relevant in this instance. Where a firm is one of the first to introduce the IoT, it may gain a first-mover advantage and also develop network effects, which can deter competitors from entering the market. Furthermore, a broader range of services on offer, where the product is directly connected to other services, has the advantage of locking the customer into a stronger relationship with the firm whilst at the same time increasing entry barriers for potential competitors.
- *Competitive rivalry*—employing the IoT has the potential to reduce competitive rivalry by offering firms opportunities for product and service differentiation and providing additional related services. For example,

some firms producing medical devices, such as pacemakers and insulin pumps, have augmented their product offerings with health monitoring services, such as allowing doctors to monitor patient health remotely. Complementing a product with value-added services provides a clear means of promoting the long-term value of a product over competitors.
- *Threat of substitutes*—the IoT can allow a firm to offer superior services to its existing products, which can reduce the threat of substitution. However, some products may be at risk of substitution by products with additional capabilities driven by the introduction of the IoT. For example, smartphones have increasingly added fitness-related apps, which have substituted many of the capabilities of wearable devices. A further substitute threat can arise from innovations in business models and the shift away from ownership to sharing-based business models. For instance, the trend toward sharing and usage-based business models has affected the overall demand for products such as cars and bicycles. These business models can also serve as substitutes for other types of transport, such as rail and bus services.
- *Supplier power*—a firm also has to consider the increasing use of the IoT in its products and how it can bring new suppliers into the market. The IoT can introduce new suppliers in areas such as software, data analytics, cloud computing and sensor technologies, and these can affect the balance of supplier power. For example, with the increasing use of the IoT in the car industry, car makers have to consider the power of suppliers such as Google, who have strong brands and considerable resources available to them.

3.11.4 Technical Considerations

The following technical issues should be considered when implementing the IoT:

Internal systems integration. The IoT implementation should be integrated with any internal systems to ensure the smooth and secure flow of data. This may involve employing application programming interfaces to establish communication protocols between IoT devices and internal systems. Implementing the IoT has implications for the technology infrastructure of a firm and will involve adapting hardware, software applications, and the operating system embedded in the product itself [27].

IoT infrastructure development. In some instances, IoT implementation may also involve building and supporting a new technology infrastructure that requires significant investment and developing a new set of skills in areas

Table 3.3 Common elements of the IoT technology infrastructure [28]

Element
Adapted hardware, software applications and an operating system embedded into the product
Network communications to support connectivity
Product cloud, the software running on the firm or a third-party server, containing the product database. This should allow aggregation, normalisation and management of real-time and historical product data
A platform for developing software applications that allows the rapid creation of smart, connected business applications using data access and visualisation tools
A rules engine and analytics platform including analytical capabilities to populate the algorithms involved in the operation of the product and obtain new product insights
Smart product applications that are not embedded in the product, running on remote servers that monitor, control and optimise the functions of the product

such as software development, data analytics and cybersecurity expertise. Table 3.3 summarises some of the common elements of an IoT infrastructure.

Product versus cloud functionality. A firm has to decide on the IoT technology and associated functionality that should be included in the product, in the cloud or in both. Integrating functionality into the product is appropriate in the following instances [29]:

- It is likely to be more appropriate where there is a need for a quick response time, such as when critical equipment breaks down and there is a need for a rapid response.
- Integrating IoT into the product means that there is less dependence on network reliability and the amount of data that must flow from the product to the cloud, thus lowering the risk of sensitive data being compromised.

Integrating more functionality into the cloud is appropriate in the following instances:

- When there is a need for product changes and upgrades, these can be done automatically.
- Where the product interface is complex, requiring frequent updates and changes, locating the interface in the cloud allows improvements to be made on a continuous basis.
- Finally, where products are located in remote or hazardous locations, locating functionality in the cloud can reduce the dangers and costs of operating the product.

3.11.5 Data Considerations

There are a number of issues that firms should consider regarding data in the IoT.

- *Data ownership*—the issue of data ownership can be a complex issue for firms. When using IoT-enabled devices, data are often generated by the actions of the user and could be considered to be their property. However, the manufacturer of the product could claim ownership of the data, as the data are collected and analysed on the servers and applications of the manufacturer or another third party. Therefore, there are a number of potential options, including firms obtaining outright ownership of the data or seeking joint ownership. There are also various levels of usage rights, including non-disclosure agreements, the right to share the data, or the right to sell it. As the IoT increases in prominence across a range of application areas, there is often no strict set of guidelines for data ownership, but only a range of caveats and considerations specific to different business sectors [30].
- *Data security and privacy* and privacy —this involves implementing robust encryption protocols to ensure data integrity between the IoT devices, the cloud and internal technology infrastructure. Unauthorised access should be prevented through device authentication and access control mechanisms. A firm should also consider the privacy and security risks for each type of data and the associated cost. Where the firm is collecting less-sensitive data, there are likely to be lower risks for breaches and transmission disruptions. Alternatively, where security requirements are high, a firm will have to put mechanisms in place to protect the data and limit transmission risk by storing data in the product itself. These mechanisms should be monitored on a continuous basis to mitigate any potential cybersecurity threats. Also, consideration should be given to any relevant legislation around IoT implementations to protect customer data.
- *Data analytics*—there should be mechanisms in place for gathering, storing and managing large volumes of data generated by IoT devices. This will serve as a basis for deploying data analytics tools to obtain insights from the data in areas such as customer behaviour, performance optimisation and predictive maintenance. These issues are considered in more detail in Chapter 5: Managing Data for Business Value in Digital Transformation.

Discussion Questions

1. Referring to the case of the smart inhaler and the power of the IoT in Sect. 3.2, select a product with IoT capabilities that you are familiar with and analyse how it develops *multi-dimensional connectivity*, *converts data into a strategic resource* and *develops a multi-dimensional and dynamic understanding of the customer*.
2. Referring to Sect. 3.4, select a product with IoT capabilities and outline how it has *connecting*, *collecting*, *monitoring*, *optimising* and *autonomising* capabilities.
3. Referring to Sect. 3.11.1, select a product with IoT capabilities and outline the way in which it creates value for customers and captures value for the firm.
4. Select a product with IoT capabilities, highlight the privacy and security risks associated with its data and outline practices that should be implemented to mitigate these risks.
5. Select a product with IoT capabilities and assess how it impacts the industry's competitive forces of buyer power, supplier power, rivalry, threat of substitutes and entry barriers.

References

1. Subramaniam, M. (2022). How smart products create connected customers. *MIT Sloan Management Review, 64*(1), 33–37.
2. Kantar. 2020. *Oxford Said Business School, Haier, IoT Ecosystem Brand White Paper, September 20*. www.sbs.ox.ac.uk/sites/default/files/2020-09/IoT%20Ecosystem%20Brand%20White%20Paper_0.pdf
3. Porter, M. E., & Heppelmann, J. E. (2014). How smart, connected products are transforming competition. *Harvard Business Review, 92*(11), 64–88.
4. Lee, I., & Lee, K. (2015). The Internet of Things (IoT): Applications, investments, and challenges for enterprises. *Business Horizons, 58*(4), 431–440.
5. See Porter and Heppelmann (2014) in reference 3 above.
6. Suppatvech, C., Godsell, J., & Day, S. (2019). The roles of internet of things technology in enabling servitised business models: A systematic literature review. *Industrial Marketing Management, 82*, 70–86.
7. Bilgeri, D., Fleisch, E., Gebauer, H., & Wortmann, F. (2019). Driving process innovation with IoT field data. *MIS Quarterly Executive, 18*(3), 191–207.
8. Bouguettaya, A., Sheng, Q. Z., Benatallah, B., Neiat, A. G., Mistry, S., Ghose, A., Nepal, S., & Yao, L. (2021). An internet of things service roadmap. *Communications of the ACM, 64*(9), 86–95.
9. See Bouguettaya et al. (2021) in reference 8 above.
10. See Kantar (2020) in reference 2 above.

11. Saarikko, T., Westergren, U. H., & Blomquist, T. (2017). The Internet of Things: Are you ready for what's coming? *Business Horizons, 60*(5), 667–676.
12. Attaran, M., 2020, July. Digital technology enablers and their implications for supply chain management. In *Supply Chain Forum: An International Journal 21*(3), 158–172.
13. Simchi-Levi, D., & Timmermans, K. (2021). A simpler way to modernize your supply chain. *Harvard Business Review, 99*(5), 133–141.
14. Fisher, M. (1997, March/April) What is the right supply chain for your product? *Harvard Business Review, 75*(2), 105-116.
15. See Fisher (1997) in reference 14 above and Lee, H. L. (2002). Aligning supply chain strategies with product uncertainties. *California Management Review, 44*(3), 105–119.
16. See Simchi-Levi and Timmermans (2021) in reference 13 above.
17. Raddats, C., Kowalkowski, C., Benedettini, O., Burton, J., & Gebauer, H. (2019). Servitization: A contemporary thematic review of four major research streams. *Industrial Marketing Management, March*, 1–17 and Baines, T., Lightfoot, H. W., Benedettini, O., & Kay, J. M. (2009). The servitization of manufacturing: A review of literature and reflection on future challenges. *Journal of Manufacturing Technology Management, 20*(5), 547–567.
18. Paiola, M., & Gebauer, H. (2020). Internet of things technologies, digital servitization and business model innovation in BtoB manufacturing firms. *Industrial Marketing Management, 89*, 245–264.
19. See Suppatvech et al. (2019) in reference 6 above.
20. See Bouguettaya et al. (2021) in reference 8 above.
21. See Suppatvech et al. (2019) in reference 6 above.
22. See Suppatvech et al. (2019) in reference 6 above.
23. Kamble, S. S., Gunasekaran, A., Parekh, H., & Joshi, S. (2019). Modelling the internet of things adoption barriers in food retail supply chains. *Journal of Retailing and Consumer Services, 48*, 154–168.
24. See Porter and Heppelmann (2014) in reference 3 above.
25. See Suppatvech et al. (2019) in reference 6 above.
26. See Porter and Heppelmann (2014) in reference 3 above.
27. Mohelska, H., & Sokolova, M. (2016). Smart, connected products change a company's business strategy orientation. *Applied Economics, 48*(47), 4502–4509.
28. See Mohelska and Sokolova (2016) in reference 27 above.
29. See Porter and Heppelmann (2014) in reference 3 above.
30. See Saarikko et al. (2017) in reference 11 above.

4

Artificial Intelligence in Digital Transformation: Capabilities, Risks and Ethics

4.1 Introduction

Artificial intelligence (AI) continues to extend its capabilities and scope across a range of fields, including law, medicine, media, retail and manufacturing. The advent of generative AI applications, such as ChatGPT, offers the capability to create new content, including music, speech, text, images and video. These applications have been used to write software code, transcribe interactions between doctors and their patients and allow customers to interact with customer relationship management systems [1]. Although these AI capabilities offer significant potential for firms to improve business performance, many managers have struggled to understand the issues surrounding the use of AI technologies in their businesses.

Employing AI involves challenges from business, technical and ethical standpoints. Business and technical challenges include managing the interaction between humans and AI models, as well as overcoming issues of user trust, security and safety. For example, the risk of harm is much lower when AI offers advice on the steps involved in a cooking recipe, in contrast to when it provides an incorrect medical diagnosis to a patient. Moreover, many of the challenges associated with AI are ethical in nature, including those related to employees and customers around privacy, fairness, discrimination, bias and surveillance [2]. Firms often prioritise technical and business issues when implementing AI and fail to pay sufficient attention to ethical issues. The aim of this chapter is to understand the business, technical and ethical issues involved in implementing AI in the context of digital transformation.

> **Learning Outcomes**
>
> - Understand AI types and technologies based on intelligence, technology and function.
> - Understand machine-learning and fixed and adaptive algorithms.
> - Understand how AI capabilities can enhance business performance.
> - Understand how AI impacts product and process capabilities.
> - Understand the risks of AI implementation.
> - Understand the practices required for effectively integrating business, ethics and technical issues into AI implementation.

4.2 AI Overview

AI simulates human intelligence through the use of algorithms, data and digital technologies. It allows software or machines to perform tasks that normally require human intelligence, including reasoning, problem-solving, learning, perception and language understanding. AI models are trained on huge amounts of data to learn to identify patterns so that they can perform tasks such as predicting whether a customer will buy a product or whether a product is likely to break down. AI models can take a set of data inputs, perform calculations and create a set of outputs. For example, a loan application can take data from a loan applicant, including earnings, outgoings and age, and produce a decision on loan approval. AI models can also take input data such as CVs, criminal records and medical symptoms from individuals, and make judgements on their interview suitability, risk of reoffending and medical conditions.

AI can be categorised on the basis of intelligence level, technology and function, as outlined below:

Intelligence level

- *Artificial narrow intelligence*—it can perform a specific task in much the same way as a human can. Examples include Amazon's Alexa and Apple's Siri, which can understand the human voice and act accordingly. ChatGPT is considered an example of narrow intelligence, as it is limited to the single task of text-based chat.
- *Artificial general intelligence*—these AI models possess human-level intelligence and exhibit characteristics of adaptability, learning and reasoning. Applications at this intelligence level are hypothetical, and achieving this intelligence level poses ongoing challenges in the field of AI research.

- *Artificial super intelligence*—once artificial general intelligence is achieved, the next stage could involve artificial super intelligence, which exceeds the cognitive performance of humans in all domains of interest. This intelligence is self-aware and conscious and could potentially make humans redundant.

Figure 4.1 illustrates potential scenarios surrounding these intelligence levels in the case of Apple's Siri.

Technology. A further category of AI is based on the technology employed to drive the AI model. These technologies include machine learning, deep learning, neural networks, natural language processing, rule-based expert systems, robotic process automation and robots. Table 4.1 provides an overview of these, along with application areas.

Function. These are a type of AI based on function and include the following [5]:

- *Conversational AI* refers to the ability of AI models to understand and respond using natural human language, including both voice—and text-based technologies. Examples include chatbots or virtual agents that users can interact with.
- *Biometric AI* employs tools to measure a person's physiological traits including fingerprints, retinas and facial image, and behavioural traits including signature, voice and keystroke rhythms. An example is facial or fingerprint recognition technology that gives a user access to a smartphone.

Artificial narrow intelligence

Weak, below human-level AI
- AI applications in specific areas
- Unable to autonomously solve problems in other areas
- Outperforms humans in specific areas

Siri can recognise a person's voice, but cannot perform other tasks such as driving a car.

Artificial general intelligence

Strong human-level AI
- AI applications in several areas
- Able to autonomously solve problems in other areas
- Outperforms humans in several areas

Siri evolves into a robot with a range of capabilities including voice recognition, writing and diagnostic problem solving

Artificial super intelligence

Self-aware, above human-level AI
- AI applications in any area
- Able to solve problems in other areas automatically
- Outperforms humans in all areas

Siri has super human capabilities such as solving complex mathematical problems or writing a best selling song

Fig. 4.1 Levels of AI [3]

Table 4.1 AI technologies and application areas [4]

Technology	Description	Application area
Machine learning	Learns from experience. Learns from a set of training data. Detects patterns in data that are not labelled and its result is not known.	Highly granular marketing analysis of sales data.
Deep learning	A type of machine learning that learns without human supervision, drawing from data that are both labelled and unlabelled.	Image and voice recognition, self-driving cars.
Neural networks	Algorithms that attempt to recognise relationships in a dataset through a process that replicates the way the human brain works.	Credit and loan application assessments.
Natural language processing	A system that is able to understand human written or spoken language.	Speech recognition, text analysis, translation and generation.
Rule-based expert systems	A set of logical rules developed from the reasoning of human experts.	Insurance underwriting and credit approval.
Robotic process automation	Systems that automate structured digital tasks and interfaces.	Credit card replacement, validating online credentials.
Robots	Automatically operated machines that automate physical tasks and manipulate objects.	Manufacturing and warehousing tasks.

- *Algorithmic AI* is based on machine-learning algorithms that can be trained on structured data and are specific to narrow task applications, such as speech recognition and image classification.
- *Robotic AI* allows robots to move beyond automation to tackle more complex tasks, such as the ability to sense their environment, act and learn. An example is an AI-enabled robot vacuum cleaner that has cameras to detect and measure the distance between objects in real time to avoid obstacles.

> **Illustration 4.1 AI and the Case of Google Search**
>
> Google Search provides a useful illustration of how AI works. When a user starts to type a few letters into the Google Search box, an algorithm can dynamically predict the full search term based on the terms that many users have typed previously and on the user's previous actions. These predictions are captured in a drop-down menu, referred to as the autosuggest box, which helps the user quickly zone in on a relevant search. Each keystroke and click is captured as a data point, and each data point is used to improve predictions for future searches.
>
> AI can generate organic search results, which are drawn from a previously assembled index from the internet and then optimised according to the clicks generated on the results of previous searches. The entry of the term also starts an automated auction for adverts that are most relevant to the user's search. Any click on or away from the search query or search results page provides valuable data for Google. The more the searches, the better the predictions, and the better the predictions, the more the search engine is used.
>
> Source: Iansiti, M., and Lakhani, K.R., 2020. Competing in the Age of AI: How Machine Intelligence Changes the Rules of business. *Harvard Business Review*, 98 (1), pp. 60–67.

4.3 Machine Learning

Machine learning is a branch of AI that involves developing algorithms to interpret, process and analyse data to solve business problems. These algorithms can extract new knowledge from enormous quantities of data, making advanced or deep machine learning the key component of contemporary AI systems. Deep machine learning augments the system's ability to solve more complex problems more efficiently and increases the accuracy of recurring task solutions [6]. These algorithms are designed so that they learn and improve over time when they are exposed to new data. Machine-learning algorithms are the basis for facial and speech recognition, as well as virtual assistants such as Alexa and Siri. Machine-learning algorithms can be categorised into the following:

- *Supervised*—these algorithms are trained with labelled datasets, which allow the models to learn and develop more accurately over time. For example, an algorithm could be trained with pictures of dogs, all labelled by humans, and the machine would learn ways to identify pictures of dogs on its own. The algorithm incorporates data and other images to determine the required solution in advance.

- *Unsupervised*—in this case, the algorithm searches for patterns in unlabelled data such as newspaper articles or photos. Unsupervised machine learning can detect patterns or trends that people have not explicitly searched for. For example, it is possible to analyse online sales data to identify different segments of customers making purchases. In contrast to supervised learning, unsupervised learning does not set the required solution in advance. Unsupervised machine learning can classify unlabelled data on the fly, which allows results to be obtained and the system to improve over time without human involvement.
- *Reinforcement*—these models are trained through trial and error to prescribe an optimal course of action through a reward system. Reinforcement learning can train models to play games or train autonomous vehicles to drive by informing the machine when it has made the correct decisions.

4.4 Fixed and Adaptive Algorithms

When employing machine learning, firms need to decide whether they should lock the algorithm and update it periodically, sometimes referred to as a *fixed algorithm*, or whether the algorithm should continuously evolve in response to a changing environment, sometimes referred to as an *adaptive algorithm*. Each of these algorithms is now explained.

Fixed algorithms. These algorithms are typically well-trained on existing datasets and provide accurate results based on known data inputs. These types of algorithms have been widely approved by medical bodies, such as the Food and Drug Administration in the United States, as they consistently produce the same result each time the same input is applied and does not change [7]. The rationale for this approval is that medical bodies do not want to endorse medical treatments that change in ways they cannot understand. Therefore, these algorithms are prominent in environments where there is minimal variation in the data that influence the decision outcome.

Adaptive algorithms. These algorithms evolve as they do not require input from developers and can improve through learning from data during use. The need for an update in the software might only become evident after the device or software has been released. An adaptive algorithm could still update and learn from real-world experience. Adaptive algorithms are likely to be selected in environments with a high level of change, as the rules and patterns recognised by the model can become obsolete. As the real-world environment of live data shifts from the training environment, the model will become less effective. Therefore, adaptive algorithms can be regularly retrained to keep abreast of evolving and changing data.

Adaptive algorithms are likely to become more prominent in a medical context as more recent and accurate data have the potential to improve new treatment options. Machine-learning models can be trained on new datasets periodically and released at certain points with the approval of medical bodies.

4.5 How AI Capabilities Transform Business Performance

Traditionally, digital technologies have been employed to automate many business processes, such as order and payroll processing, by codifying largely repetitive tasks and eliminating the need for human involvement [8]. Firms have employed digital technologies to integrate and standardise many processes, which has also enhanced business decision-making through business intelligence and data analytics tools.

Although AI has been used to automate many business tasks, it is doing so in a different and more powerful way [9]. Conventional digital technologies largely automate tasks in a manner explicitly programmed by humans. For example, management information systems processed data in ways determined by humans. Early generations of AI were also rule-based applications, replicating the knowledge of an expert in a field such as machine fault diagnosis.

However, AI tools are now generating and making decisions not simply by following the rules laid out by humans, but in some cases acting autonomously and outperforming humans by controlling and learning from information in a range of domains. For example, Apple's Siri tool routinely makes autonomous decisions for users in a range of domains. These developments in AI have created the key capabilities of *autonomy* and *learning,* and each of these is now outlined.

- *Autonomy*—many AI tools have the capability to make autonomous decisions and operate without human intervention. Loan applications in banks can process loans, and medical applications can make diagnoses related to certain diseases without human involvement. As AI extends its reach to a wider range of fields, the decision between human and automation

involvement in tasks is blurring. For example, firms are employing AI tools in the new product development process to generate design ideas—time-consuming tasks traditionally performed by humans. Although AI is not replacing humans, it has become an integral part of supporting humans in the design process [10].
- *Learning*—many AI tools have a learning element developed through data analysis and experience. These learning capabilities have allowed AI to be applied in more complex contexts involving audio, speech and object recognition. Moreover, AI is no longer limited to accessing internal corporate data but can access data from a range of external sources outside the firm, including the cloud.

Autonomy and learning AI capabilities have led to the following developments for firms in the application of AI [11]:

- *Increasing in performance*—AI is creating higher performance levels across a wider range of tasks, driven by advances in technologies such as machine learning and cloud computing. These advances are allowing AI to be applied in a wider range of contexts, including medicine, engineering and energy.
- *Increasing in scope*—this refers to the increasing range of contexts to which AI is applied. At the same time, AI is being applied to more complex tasks. AI is being employed to select films to stream, search for internet content and control temperatures in the workplace and at home.

Illustration 4.2 The Increasing Performance and Scope of AI in the Circular Economy

As consumers become more conscious about shopping sustainably, firms have been employing AI to enhance their contribution to the circular economy, where firms recover or recycle resources used in the value chain. Barriers to the circular economy have included the low residual value of used products, an inability to collect materials, high costs of separating and processing materials, and poor traceability of products and materials being recycled. However, the increased performance and scope of AI mitigate some of these barriers and positively impact the following areas of the circular economy:

- *Material use reduction*—AI can help reduce the overall use of materials in products, particularly in product design, where almost 80% of the environmental impact of a product is determined. Generative design, enhanced by

AI, has contributed to sustainability in manufacturing by using AI algorithms to quickly analyse data and generate infinite design iterations that far exceed the capabilities of humans. This allows users to establish goals for product design, such as being lightweight or having cost limits, and the AI tool can then present the user with a range of options. For example, AI has been used in garment design to create mock-ups that generate less pre-customer waste from offcuts during the production process. This has led to almost zero waste in fabric, as opposed to 10–30% waste in the conventional design of garments.

- *Improved resource efficiency*—AI and real-time data access can improve the efficiency of production resources across business sectors. For example, in the agriculture sector, firms have been integrating and analysing data from weather stations, soil sensors and farm equipment, along with AI tools, to provide guidance on planting, irrigation and harvesting. This has allowed farmers to reduce water and fertiliser waste, improve crop yields and drive better use of resources. AI can also drive predictive maintenance by reducing waste from decommissioned equipment, lowering carbon emissions and improving resource efficiency.
- *Improved recycling process*—AI, along with robotics and computer vision, can enhance a firm's understanding of the breakdown of materials at the end of a product's life for identifying and sorting materials for recycling. These technologies allow waste management firms to scale recycling whilst monitoring material purity and optimising processes in real time. Firms can generate revenue from this recycling process by selling spare parts and offering repair services. Using more recycled materials can also improve 'materials security', which is important for industries that depend on rare minerals such as cobalt and lithium.
- *Better customer demand forecasting*—AI technologies can be employed to better predict actual customer demand in the supply chain. A major sustainability problem in supply chains is the overstocking of products, which is a particular issue in food supply chains, where the perishable nature of food items means there is a lot of waste. However, retailers have been employing AI technologies to better anticipate customer demand and the actual number of products they need, thus reducing waste and positively impacting their sustainability goals.

Source: Kumar, M. (2025, February 21). Monetising sustainability: how AI and data drive the circular economy. *Forbes*. Retrieved from https://www.forbes.com/councils/forbestechcouncil/2025/02/21/monetizing-sustainability-how-ai-and-data-drive-the-circular-economy/ and Lu, S., and Serafeim, G. (2023, June 12). How AI will accelerate the circular economy. *Harvard Business Review*. Retrieved from https://hbr.org/2023/06/how-ai-will-accelerate-the-circular-economy

4.6 How AI Transforms Process and Product Capabilities

AI has an important impact on firm capabilities, as shown in the framework in Fig. 4.2 [12]. This framework focuses on AI-enabled transformation at both the product and process levels. An AI-enabled *product* transformation involves adding intelligence to products, such as robotic lawnmowers that can adapt to their operating environments. An AI-enabled *process* transformation involves applying AI to historical purchasing data to detect patterns that predict future customer purchases, thus improving the accuracy of predictions and leading to better marketing decisions.

A further dimension of the framework involves considering whether these transformations destroy or enhance the capabilities of a firm. Transformations enabled by AI that make existing knowledge and skills obsolete can destroy capabilities at both the product and process levels, and this can have an impact at both the firm and industry levels. For example, at the product level, AI-enabled robots are replacing production and warehousing tasks by providing autonomous trucks for moving, loading and unloading products in production facilities.

Alternatively, transformations enabled by AI can enhance the capabilities, skills and knowledge of the firm. For example, AI applications can rapidly analyse data in drug-discovery processes, which enhances the capabilities of

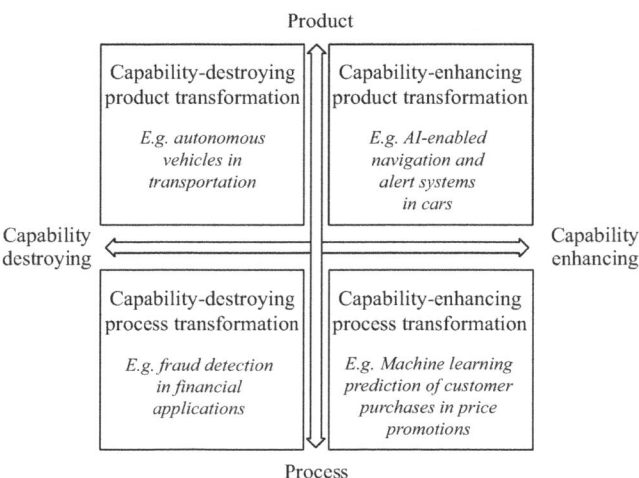

Fig. 4.2 The transformational impact of AI on firm capabilities [13]

a biochemist in interpreting the AI-generated data. In summary, capability-destroying transformations displace current skills and knowledge, whilst capability-enhancing transformations build upon and improve current capabilities.

Combining these two dimensions can provide managers with an understanding of how AI can lead to four different types of transformations at the product and process levels, as illustrated in the following examples:

- *Capability-enhancing process transformations*—these lead to improved process performance. For example, machine-learning models are transforming the marketing process through analysing images, deciphering text, segmenting customers and predicting how customers will react to promotions [14]. Machine learning already drives purchasing in online advertising, recommendation engines and purchase behaviour in customer relationship management systems.
- *Capability-enhancing product transformations*—in this case, AI creates capabilities that lead to transformations that improve product performance. These innovations can make some of the capabilities redundant for manufacturing the product, whilst not affecting other capabilities. Although automakers can integrate AI-enabled navigation and driver alert systems into the car to improve the driver experience, these innovations do not change the many other capabilities required to design and manufacture the car.
- *Capability-destroying process transformations*—these lead to a new way of performing the process and make existing capabilities in the process obsolete. For example, AI has led to the replacement of many finance tasks, such as fraud detection through the analysis of financial data. These transformations can radically alter the capabilities and technologies required to compete in an industry.
- *Capability-destroying product transformations*—these create a new product or act as a substitute for an existing product. For example, autonomous vehicles have the potential to destroy the capabilities of taxi drivers and other transport providers. Again, these types of innovations can radically change the capabilities required to compete in an industry.

This framework can be used to analyse how AI technologies are likely to impact products and processes in a firm, and, in turn, its current capabilities. This will also allow a firm to consider the risks and opportunities associated with implementing AI technologies. This could involve tracking whether AI technologies are likely to create value or destroy value in its current portfolio of products and processes within the industry, and, in turn, could influence AI technology investment decisions around certain products and services.

> **Illustration 4.3 How AI Is Transforming the Legal Profession**
>
> AI has increasingly been employed to perform a range of legal tasks, including scrutinising documents, due diligence, research and data analytics. Much of this involves extracting information from text documents and answering questions about their contents. Legal firms have been using generative AI tools to improve legal research and document review, and this has included contract analysis, due diligence and preparation for litigation.
>
> However, there are risks associated with applying AI in the legal field. For example, some AI tools can confidently express inaccurate information and may inadvertently process information that is subject to lawyer–client privilege. Despite these risks, AI is still likely to transform the legal profession in the following ways:
>
> - Firstly, it could reduce the people advantage that large law firms have, particularly in the case of complex lawsuits. These normally require legal associates to read large documents to respond to queries from senior lawyers. AI now allows smaller law firms to upload these documents into tools that can perform many of these queries.
> - Secondly, AI could potentially change the revenue model for some legal services, as AI can automate tasks currently undertaken by large numbers of junior lawyers. Some legal services may have to be charged on a flat fee based on the service provided, rather than on billable hours spent delivering it.
> - Thirdly, in the longer term, AI is likely to lead to a reduction in headcount in law firms, as AI can perform many legal tasks in a fraction of the time compared to humans. AI could reduce the cost of legal services and make them more accessible to smaller firms that have previously struggled to afford such services. Furthermore, recent graduates in the legal field could use AI to quickly establish their own practices.
>
> Source: Anonymous. (2023, June 10). First thing we do, let's bot all the lawyers. *The Economist*, pp. 57–58.

4.7 Risks of Applying AI

Although the increasing capabilities of AI offer considerable benefits to firms, there are also potential risks associated with applying AI, as outlined below in this section.

4.7.1 Algorithmic Transparency

The concept of algorithmic transparency refers to the extent to which the factors influencing an AI decision or recommendation are evident to the users. This relates to factors such as how the AI model has been trained, what data was used for training, how the data inputs affected the output and how the decision would change under different circumstances. Many AI tools are 'black boxes' that fail to fully explain how they arrived at a decision outcome.

Previously, rules-based AI models were designed around eliciting knowledge from an expert in a problem domain and converting it into a set of rules where the expert could explain the reasoning for the decision outcome. However, many machine-learning models programme themselves, and the decision outcome is often incomprehensible to humans. Some progress has been made in interpreting decision outcomes through reverse engineering AI models that attempt to map individual parts of the model to specific patterns in the training data. The downside of this approach is that it becomes less effective with larger models. Moreover, this lack of transparency in the decision outcome can lead to a loss of trust and potential legal action in evidence-based contexts such as medicine and law.

4.7.2 Algorithmic Bias

Algorithmic bias has been an ongoing problem with AI applications, with criticisms of discrimination around gender, race and age. This risk is sometimes referred to as algorithmic bias, as the algorithm inherits biases from the training data. Since many AI models learn from historical data, any bias present in the data can lead to unfair treatment for certain groups or individuals. For example, some human resource AI systems have been found to discriminate against older job seekers, whilst healthcare algorithms employed by health insurance companies have been found to disadvantage older people based on age, even though these people may be healthy. There are a number of causes of bias in AI models:

- *Selection bias*—this occurs when there is under or over-sampling from the population used to train the algorithm, which can inadvertently favour certain groups or exclude others. For example, a human resource recruitment algorithm can be trained predominantly on the CVs of younger workers and fails to adequately consider the skills and experience of older workers. Also, consider an AI application that tracks smartphone

geolocation data to analyse the commuting patterns of people to determine travel schedules for public transportation. This application is likely to fail to consider people who are less well-off and do not own a smartphone, which, in turn, will lead to decisions around public transportation favouring more well-off people in a particular area [15].
- *Proxy bias*—this occurs when training data include variables that act as proxies for sensitive attributes such as race, age or gender. Although these sensitive attributes are not included in the data, the algorithm may indirectly infer them from the proxy variables and thus lead to bias. In many instances, occupation can act as a proxy for gender, and location can act as a proxy for ethnicity. Furthermore, when an algorithm uses postal codes as a proxy for economic status, it can potentially disadvantage groups whose postal codes are associated with certain racial demographics.
- *Temporal bias*—it involves bias due to changes in circumstances, norms or regulations over time. When the training data do not represent current reality and become outdated, the AI model is likely to provide decisions that are biased. For example, this decision bias can occur on the basis of not being aligned with current legislation. Additionally, when the AI model contains outdated data that reflect discriminatory practices, it is likely to produce decision outcomes that discriminate against certain groups.

4.7.3 Changing Operating Environment

The operating environment for the machine-learning application may evolve or differ from the environment in which the machine-learning application was originally trained. This can occur in the following ways:

- *Concept drift*—this refers to a situation in which the inputs into the machine-learning model are not stable or have been poorly specified. As the model has been trained on static training data, the evolution in the data can affect the prediction of the model. For example, a machine-learning model for predicting buyer behaviour may fail to account for wider economic factors and how they influence buyer behaviour. Emerging economic trends, not considered in the original model, will impact the accuracy of the model.
- *Covariate shift*—this refers to a situation where the data inputs used to train the machine-learning model have changed in the live operating environment. This drift in the evolution of the data can invalidate the

predictions of the machine-learning model. For example, credit-scoring, machine learning models that have been trained using data only from a growing economy are likely to make incorrect predictions in the case of an economy in recession. In a medical context, models that have been trained only on certain categories of patients are likely to be invalid. A medical machine-learning model application that has been trained only using data from patients in their 20s will not be accurate when screening patients in their 60s.

4.8 Practices for Integrating Business, Ethics and Technical Issues Into AI Implementation

The analysis so far has highlighted the capabilities and risks of applying AI technologies. This section presents a framework that integrates the business, technical and ethical issues involved in implementing AI in a digital transformation context, as shown in Fig. 4.3. The framework involves the phases of planning, implementation and evaluation, with each stage having a number of practices. The framework highlights how firms can exploit the benefits of AI whilst, at the same time, mitigating the potential risks.

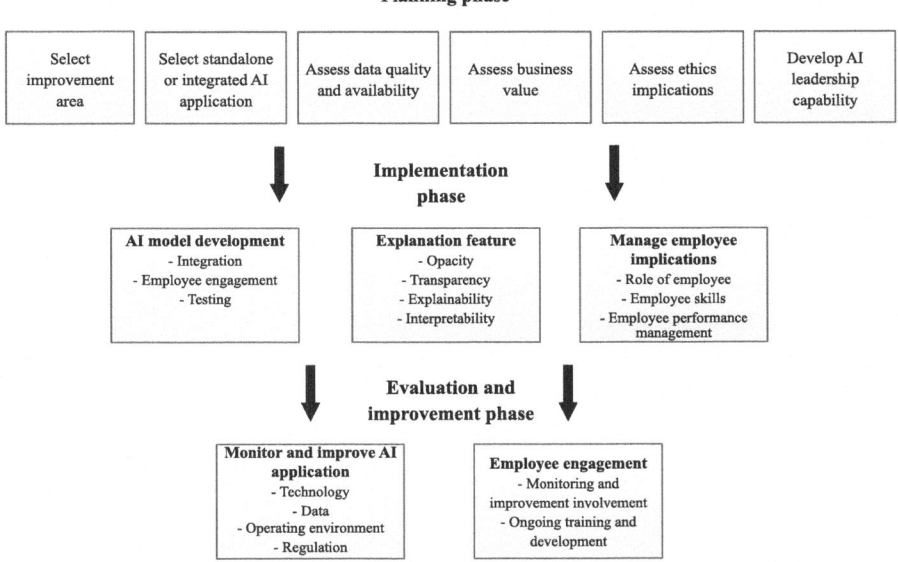

Fig. 4.3 A framework for integrating business, technical and ethical issues into AI implementation

4.8.1 The Planning Phase

Select improvement area. This involves selecting a process or task that can be improved through applying an AI technology. A key consideration here is the complexity of the potential improvement area. AI is a powerful tool for finding trends, identifying patterns and making predictions for well-structured problems, whilst at the same time, it can struggle to deal with context, emotional intelligence and business ethics issues. AI is also likely to be a more powerful tool for analysing discrete tasks rather than complex, integrative problem areas.

Consider the application of generative AI in the software development process. Software that offers value through integration with other products or services is less likely to be at risk from disruption by AI than more discrete tasks such as coding. For example, the payment platform Stripe is built on complex, highly secure connections to financial institutions that are very difficult for AI technologies to replicate [16].

AI can be employed in the following ways based on process complexity:

- *Task automation*—in this instance, AI can be employed to perform repetitive and structured tasks that follow a set of rules and a pre-determined sequence of operations. Simple chatbots operated by social media firms that automatically send email welcomes to new customers are an example of this application [17]. This option is likely to be chosen when there are low risks associated with the AI tool delivering an inaccurate outcome.
- *Task augmentation*—alternatively, in the case of more complex tasks and processes where the cost of making errors is high, the AI application is likely to be chosen to augment the human decision-maker. For example, in a medical context, AI applications are often used as a support tool for physicians rather than autonomous tools due to the high complexity and risks of inaccurate diagnoses of serious illnesses.
- *Tasks that AI cannot perform*—these are typically tasks that are too complex for AI to analyse and/or where the risks from inaccurate outcomes are too high. For example, AI models cannot make decisions on complex moral or ethical issues.

> **Illustration 4.4 Selecting an Improvement Area for AI at a Medical Device Manufacturer**
>
> This case provides an illustration of how a medical device manufacturer differentiated between tasks when applying ChatGPT [18].
>
> - *Task automation*—an area identified involved the labour-intensive task of emailing external parties to request contract changes. ChatGPT could automatically generate emails by reading through revised contracts.
> - *Task augmentation*—a sample task identified involved ensuring contracts accurately reflected requests for proposals (RFPs). ChatGPT could develop a draft contract based on the terms of agreement by reading through an RFP and a standard template. Employees reviewed the draft to highlight any areas of concern that needed to be amended.
> - *Tasks that AI cannot perform*—these include tasks that must comply with government policy and tasks involving intellectual property when working with external consultants.
>
> Source: Leonardi, P. (2023). Helping Employees Succeed with Generative AI: How to manage performance when new technology brings constant and unpredictable change. *Harvard Business Review*, pp. 49–53.

Select stand-alone or integrated AI application. Firms have to consider whether AI applications should be stand-alone or integrated with other internal applications within the firm.

- *Stand-alone applications*—these applications are separate and clearly segregated from existing internal systems inside the firm. They are distinct from the channels through which customers learn about, buy or get support for using a firm's products or services, as well as the channels employees use to market, sell or service these offerings [19]. For example, ChatGPT can offer significant functionality without needing to be integrated into the existing internal systems of the firm.
- *Integrated applications*—these are embedded within the existing systems of the firm and are often not visible to customers. For example, machine-learning algorithms employed by Netflix to offer programme recommendations for viewers, based on real-time analysis of viewing habits, are integrated into existing internal systems and are invisible to the viewer. When developing integrated AI applications, firms must consider the costs and time required for integrating them with existing internal systems.

Assess data quality and availability. The success of an AI application will depend upon the availability, quantity and recency of the data accessed. Data availability involves ensuring that there is an adequate amount of data accessible to the AI application. Data quality involves considering the quality of data used to train the AI application. Where training data is sourced from limited, non-representative or poorly defined sources, it is likely to deliver poor predictions. A firm will have to be careful in ensuring that any data it is sourcing comply with ethical and legal compliance rules.

Assess business value. Consideration should be given to the impact the AI application will have on the performance of affected tasks and processes. This will involve assessing how critical AI is to the overall strategy of the firm and the technical and organisational issues associated with implementation. This will also involve comparing the potential benefits of the AI application relative to the costs of implementation. The potential benefits are likely to include cost reductions, improved employee productivity, better customer service and higher customer satisfaction, whilst the costs are likely to include hardware and software costs, training and employee development initiatives. This analysis should help to prioritise AI implementation according to which applications offer the most short—and long-term value and indicate the resources required to implement the AI application.

Assess ethics implications. Ethics issues around bias, privacy and transparency have to be managed, along with the associated risks. Firms need to have practices in place to both identify potential ethical risks and implement practices for mitigating them. A key aspect of this effort involves integrating expertise from both inside and outside the firm. The following areas of expertise are important for managing AI ethics issues [20]:

- *Ethics expertise*—this includes people with qualifications and experience in ethics. They should have knowledge and experience of ethical risks in a range of business contexts and be able to help the firm objectively assess ethical issues. For example, ethics experts should be able to detect when a financial service loan application discriminates against certain customers based on demographics.
- *Legal expertise*—it is necessary to consider what is legally permissible. Legal expertise is necessary for assessing whether applying a particular metric in the AI model impacts different sub-groups and whether it could be viewed as discrimination under the law. Moreover, as AI blurs the accountability boundaries between AI and human elements in certain tasks, legal expertise is required to understand who is liable when something goes wrong.
- *Business strategists*—a firm must strike a balance between the benefits of employing AI and the investments in resources required to deal with the ethical risks that may arise. For example, a firm is unlikely to pursue an AI

opportunity where the benefits are not significant and where the ethical risks are high. Alternatively, where there are significant benefits and complex ethical issues, business strategists will have to make judgements around the balance between business value and ethical risks.

- *Technical expertise*—this can help the firm understand the technology embedded in the AI model and potential risk mitigation strategies. For example, this could involve assessing whether it is possible for the AI model to be retrained in response to changes in the operating environment.
- *Subject matter experts*—these people are important for detecting any flaws or biases in the decision outcomes of the AI model. They should have in-depth knowledge of the decision-making context and be involved both during the initial implementation stages and when the AI model goes live.

Develop AI leadership capability. This will involve having a leader in place who understands the capabilities of AI and how it can impact the processes, products and business models. Crucially, this leadership will involve developing a culture that highlights the importance of data-driven decisions and inspiring enthusiasm amongst employees about the potential for AI to improve business performance. There are a number of attributes that such a leader should possess [21]:

- Firstly, the leader should be familiar with digital technologies and AI, as well as their transformational impact across a range of business processes.
- Secondly, they should be willing to participate in some AI project development initiatives to signal the importance of AI to the business. This should help motivate employees and encourage them to develop new skills.
- Finally, the leader should have the power to ensure the required resources are committed by the firm to ensure AI is developed and deployed effectively on an ongoing basis.

4.8.2 The Implementation Phase

AI model development. This involves working with affected stakeholders of the AI model to determine how AI can be employed to develop and improve the selected process. Some of this activity involves data scientists going through multiple iterations of finding and cleansing data that will be input into the AI model. Exploratory data analysis can then be performed and used as a basis for training and assessing outcomes from the AI model. Where the model has been found to deliver the desired accuracy level, the model should be fully developed. There are a number of key issues around moving to full development:

- *Integration*—where the firm has opted for an AI-integrated model, the next step will involve integrating the AI model into the business processes and workflows of the firm. Business processes and workflows may have to be redesigned to ensure that the AI model and employees complement one another's capabilities. Affected employees and data scientists will have to work closely to align the AI capabilities with employee needs. For example, integrating AI into customer service workflows will require an in-depth understanding of the associated processes, knowledge that is only held by experienced customer service employees.
- *Employee engagement*—employees impacted by the AI model should work closely with data scientists to determine how processes can be improved via AI. The outcome of this effort should involve the development of an AI model that can be deployed by employees. This can involve developing user interfaces and/or integrating the AI applications with other IT systems and business processes.
- *Testing of the AI model*—this could involve carrying out random tests on the AI model to ensure it is accurate and free from bias. For example, this could involve analysing decisions around products in the actual market, where there are various types of users, to determine whether the quality of decisions differs across them [22]. Firms could compare the accuracy of decisions made by the AI model with those made in the same instances where AI has not been employed.

Explanation feature. Where possible, the AI tool should incorporate an explanation feature to outline the rationale for reaching a decision or recommendation. This feature is particularly important in evidence-based contexts, such as medicine, where the user needs to understand the inputs and reasoning that were used to make the recommendation regarding medical procedures. Explanation features have become more prominent in contexts where the conclusion could be challenged legally for being unfair, illegal or discriminatory. There are a number of interrelated elements that should be considered here [23]:

- *Opacity* refers to the lack of visibility in an algorithm. In some instances, the logic of machine-learning algorithms is not even accessible to the AI model developers.

- *Transparency* refers to the willingness of the owners of the AI model to disclose how it reached the decision outcome—for example, when secrecy is required.
- *Explainability* refers to the ability to understand the reasoning behind how the AI model arrived at the decision outcome. The explanation should be outlined in language understandable to the user.
- *Interpretability* refers to the understandability on the part of the human, where a person can understand the reasoning of the algorithm; there is strong interpretability. Interpretability will depend on the person's knowledge of the algorithm and the domain area.

When integrating an explanation feature into the AI model, firms have to strike a balance between exploiting the capabilities of AI whilst, at the same time, risking not losing the trust of users and customers. In instances where there is uncertainty around the decision outcome from AI models, this could be communicated to the user, which could allow users to validate it. For example, in the case of generative AI, this could be done through citing sources where the model has extracted the data from to lead to the decision outcome [24]. The AI model could also explain how it arrived at the decision outcome and, where appropriate, highlight the uncertainty around the outcome.

Manage the employee implications
Implications for the role of the employee. AI has important implications for the roles of employees, as it allows firms to complete tasks more quickly through either task augmentation or task automation. AI is already impacting the medical, information technology and legal fields, where expertise, judgement and creativity are highly valued and considered irreplaceable [25]. Although AI will not lead to the disappearance of these fields, it has already been impacting the traditional roles of employees in these fields. There are a number of important issues that firms must consider regarding the changing role of the employee:

- *Over-dependency on AI*—as firms use AI to augment more tasks and decisions, they will become increasingly dependent on AI tools. This over-dependency may have a detrimental impact on skills and capabilities, as employees may struggle to deal with more complex tasks [26]. Moreover, there is a risk that firms may lose important employee knowledge when they automate certain processes.

- *Balancing AI model autonomy and human involvement*—as AI technologies advance, they will be able to automate an expanding range of tasks that employees currently perform. Firms must constantly assess the balance between which tasks should be automated and those that should involve employees.

There are two approaches firms can take to deal with the changing roles of employees impacted by AI [27]:

- *Deepening employee roles*—this allows employees to devote more time to tasks than they were previously able to. For example, employees can use AI to speed up certain tasks, such as handling customer queries and resolving issues, and thus limit the need for human involvement.
- *Upgrading employee roles*—this allows employees to take on more critical, value-adding tasks. For example, AI can automate routine administrative tasks such as sorting emails, summarising text documents and developing reports, thus allowing employees to focus on more creative and collaborative-type tasks.

Employee skills. Changing employee roles will also have implications for employee skills development. Where firms decide to upgrade employee roles, training and development will have to be put in place to allow employees to transition to these new roles. Employees will have to develop skills in collaborating with AI that allow them to effectively harness the optimum power of AI—sometimes referred to as AI fusion skills. Three types of fusion skills are associated with employing generative AI tools that are relevant to the analysis here [28].

- *Intelligent interrogation*—this involves giving AI tools, such as ChatGPT, instructions that will lead to better reasoning and outcomes. For example, a salesperson might use it to find an answer to a complex customer service query.
- *Judgment integration*—this involves employing human judgement to supplement the outcome of the AI application where there is uncertainty around the accuracy and explainability of the outcome. This requires an understanding of the accuracy and explainability of the outcome, and sensing where, when and how to intervene.
- *Reciprocal apprenticing*—this involves helping AI learn about the tasks and needs of a firm by integrating data and knowledge into the prompts given to it, thereby training it to be a co-creator. Essentially, this skill involves

customising generative AI applications to a specific firm context so that it can achieve the desired outcomes. Although data scientists have developed similar capabilities when building AI models, reciprocal apprenticing has become more important for employees in non-technical roles.

Firms will have to develop these skills in their employees on an ongoing basis, as AI tools and applications are constantly changing. Employees need to understand how AI tools work, how to train AI, how to create effective prompts and how to assess the accuracy of the outcomes [29].

Employee performance management. In some instances, the performance of employees is being evaluated by AI tools, often with little understanding of the variables determining the outcome. Such changes in the values of firms not only impact how firms manage their employees but also have a detrimental impact on employees as well [30].

> **Illustration 4.5 The Consequences of an AI Loan Application at a German Bank**
>
> This case focuses on a high-street German bank that implemented an AI application to act as a substitute for the human decision-making process for personal loans. Prior to implementation, loan consultants advised customers and made the decisions on granting loans. The AI application now autonomously decides on loan approval, providing the consultant with a final and irreversible decision. This implementation had the following consequences for the bank:
>
> - *Loss of critical thinking*—transferring decision-making authority to the loan application led to employees losing the ability to critically reflect on their work. They lacked the opportunity to reflect on loan decisions, as the system had taken over the decision-making process.
> - *Knowledge outsourcing*—the new arrangement meant that knowledge around loan approval was outsourced to the AI application. Loan consultants no longer understood the loan process, which prevented them from answering customer queries about loan decisions. Additionally, this transfer of knowledge led to consultants being unable to identify system errors or areas for improvement.
> - *Loss of expertise*—the bank was at risk of losing highly experienced loan consultants, who offered specialist advice to customers and were difficult to replace. Also, as the bank had to sell other financial products to loan customers, it needed experienced consultants who could offer advice on a range of financial matters.
> - *Exclusion of certain customers*—the system excluded customers based on social status, origin or place of residence. Even though customers may have matching profiles in terms of payment behaviour and debt levels, the system may have excluded a customer based on place of residence alone.

> - *Loss of firm's unique selling point*—the bank risked losing its unique selling point of offering customised advice as the loan process was automated, and the loan consultant had a limited role to play. Current customers lost the benefit of availing tailored advice and thus perceived the bank as no different from an online bank with standard and cheaper conditions.
>
> Source: Mayer, A.S., Strich, F., and Fiedler, M. (2020). 'Unintended Consequences of Introducing AI Systems for Decision Making'. *MIS Quarterly Executive*, 19(4).

4.8.3 The Evaluation and Improvement Phase

Monitor and improve AI application. As many AI applications operate in environments that are constantly evolving and changing, firms must have monitoring practices in place to ensure that the model is operating as intended and, where appropriate, make improvements. The following influences on the AI application should be considered in this process:

- *Technology*—AI tools and technologies are evolving in terms of reduced costs and increasing capabilities. Post-implementation, a firm may find that there are more suitable AI technologies available than their current choice of AI application.
- *Data*—it should be recent and well-indexed, particularly in operating environments where there is considerable change. Where data have become outdated, it will lead to a decline in performance from the application. For example, where a firm has developed an AI model to predict customer buyer behaviour, the performance of the application will drop if customer preferences or market conditions change over time.
- *AI model operating* environment—as has already been highlighted, the operating environment for the AI application may evolve or differ from the environment in which the AI model was originally trained. For example, pricing and credit evaluations face a shifting market context when the business cycle enters a new phase, such as a recession.
- *Regulation*—AI has been attracting the attention of regulators, and firms need to be aware of ongoing changes in regulation and how it affects AI applications. Compliance around data privacy regulation is an issue that firms need to be mindful of, particularly when they are collecting customer data on an ongoing basis. Although firms want to learn as much as

possible about customers in an AI context, they must ensure that they are protecting the privacy of customers and complying with the law.

A challenge is ensuring that the AI application and the environment are developing in a way that allows the model to make appropriate decisions. Although it is prudent to regularly retrain AI models on fresh data, this can be an expensive process. Firms should put in place practices for monitoring and alerting managers to changes in the performance of the model that highlight the need for retraining.

Employee engagement. Firms should engage with employees on an ongoing basis to ensure the AI application is meeting the business objectives and, where necessary, highlight areas for improvement. There are a number of important elements to this process:

- *Monitoring and improvement involvement*—employees should be involved in monitoring and improving the AI application when it is in use. Many AI applications cannot understand emotion and sentiment in a business context. Employees have strengths that are more appropriate for assessing the outputs of the AI model for accuracy, ethics, bias issues and the potential impacts on customers. For example, evaluation and improvement could involve the firm engaging with employees and customers on a one-to-one basis to gauge their opinions and feelings about the firm's use of AI.
- *Ongoing training and development*—this is necessary for ensuring that employees are realising their full potential from the current AI application and also increasing awareness of other potential developments in AI. This could also involve investing in ethical AI training across the business to include data scientists, department managers and senior management. Integrating the human element into the AI model evaluation process should consider whether AI tools are employed in a way that enhances, rather than diminishes, the experience of employees and their customers. The actions of the firm will be influenced by its stance towards the responsible use of AI to maintain accuracy, safety and honesty, mitigate risks, and eliminate biased outcomes [31].

Discussion Questions

1. Referring to Sect. 4.2, highlight how the four functions of AI are being employed to improve performance across the healthcare, entertainment and manufacturing sectors.
2. Referring to Sect. 4.3, select a firm with which you are familiar and outline how it employs machine-learning algorithms for *supervised*, *unsupervised* and *reinforcement* learning to enhance business performance.
3. Referring to the framework in Fig. 4.2, highlight examples from a range of business sectors of how AI is impacting the four categories of product and process capabilities.
4. Compare and contrast the explanation features of three generative AI applications, such as ChatGPT and Microsoft Co-pilot, and critically evaluate how they provide the elements of *opacity*, *transparency*, *explainability* and *interpretability*.
5. Select a firm that is employing generative AI and consider how it is embracing the concept of AI fusion skills, including *intelligent interrogation*, *judgement integration* and *reciprocal apprenticing*.

References

1. McAfee, A., Rock, D., & Brynjolfsson, E. (2023). How to Capitalize on Generative AI: A guide to realizing its benefits while limiting the risks. *Harvard Business Review*, *101*(6), 43–48.
2. Berente, N., Gu, B., Recker, J., & Santhanam, R. (2021). Managing artificial intelligence. *MIS Quarterly*, *45*(3).
3. Kaplan, A., & Haenlein, M. (2019). Siri, Siri, in my hand: Who's the fairest in the land? On the interpretations, illustrations, and implications of artificial intelligence. *Business Horizons*, *62*(1), 15–25.
4. Benbya, S., et al. (2020) in reference 4 above.
5. Benbya, H., Davenport, T. H., & Pachidi, S. (2020). Artificial intelligence in organizations: Current state and future opportunities. *MIS Quarterly Executive*, *19*(4).
6. Lee, I., & Shin, Y. J. (2020). Machine learning for enterprises: Applications, algorithm selection, and challenges. *Business Horizons*, *63*(2), 157–170.
7. Babic, B., Cohen, I. G., Evgeniou, T., & Gerke, S. (2021). When machine learning goes off the rails. *Harvard Business Review*, 21–32.
8. See Benbya et al. (2020) in reference 4 above.
9. See Berente et al. (2021) in reference 2 above.
10. Zhang, Z., Yoo, Y., Lyytinen, K. & Lindberg, A. (2021). The unknowability of autonomous tools and the liminal experience of their use. *Information Systems Research*, *32*(4), pp. 1192–1213.
11. See Berente et al. (2021) in reference 2 above.

12. Paschen, U., Pitt, C. & Kietzmann, J. (2020). Artificial intelligence: Building blocks and an innovation typology. *Business Horizons*, 63(2), pp.147–155.
13. This figure has been adapted from Paschen et al. (2020) in reference 12 above and augmented with examples.
14. Davenport, T., Guha, A., & Grewal, D. (2021). How to design an AI marketing strategy. *Harvard Business Review*, July-August, 42–47.
15. Blackman, R. (2022). Why You Need an AI Ethics Committee. *Harvard Business Review*, *100*(4), 118–125.
16. Cook, S., Hagiu, A., & Wright, J. (2024). Turn generative AI from an existential threat into a competitive advantage. *Harvard Business Review*, *102*(1), 118–125.
17. See Davenport et al. (2021) in reference 14 above.
18. Leonardi, P. (2023). Helping Employees Succeed with Generative AI: How to manage performance when new technology brings constant and unpredictable change. *Harvard Business Review*, 49–53.
19. See Davenport et al. (2021) in reference 14 above.
20. See Blackman. (2022) in reference 15 above.
21. Davenport, T., Guha, A., & Grewal, D. (2021). How to design an AI marketing strategy. *Harvard Business Review*, July-August, 42–47.
22. See Babic et al. (2021) in reference 7 above.
23. Vimalkumar, M., Gupta, A., Sharma, D., & Dwivedi, Y. K. (2021). "Understanding the Effect that Task Complexity has on Automation Potential and Opacity: Implications for Algorithmic Fairness", AIS Transactions on Human-Computer Interaction (13:1), pp. 104–129.
24. Baxter, K. & Schlesinger, Y. (2023). Managing the risks of Generative AI, *Harvard Business Review*, Winter, 137–139.
25. See Benbya et al. (2020) in reference 4 above.
26. Bogert, E., Schecter, A., & Watson, R. T. (2021). Humans rely more on algorithms than social influence as a task becomes more difficult, *Nature Scientific Reports*, *11*(8028) https://doi.org/10.1038/s41598-021-87480-9
27. See Leonardi. (2023) in reference 18 above.
28. Wilson, H.J., & Daugherty, P.R. (2024). Embracing gen AI at work. *Harvard Business Review*, pp. 151–155.
29. See Leonardi. (2023) in reference 18 above.
30. See Benbya et al. (2020) in reference 4 above.
31. See Baxter and Schlesinger. (2023) in reference 24 above.

5

Managing Data for Business Value in Digital Transformation

5.1 Introduction

Digital technologies such as the internet of things (IoT), cloud computing and data analytics tools have radically altered the business landscape by making a vast amount of data available to firms. Advances in storage and analytics technologies have allowed firms to make quick decisions based on detailed insights rather than relying on hunches or guesswork. The collection and analysis of data allow firms to predict trends in buyer behaviour to drive more targeted marketing and improve operational performance. Despite considerable investments in data analytics, many firms have struggled to achieve the potential benefits and have encountered significant challenges.

Consider the case of a large Asia–Pacific bank that adopted a radical approach to implementing data analytics across its business, which involved attempting to meet the needs of each analytics development team and data end users [1]. It developed pipelines to extract all the data from its systems, clean it and aggregate it into a data lake in the cloud. However, it paid insufficient attention to aligning these efforts with the needs of business users. Three years into the implementation, it found that the system was only useful to some users, such as those seeking raw historical data for ad hoc analysis, and many potential applications, such as real-time data feeds for personalised customer offerings, had not been included.

A further challenge firms have encountered is related to data privacy and data protection issues in their data analytics practices. Reports on how data analytics, enabled by AI tools, have led to discrimination against minority groups in credit card approvals and healthcare diagnoses have raised concerns amongst consumers about how firms collect and analyse personal data [2]. At the same time, governments are enacting stronger legislation to compel firms to change their data management practices. This chapter addresses these management challenges by providing an understanding of how firms should manage data to create value in digital transformation.

> **Learning Outcomes**
>
> - Distinguish between business intelligence, business analytics and data analytics.
> - Distinguish between the 3 V's of volume, velocity and variety in big data.
> - Understand the concept of digital data streams and data network effects.
> - Understand the challenges of managing data.
> - Understand the issues involved in managing and analysing data to create value.
> - Outline data analytics applications, including descriptive, diagnostic, predictive and prescriptive.
> - Understand how data analytics tools can be used to analyse text, audio, video and social media.
> - Understand how firms can build trust and transparency in their data management practices.

5.2 Business Intelligence, Business Analytics and Data Analytics

Business intelligence is a technology-driven process for collecting, managing and analysing data to generate insights that can improve the business strategies and operations of a firm. Business intelligence encompasses a range of intelligence around competitors, customers, markets, products, strategy and technology [3]. It involves applying visualisation and analytics tools. Visualisation tools, such as digital dashboards, provide graphic representations of data to develop visual and useful information to assist with decision-making.

Business analytics is a subset of business intelligence and includes visualisation, statistics, statistical analysis and modelling applications. Whereas business intelligence tends to be descriptive, employing current business data to improve business decisions, business analytics tends to focus on prescriptive, future-driven analysis.

Data analytics refers to the practice of using techniques to analyse and acquire intelligence from data to allow firms to make data-driven business decisions.

5.3 Big Data

Big data is a term often used in the context of data analytics and refers to large and diverse collections of structured and unstructured data managed by a firm. Big data is characterised by the 3 V's: volume, velocity and variety.

Volume refers to the magnitude of data and can vary based on factors such as time and the type of data [4]. The volume of data will continue to grow as firms employ digital technologies to manage their operations and engage in the collection and analysis of data to support their business activities. Although firms have been managing an increasing volume of internal data, a significant development has been the dramatic growth in the volume of external data. For example, digital technologies can provide data on usage patterns by customers, the devices they are using, where they are located, and whom they are with.

Velocity refers to the speed at which data are generated and the speed at which data can be delivered. Examples of high-velocity data include real-time data from smartphones, clickstream data from internet retailers and financial data on stock markets. The proliferation of digital devices such as smartphones and IoT devices has led to the real-time generation of data, which in turn has driven the need for data analytics in real time. Data from these devices produce information on customers' location, demographics and previous buying behaviour that can be analysed in real time to better customise products and services to the needs of customers.

Variety refers to the different sources and formats that data can come in. Table 5.1 provides examples of data variety along the dimensions of source and format. Data sources include devices such as smartphones and industrial equipment on the IoT, as well as data generated from users, such as website interactions and purchases by customers. The format of data can be in the following categories:

- *Structured* data tend to be tabular, numerical data stored in spreadsheets or database applications and it is readily searchable by search engine algorithms.
- *Unstructured* data include text documents, email, financial transactions, images, video and audio, and as this type of data is poorly structured, it is more challenging to analyse. However, the emergence of innovative analytics technologies enabled by AI is breaking down the barriers to analysis. For example, facial recognition technologies and in-store location

Table 5.1 Data variety examples

	Structured data	Unstructured data
Machine generated	Usage metrics from web pages and social media channels including time of postings, etc. Product purchase data from systems Sensor data automatically tracked on RFID tags, meters medical and Global Positioning System (GPS)-enabled devices Financial data on sales, production rates, quality levels, etc	Weather data Video and photographic data for surveillance, security, etc. Sonar data
Human generated	Number of tweets or likes on social media channels Clickstream data generated by humans on websites Customer ratings on retail marketplaces Any data input by users including forms, surveys, etc.	Internal text data including emails, letters, text messages, and reports Text data from social media platforms Customer and employee reviews Voicemails Comments in online forums

analytics have allowed retailers to develop intelligent insights into the in-store movements of different customers to influence the positioning of product categories.

5.4 The Concept of Digital Data Streams

The concept of the digital data stream is useful for understanding the power of data analytics and how it can improve firm performance and decision-making [5]. A digital data stream includes the transmission of digital representations of events, such as when a customer tweets about a purchase or where a customer made a purchase. Analysis of digital data streams allows firms to analyse events in real time and develop a deeper understanding of customers. A digital data stream can capture up to six elements of an event [6]:

- *When*—the time at which the data segment was created. For example, this could involve the date, time and location of a purchase made by a customer.

- *Where*—the location of the entity when the data segment was created. For example, this could be the GPS coordinates of the location.
- *Who*—the unique identifier of the entity that created the data segment. For example, this could include the customer number or the URL address of a website.
- *What*—the activity that caused the segment to be created. For example, this could include the unique identifier of an item in a purchase transaction.
- *How*—this refers to how the event was initiated and completed. For example, this could include the credit card number used for the purchase transaction.
- *Why*—this involves understanding the motive for the action related to the data segment creation. For example, this could include a birthday gift.

Advances in digital technologies mean that considerable value can be created from analysing these events and the relationships between them. Location features and electronic wallets on smartphones allow firms to clearly measure the *where* and *who*. The GPS technology on a smartphone can provide a person's coordinates in terms of latitude and longitude, whilst electronic wallets provide precision on who is making the purchase. The *what* and *how* are common elements in a transaction. For example, this is evident in a tweet that contains metadata to indicate when the tweet was posted, where it was created and details of the author through their URL. The *why* is still a challenge, as individuals do not reveal their motives—for example, why they are purchasing a product?

5.5 Data Analytics and the Time Dimension

Data analytics can be performed on either real-time data or stored data [7]. Real-time data analysis allows firms to make immediate decisions. An example of real-time data analytics could involve an insurance company analysing current weather patterns and then messaging customers about weather conditions. The real-time weather data could be combined with static data in databases, including customer addresses. This would allow the insurance company to quickly alert customers to adverse weather in certain locations and reduce the likelihood of accidents amongst its customers.

Data analytics on stored data involves merging and analysing various datasets to provide insights into business areas. For example, retailers merge and analyse data from sources on store locations, demand patterns and product types to attempt to forecast future demand. Analytics on stored data is not based on immediate action but on deriving actionable insights for decision-making.

5.6 Data Network Effects

Data network effects occur when data generated by users of a product or service increase the value for other users [8]. As the digital platform collects and analyses more data from users, the more valuable it becomes to each user, and the more likely the user is to stay with the platform. For example, the more Google learns about users through the searches they undertake, the more it can personalise the user experience, which makes Google's search engine more valuable to each user. Data network effects do not require additional users to enhance the value of the platform, which contrasts with direct network effects, where the value of the platform grows as more users join it.

Continuous interaction with the platform by users allows the firm to collect and analyse a wider and deeper set of data, which enables the development of a more personalised experience for the user. For example, as people listen to more songs on Spotify, the more straightforward it becomes for Spotify to personalise its recommendations, and the more valuable it becomes to the listener.

> **Illustration 5.1 Data Network Effects as a Competitive Weapon**
>
> The breadth and depth of data that large technology firms such as Google and Facebook hold on users have become a significant part of their competitive power. Previously, the attention of regulators had largely focused on data in a privacy and security context. More recently, data as a competitive weapon have begun to come to the attention of regulators in a way that was not considered previously.
>
> In 2020, Google's acquisition of the wearables company Fitbit attracted the attention of European Union (EU) regulators over fears that Google might use the health data generated by its millions of users to target consumers with adverts. As part of the acquisition agreement with the EU, Google agreed not to use Fitbit's data to target users with adverts for a decade.
>
> EU regulators also focused their attention on data when Amazon attempted to acquire iRobot, the Roomba-maker. They considered whether the acquisition would give Amazon an unfair advantage over competitors. As well as having privacy concerns, critics also pointed out that, as the robotic vacuum cleaner

> moves through the homes of customers, it would gather critical data that could tilt competition in its favour. Anti-monopoly campaigners have also challenged this acquisition, arguing that it would allow Amazon to further deepen the depth of data it has on retail and consumer preferences by allowing it inside the living rooms of consumers.
>
> It is worth pointing out that few acquisitions or alliances have been blocked on data concerns alone, as there is skepticism amongst some that data can be a source of considerable competitive advantage. However, this is an area where regulators will continue to focus, as there is a lot of pressure coming from lobby and consumer groups to act.
>
> Source: Espinoza, J. (2023, Mar 9). The harvesting of personal data rises up EU's antitrust agenda. *Financial Times*. Retrieved from https://www.proquest.com/newspapers/harvesting-personal-data-rises-up-eus-antitrust/docview/2797447243/se-2.

5.7 Data Management Challenges

There are a number of challenges in managing data that prevent firms from achieving the anticipated benefits of their data analytics efforts.

- *No formal data management strategy*—firms often have no formal strategy for managing data at the corporate level, with data often being collected and stored as a result of technology investments at the functional level. This problem is further compounded as data have become more ubiquitous, coming from a wide range of sources.
- *Lack of data integration*—data are often collected by different systems and, thus, are disjointed, creating difficulties in matching different data. For example, although data from smartphones and data from personal computers can show similar customer browsing behaviour, if the data from both cannot be matched, it is likely to be difficult to effectively determine browsing behaviour. Understanding how data are integrated should be undertaken before data are collected, as this will reduce matching costs [9].
- *Data-rich, information-poor*—this refers to a situation where firms are rich in data but lack the capabilities to analyse this data to produce meaningful information that can be used in business decision-making. This has been an enduring challenge for firms throughout the history of information technology, as firms often have too much data and too little information. Data are now produced at an ever-increasing speed and in an expanding array of formats via the IoT, thus further compounding this challenge.

- *Processing difficulties*—with firms having enormous amounts of data, there can be difficulties in processing it in a timely manner or verifying its accuracy. In some instances, this leads to a lack of transparency regarding the methods by which data are collected. Integrating data from different sources and formats can be challenging, along with the costs of storing such data. These difficulties are further exacerbated in the case of firms with datasets dispersed across global locations.

5.8 A Framework for Managing and Analysing Data to Create Value

Employing data analytics to create value involves a number of elements, as shown in the framework in Fig. 5.1. Each of these elements is now discussed.

5.8.1 Data Preparation

There are a number of steps in data preparation, including data acquisition, data quality assessment, data cleansing and data warehousing, as outlined below:

Data Acquisition. Data acquisition involves the processes and technologies required to acquire, store the data and retrieve it for analysis. These data can be structured or unstructured and are normally transferred into a data warehouse.

Data Quality Assessment. A key aspect of analysing data is ensuring data quality. Data quality is affected by how data are collected, input into systems, stored and managed. Effectively managing data quality should ensure consistency, particularly when combining data from different datasets. There are a number of indicators of data quality, including the following:

- *Accuracy*—this refers to whether the data are correct and free from errors. For example, the email address of a customer should match the actual email of the customer in a database.
- *Completeness*—this refers to how comprehensive the data are. Where the data are incomplete, it is likely to be unusable. For example, a customer record for an online retailer should include the customer's name and address, as well as email address and phone number.

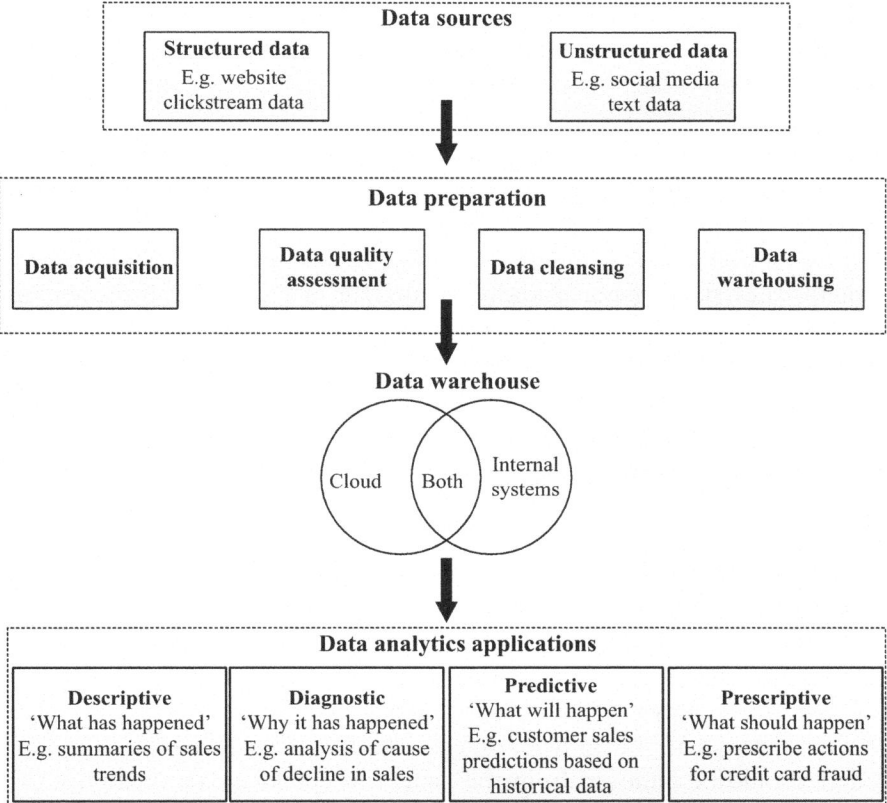

Fig. 5.1 A framework for managing and analysing data to create value

- *Traceability*—this refers to whether the data can be traced to its source, thus allowing the origin to be verified. The opaque way in which data are collected can raise issues around completeness and accuracy. Without knowing how data are generated, it is not possible to verify whether the assumptions around the data are correct.
- *Reliability*—this means that data do not contradict other data in a different database or system. For example, a person's age may be recorded differently across different databases, which affects the reliability of the data.
- *Relevance*—this refers to whether the data being collected are useful for the specific intended purpose. For example, firms often collect data without establishing how it will create value in decision-making.

- *Timeliness*—this refers to how up-to-date the data are. For example, when a firm in the fashion retail industry uses data from five years ago, it is likely to be of little value.

Data Cleansing. Data cleansing involves detecting and removing errors, inconsistencies, duplications and missing entries from datasets. Data quality and data cleansing are often considered together, as ensuring data quality is critical and necessary for undertaking effective data analytics initiatives [10]. In many cases, data are not accessible to analysts in a form that is ready to use and must be cleaned to make it suitable for analysis. Data cleansing involves removing errors, resolving inconsistencies and transforming the data into a consistent format. As a result of the explosion in data, manual data cleansing is extremely challenging, as it is time-consuming and prone to errors. Typical approaches to data cleansing will involve addressing the following:

- *Empty or missing values*—as datasets often have missing values or empty data points, data analysts will employ techniques to fill these gaps with estimates. For example, where a data point is missing, the data analyst may replace it with the average for that data point in the overall dataset.
- *Duplicates*—datasets often include duplicates of the same data, particularly when datasets are integrated from different sources. Therefore, duplicate data should be removed from the dataset to enhance data quality.
- *Outliers*—this refers to abnormal data compared to the values in the rest of the dataset. For example, in the case of customer sales data, where the average purchase is ten items per week, an outlier would be purchases of three hundred items per week. This can skew the results of data analytics, and thus, dealing with outliers is important for ensuring data accuracy. Although outliers can be removed manually, there are software tools available to identify and remove outliers in datasets.

Data Warehousing. A data warehouse is a repository of data extracted from one or more systems and organised to allow the application of data analytics tools. Data warehouses can be stored on a firm's internal systems, in the cloud or a combination of both. The cloud has become more prominent as a storage option because the volume of data has been growing exponentially for firms. Firms may also opt for a data lake to store large volumes of unformatted and unstructured data from multiple sources. The difference with the data warehouse is that the data lake has no pre-determined structure, which allows data scientists to develop exploratory models, queries and applications that can be continuously refined.

5.8.2 Data Analytics Applications

There are four types of data analytics applications that firms can apply, including descriptive, diagnostic, predictive and prescriptive analytics, as shown in Fig. 5.1. Each of these types is now outlined.

Descriptive analytics. Descriptive analytics focuses on questions related to what is happening or what has happened. It can be used to identify trends in a range of business data, including marketing, finance and operations. Descriptive analytics tools include summarisation tools, query and reporting tools, and digital dashboards to analyse performance. Although these tools can be simple, they can be extremely powerful, allowing firms to make quick and effective decisions about their business operations.

Diagnostic analytics. Diagnostic analytics involves analysing historical data to identify the causes of specific events. It can be viewed as a logical next step after using descriptive analytics to identify trends. Diagnostic analytics can drill down into data and develop insights into why certain situations occurred and the associated causes. Typical marketing issues addressed with diagnostic analytics include understanding why sales decreased over a particular time period or why there was an increase in customer churn. Additionally, human resource managers can use diagnostic analytics to understand which departments have high staff attrition rates and the reasons for this attrition.

Predictive analytics. Predictive analytics focuses on predicting what will happen in the future and providing reasons for why it may happen. It can involve employing mathematical algorithms and AI-enabled technologies, such as machine learning, to develop explanatory and predictive patterns in data. Predictive analytics has been applied to a range of business areas, including predicting the failure of industrial equipment based on data streamed from sensors, along with predicting customer buyer behaviour based on historical purchasing behaviour. There are a number of methods associated with predictive analytics, as outlined below:

- ***Association***—it involves finding correlations and rules between different datasets. Association has been applied in market basket analysis, where a database of customer transactions is analysed to identify groups of items that are often purchased together. An often-cited example of the association method is a supermarket in the United States that found men purchased beer at the same time as they bought nappies. The supermarket then positioned nappies near beer refrigerators in its outlets, and sales increased considerably.

- *Classification*—it involves analysing historical data to derive future inferences for decision-making. This involves analysing a dataset to predict which class an individual in the dataset belongs to. Consider a credit card company that needs to detect which customers are likely to default. The class, in this case, is the set of customers who are likely to default. The classification tool should then identify the indicators, sometimes referred to as independent variables, which are likely to highlight the likelihood of default. These could include missed payments, only paying off the minimum amount on the card each month, high credit card balances or a sudden reduction in income. A further example application is in the area of healthcare. Patient data, such as smoking, alcohol consumption and blood pressure, can be trained with machine-learning models to generate different classes, such as those at risk of heart attacks.
- *Clustering*—it is employed to group sets of items on the basis of similarities, with items in the same cluster being more similar to each other than those in other clusters. Market segmentation is a long-established example of clustering, where firms divide customers into distinct groups based on similarities in purchases normally made. Developments in data analytics tools have increased the potential of clustering in the marketing domain by allowing firms to provide personalised products and services. For example, Netflix has employed clustering techniques to segment its more than 250 million global subscribers into over 1000 'taste communities' of members with similar movie and television show preferences [11]. Netflix then recommends movies that share subjects popular within those communities. Additionally, grocery retailers have employed clustering to direct more targeted adverts to customers based on clusters of fresh food shoppers or convenience shoppers.

Prescriptive analytics. Prescriptive analytics focuses on what action should be taken next. It uses tools to analyse data to recommend decision outcomes. An example is a credit card company that needs to detect potential credit card fraud on customer accounts. Prescriptive analytics can identify certain instances of behaviour that are likely to highlight the potential for fraud and, in turn, recommend particular courses of action. For example, the following data are likely to raise concerns for potential fraud:

- The credit card customer makes a purchase on a device for the first time.
- A significant increase in normal monthly customer expenditure.
- Many purchases were completed from different devices in a short period of time.
- A large purchase was made in an unusual location.

Machine-learning tools can rapidly sift through large amounts of data to infer relationships between items, such as a large purchase and many purchases made from different devices. This will then allow the credit card company to highlight anomalies and cancel the credit card where appropriate. It is worth highlighting that prescriptive analytics tools are often employed as a complement to human judgement in important business decision contexts.

5.9 Data Analytics Tools for Unstructured Data

There are a number of sources of unstructured data in firms that data analytics tools can analyse to generate meaningful insights for management decision-making, as outlined below.

5.9.1 Text Analytics

Text analytics involves applying techniques to extract meaning from text. Typical text data analysed include social media feeds, customer product reviews, emails, survey responses, business documents and news feeds. Text analytics can convert large volumes of data into meaningful summaries that can be used for decision-making. Also, text analytics can be fully automated and consistent, thus allowing firms to act quickly on the insights generated. For example, text analytics can allow a retailer to immediately detect negative reviews on social media posts and take corrective action.

Text analytics involves training software tools to associate words with meaning and understand the semantic context of unstructured data by applying deep learning and natural language processing. Deep learning is a branch of machine learning that uses techniques such as neural networks to mimic the human brain and powers text analysis software to read text in a manner similar to the human brain. Natural language processing allows software to derive meaning from text, employing linguistic models and statistics to train the deep-learning technology to process and analyse text data to extract meaning. These tools drive the following types of text analytics:

- *Sentiment analysis*—this technique employs analytics tools to analyse text to reveal positive, negative, neutral or ambivalent views. Sentiment analysis can be used to analyse customer reviews on social media channels to determine whether customers are satisfied with purchases. It can also track changes in opinion and potentially identify causes of any negative reviews.
- *Text summarisation*—this involves creating a brief and accurate summary of a text document. It can be either *extractive,* which involves extracting unmodified sentences from the text, or *abstractive,* which involves generating summaries using sentences not found in the text.
- *Question answering*—this technique provides answers to questions posed in natural language. Amazon's Alexa and Apple's Siri are examples of this technique.

5.9.2 Audio Analytics

Audio analytics involves analysing and extracting insights from unstructured audio data. Audio analytics examples include analysing customer satisfaction from customer help desk calls, medical diagnostic aids and patient monitoring, and assisting patients with hearing problems. Audio analytics can analyse large volumes of recorded calls in a customer contact centre to assess advisor performance, improve customer experience and gain insights into customer behaviour.

Audio analytics have also been employed by music streaming platforms to analyse elements of sound such as melody, harmony, rhythm and tempo. The analysis can be used for song recognition, music classification and genre classification, which can be employed for music recommendation features. Audio analytics also uses sentiment analysis to detect intent, sentiment and emotion in audio.

5.9.3 Video Analytics

Video analytics involves employing techniques to monitor, analyse and extract useful insights from video streams. For example, using spatial parameters in video analytics can detect objects or individuals entering or leaving defined zones, or abnormal movement that differs from normal behaviour, and then issue appropriate alerts. There are three types of video analytics:

- *Fixed algorithm analytics*—this employs an algorithm to perform a task or identify a specific behaviour such as a shopper moving to a different part of a store.

- *AI learning algorithms*—these algorithms begin by connecting to a video stream over a number of weeks, during which they observe behaviour. During that time period, they start to learn what is normal during the day, night and at different times of the day. Over time, the system starts to issue alerts on behaviour that is inconsistent with what was observed during those different days and times.
- *Facial recognition systems*—these are used for access control or to identify individuals by matching points on the face of a person with a sample stored in a database.

The primary use of video analytics in a business context has been in surveillance functions such as recognising suspicious activities, identifying objects being removed and detecting camera tampering. Video analytics has been increasingly used in retail to develop insights into customer behaviour. For example, it can be used to develop heat maps of customer journeys through stores to identify store areas ignored by customers. These insights can also be combined with demographic data to make decisions on store layout, product placement, promotions and staffing allocations. Video analytics has also been employed to manage office usage as firms increasingly adopt remote working. Firms can monitor the occupation and usage of office space to develop heat maps of office spaces to decide on resource allocation in terms of heating and security personnel.

5.10 Data Analytics Tools for Social Media

Data analytics tools have been employed to analyse structured and unstructured data from social media channels such as Facebook, Instagram, LinkedIn, X and YouTube. Social media analytics includes metrics such as likes, follows, retweets, previews, clicks and impressions from individual channels. Data analytics and social media have focused on the areas outlined below.

5.10.1 Customer Analytics

Social media analytics can be used to determine customer sentiment around products and services, monitor the response to social media communications and identify trends around certain brands. The association, classification and clustering techniques already highlighted in this chapter have been used as tools to perform analytics on social media data. For example, clustering can be used to categorise social media users by age, gender, marital status, parent status and location. Influencers can then use these categories to better target messages, responses and initiatives. Moreover, classification can be used to determine behavioural types such as user, recommender, potential user or detractor.

Sentiment analysis has also been used to assess the tone and intent of social media comments. It can be employed to aggregate Facebook posts, X tweets and Amazon product reviews to understand customer pain points and desired features, as well as to gauge opinions on a new product just introduced to the market. Sentiment analysis can continually monitor positive or negative views around a brand, and these insights can be used to reposition or redesign features of the product or service.

5.10.2 Competitor Analytics

Firms have been increasingly using social media to analyse data on their competitors. This has included analysis of how positive, negative or neutral the content about competitors is, as well as the relevance of the content about the competitor. A firm needs to understand how competitors are using social media channels to effectively employ data analytics [12]. For example, a firm can monitor the frequency and sentiments of customers' postings about a competitor on social media channels and compare them against their own firm. Trend analysis of customer perceptions of competitor products can also provide ideas for new products.

5.11 Practices for Building Trust and Transparency in Managing Data

Managing customer data has become a key concern for firms in light of the damage it can do to corporate reputation. Whilst many firms are open about their data practices, other firms lack transparency and often collect and analyse data without the consent of customers. Proactive firms are recognising that it is not enough to provide end-user licensing agreements or present the customer with opaque terms and conditions for data use at user sign-up for a new service.

There is increasing evidence to show that winning the confidence and trust of customers is key for firms if they are to use data as a source of competitive differentiation. This can involve being transparent about what data are being collected, allowing customers to have control over their data and offering customers something in return for sharing their data [13]. There are a number of critical practices that firms should consider in building trust and transparency into their data analytics efforts, as now outlined below.

> **Illustration 5.2 Surveillance Capitalism**
>
> Concerns have been highlighted around privacy and the societal implications of the ever-increasing collection and analysis of data by technology firms on human behaviour. Some of these concerns have been grouped under the term 'surveillance capitalism'. Individuals are unwittingly allowing firms to collect data on their behaviour without fully understanding who is accessing the data and how the data are being used. They are engaging continuously with technology platforms that appear to offer free services, whilst in reality, these platforms are manipulating user behaviour to benefit other third parties. For example, social media platforms have been accused of using algorithms to modify the behaviour of individuals, including children, where individuals are receiving customised and continuously adapted influencing posts and advertising, which leads to subtle manipulation and addiction.
>
> The privacy of individuals has also been compromised by digital platforms as they invite more apps and third parties onto their platforms. For example, by expanding the number of third-party apps on its platform, Facebook released sensitive data on millions of people through mass data leaks. Despite the presence of regulation, it can still be quite challenging for individuals to obtain access to the data that firms hold on them. Privacy risks can extend into unforeseen consequences, such as inferences being made about individuals through the increasing use of algorithms and predictive analytics tools. For example, an angry father challenged Target, the US retailer, on why it had been sending his teenage daughter coupons for pregnancy products. Target's analytics tools had correctly inferred from his daughter's online activities that she was pregnant, something the father was unaware of.
>
> *Sources:* Zuboff, S., 2023. The Age of Surveillance capitalism. In *Social Theory Re-wired* (pp. 203–213). Routledge; and Gawer, A., 2022. Digital Platforms and Ecosystems: remarks on the Dominant Organizational Forms of the Digital age. *Innovation*, *24*(1), pp. 110–124.

5.11.1 Determine Data Origin and Source

Firms need to consider the origin and source of the data, which involves considering where the data came from, whether it was legally obtained and whether the appropriate consent from customers was obtained. Taking these actions will prevent the following problems arising [14]:

- *Collecting data without customer consent*—this involves collecting personal and sensitive data without consent and failing to ensure data accuracy. For example, in 2021, Amazon received a fine of €746 million from the Luxembourg National Commission for Data Protection in relation to consent. An investigation revealed how Amazon processed personal customer data and found that its advertising targeting system had not secured proper consent from customers.
- *Collecting data under deception*—this involves seeking consent to collect data from a person whilst not fully disclosing the purposes for which the data are being used.
- *Dark data*—firms often collect dark data, which refers to data that are rarely used and often forgotten. For example, these data tend to be unstructured and can include emails, text documents, social media posts, photographs and surveillance video footage. With the advent of advanced AI and other analytics tools, firms have been able to generate insights from these data without considering the ethical implications of doing so.

5.11.2 Communicate the Purpose of Data Analysis

A firm should seek the consent of the customer for collecting data for a specific purpose. It will be difficult to build trust if customers are unaware of why their data are being collected and analysed. Firms need to ensure that data are being analysed for the intended purpose, and whether the customer has agreed that it be used for that purpose. In particular, they should ensure that data are not being used for a purpose that was not originally implied when consent was given. Taking these actions will prevent the following problems arising [15]:

- *Collecting data for a different purpose*—this involves firms collecting data for one purpose and then employing analytics tools for another purpose. For example, a firm may analyse employee emails to gain insights into human resource-related issues, such as relationships with other employees, even though the email was originally intended as a communication tool only.
- *Selling data to third parties*—some firms have been collecting data and selling it on, often without the consent of the data provider. For example, the Australian postal service was sanctioned by the Australian government for selling names, addresses, ages and, in some cases, the political

affiliations of its customers. Whilst the data were being collected for postal purposes, it was then being sold on for use for another purpose.

5.11.3 Implement Effective Data Protection Mechanisms

A key aspect of building trust with customers involves ensuring that customer data are protected and not accessible to unauthorised parties. There have been some high-profile data protection failures that have led to significant fines for firms. For example, in May 2023, the Irish Data Protection Commission fined Meta, the US parent company of platforms including Instagram and WhatsApp, €1.2 billion. This fine was imposed as a result of Meta transferring the personal data of users in Europe to the United States without putting in place appropriate data protection mechanisms. Firms should also consider how data are protected both from malicious access and from accidental loss. This will also involve being able to restore data in the event of any damage or loss. It is also necessary to determine how long the data will be available and who has responsibility for destroying it.

5.11.4 Ensure Data Privacy

Data privacy is based on the principle that a person should have control over their personal data, such as how firms collect, store and use their data. Some of the recommendations already highlighted are relevant here, including obtaining user consent around collecting and analysing data and protecting data from misuse. It is worth noting that firms may benefit from implementing technical solutions around privacy protection, as these can also act as defences against malicious access by hackers.

One approach that firms employ to reduce data privacy risks is anonymising the data, which involves obscuring or removing personally identifiable information from a dataset. For example, credit card numbers can be replaced with either meaningless characters, digits or symbols, sometimes referred to as *data masking*. Other techniques include aggregating data through summaries or averages and approximating values, such as using ranges rather than actual ages. Data anonymisation has been used along with data analytics applications in healthcare to secure medical history, personal and treatment data.

However, there is often a trade-off with data anonymising as not enough anonymising may fail to comply with legislation [16]. At the same time, too much anonymising may render the data of no value for decision-making as a result of removing important data elements. Even anonymised data are potentially identifiable by cross-referencing data from other datasets. Firms need to consider how the data will be anonymised, who will have access to anonymised data and who will have access to data that can be used to identify the person.

5.11.5 Offer Customers Value in Exchange for Data Sharing

Research has found that customers will willingly share their data if firms provide them with value in return [17]. For example, customers are more likely to share data if it leads to enhancements in the product or service or results in price reductions. Smartphone providers use data to automatically add contacts that users interact with most often to their favourites list. Most customers value and opt into this feature, thereby agreeing to share their data for enhanced service.

Firms with trusted brands are more likely to find that consumers are willing to share their data. For example, users of music streaming services such as Spotify share their data so that these services can develop a user profile, allowing songs to be streamed to them that are tailored to their specific musical tastes. Where there is a clear link between the data collected and the resulting services provided, users will become more comfortable with sharing data as they increasingly use the service.

5.11.6 Give Customers Control Over Their Data

Some firms have started to build trust by giving customers control and access to the data held on them. Some healthcare digital services, such as cardiac monitoring, allow patients to view their own data and control how much data go to whom, using a browser and an app [18]. Patients can set up networks of healthcare providers, family and friends, or fellow users and patients, and send each different data. This contrasts with many healthcare services where the patient does not own the data or is unable to access it.

Illustration 5.3 Government Regulation and Data Access

Governments have been increasingly requesting access to data held by technology firms for security and law enforcement purposes. Technology firms such as Apple, Google and Meta, and have been accused by some governments of preventing access to personal data on criminals, terrorists and child abusers that could be used as evidence for prosecutions and intelligence for national security purposes.

The dispute between the UK government and Apple regarding one of its cloud services provides insights into the issues at play here. Apple received a demand from the UK government to grant access to its most secure cloud storage systems in order to access data held on individuals. In response, Apple mounted a legal challenge and withdrew its Advanced Data Protection system for iCloud in the UK rather than comply with the demand. Apple argued that this would create a 'back door' or cyber vulnerability by allowing law enforcement or security services to access its systems.

Cybersecurity experts have argued that encryption is necessary for protecting users from the increasing prevalence of fraud, identity theft and other attacks by hackers. They have also raised concerns that, by targeting a little-known Apple service, the UK government could set a precedent for compelling technology firms to create back door access to more popular apps. However, the UK government believes that breaking through the shield of encryption systems of Apple and Meta, including messaging apps, is critical for protecting citizens from terrorism and child abusers. The UK government argues that the legislation includes safeguards and independent oversight to protect privacy and security, and that data are requested only in exceptional circumstances.

Source: Bradshaw, T., Fisher, L., and Rathbone, J. (2025, Feb 7). UK orders Apple to give it access to encrypted cloud data, *Financial Times*.

Discussion Questions

1. Select a sector, such as financial services or transportation, and analyse how data analytics is transforming the sector. Identify examples of data analytics applications, types of data being collected and analysed, and the benefits and challenges of applying data analytics.
2. Select a firm that is using data network effects to strengthen its competitive position. Identify the types of data it is collecting and how it is using these data to lock-in customers and reduce switching costs. Highlight the regulatory implications around the way the firm handles data.
3. Select a digital platform such as Uber or eBay and assess how it employs predictive and prescriptive analytics to enhance service and create more personalised offerings for users.
4. Undertake research in a healthcare setting and analyse how audio and video analytics can be employed to deliver better health outcomes for patients.
5. Select a firm with which you are familiar and analyse the practices the firm uses for building trust and transparency in managing data, as set out in Sect. 5.11. Highlight any weaknesses in its approach and critically assess how the firm can improve its approach to managing data.

References

1. Desai, V., Fountaine, T., & Rowshankish, K. (2022). A better way to put your data to work. *Harvard Business Review, 100*(4), 100–107.
2. Segalla, M., & Rouziès, D. (2023). The ethics of managing people's data. *Harvard Business Review, 101*(4), 86–94.
3. Kimble, C., & Milolidakis, G. (2015). Big data and business intelligence: Debunking the myths. *Global Business and Organisational Excellence, 35*(1), 23–34.
4. Gandomi, A., & Haider, M. (2015). Beyond the hype: Big data concepts, methods, and analytics. *International Journal of Information Management, 35*(2), 137–144.
5. Pigni, F., Piccoli, G., & Watson, R. (2016). Digital data streams: Creating value from the real-time flow of big data. *California Management Review, 58*(3), 5–25.
6. See Pigni et al. (2016) in reference 5 above.
7. See Pigni et al. (2016) in reference 5 above.
8. Govindarajan, V., & Venkatraman, N. V. (2022). The next great digital advantage. *Harvard Business Review, 100*(3), 55–56.
9. Mela, C. F., & Moorman, C. (2018). Why marketing analytics hasn't lived up to its promise. *Harvard Business Review, 108*(5), 1–7.
10. Ridzuan, F., & Zainon, W. M. N. W. (2019). A review on data cleansing methods for big data. *Procedia Computer Science, 161*, 731–738.
11. Lee, I., & Shin, Y. J. (2020). Machine learning for enterprises: Applications, algorithm selection, and challenges. *Business Horizons, 63*(2), 157–170.
12. Lee, I. (2018). Social media analytics for enterprises: Typology, methods, and processes. *Business Horizons, 61*(2), 199–210.
13. Morey, T., Forbath, T., & Schoop, A. (2015). Customer data: Designing for transparency and trust. *Harvard Business Review, 93*(5), 96–105.
14. See Segalla and Rouziès (2023) in reference 2 above.
15. See Segalla and Rouziès (2023) in reference 2 above.
16. See Segalla and Rouziès (2023) in reference 2 above.
17. See Morey et al. (2015) in reference 13 above.
18. See Morey et al. (2015) in reference 13 above.

6

Digital Innovation

6.1 Introduction

Digital technologies have become a major aspect of innovation and new product development activities, allowing firms to collaborate externally with customers, technology suppliers and digital start-ups to create new products and services. Innovation has now become a truly collaborative process, where value is created by different players in the innovation process. The availability of large quantities of structured and unstructured data, such as text, images, video, audio and facial recognition data, has become an essential ingredient of innovation and new product development activities. Data gathered from sensors on products via the internet of things (IoT) can be analysed in real time both to improve customer experience and to generate insights into how the product can be redesigned for improvement. For example, the sensors in many cars can transfer performance data back to the manufacturer and can be used as a vital ingredient in future new product development activities.

Advances in digital technologies have allowed firms to pursue digital innovation, which involves adopting practices and processes to employ digital technologies to create new and improved products and services. Although these developments offer significant benefits to firms and their customers, they also present significant challenges. Many established firms do not have advanced digital services embedded in their products and lack an understanding of the

---

The original version of the chapter has been revised. A correction to this chapter can be found at https://doi.org/10.1007/978-3-031-99258-2_11

capabilities required for innovation in this context. Integrating digital services into a product is difficult due to the changing nature of digital technologies, and it is often not possible to predict the services customers will want in the future. Therefore, firms must rethink their current practices and processes regarding innovation and new product development. This chapter provides an understanding of the issues involved in digital innovation.

> **Learning Outcomes**
> - Understand the relationship between innovation, creativity and design.
> - Outline how digital technologies drive innovation.
> - Understand how digital technologies transform the design process.
> - Understand the concept of digital innovation.
> - Understand how data drive digital innovation.
> - Understand the challenges of digital innovation.
> - Understand the stages in the digital innovation process.
> - Understand the enablers of the digital innovation process.

6.2 Innovation

Innovation refers to a new way of doing something, such as the introduction of a new product or business process. Innovation can involve transforming ideas into something that is not only novel but also practical can provide a commercial return, and can come in the following forms [1]:

- It can be in the form of an invention, where the focus is on the use of resources such as people and equipment to develop a new product, service or a new way of doing things.
- It can lead to either incremental or radical changes in the way a firm creates and delivers a product or service.

There are a number of related aspects to innovation, including creativity and design, that provide an understanding of the concept of innovation, as shown in Fig. 6.1. Each of these is now outlined:

- *Creativity* is an essential ingredient of innovation, which involves developing new and useful ideas and going beyond conventional ideas or assumptions. Being creative can also involve putting existing or new ideas together into different combinations to create something new and useful.

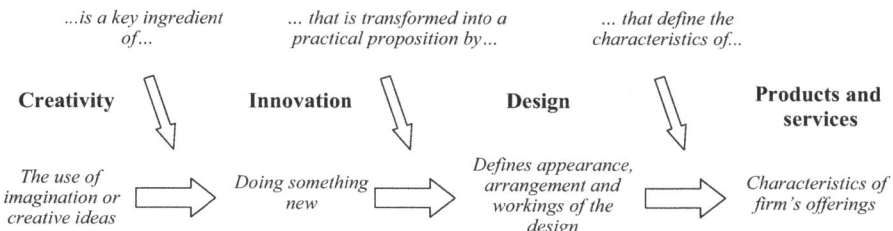

Fig. 6.1 The relationship between creativity, innovation and design [2]

- *Design* is the process of transforming innovative ideas into something more tangible. The design offers a road map of how the idea will work in practice. For example, this could be in the form of a design specification for a product or a process map for a new business process.

6.3 How Digital Technologies Drive Innovation

Innovation is recognised as a key driver of economic productivity, both at the national and firm levels. The proliferation of digital technologies is further improving and changing the innovation process. Erik Brynjolfsson has identified four ways in which digital technologies are revolutionising innovation [3].

6.3.1 Measurement

Firms can use data analytics technologies to analyse data from a range of sources, including clickstream data, Google Trends, product sensor data and data in enterprise resource systems. A more informed understanding of these data can allow companies to gain better knowledge of their customers, their business processes, and product and service quality. For example, Spotify places significant emphasis on measuring data around subscriber retention. It tracks subscriber retention rates to assess the effectiveness of its user acquisition and retention strategies, thus informing process improvements and customer experience initiatives. It also measures the conversion rates of free users moving to premium subscribers and the impact of ad-supported accounts on the success of its revenue models and marketing efforts [4].

6.3.2 Experimentation

When firms measure data, it allows them to experiment with how they sell to customers and improve the customer experience. Amazon conducts 'A/B experiments' with its customers, which involve testing its web pages by delivering different versions of the same page at the same time to different visitors, monitoring customer experience and follow-through. Spotify's approach to creating playlists employs a continuous cycle of experimentation to refine the listener experience. Spotify carries out experiments to develop and optimise suggested playlists for individual listeners by collecting data on their listening habits and preferences. It uses algorithms to analyse listener behaviour and feedback to dynamically alter playlist recommendations, thus ensuring they are tailored to the unique tastes of listeners [5]. This iterative process of experimentation allows Spotify to continually test and adapt listener playlists and deliver the most relevant and engaging experience to its audiences.

6.3.3 Sharing

Digital technologies make it possible to share data, insights and innovations. For example, firms can readily share information between employees on a range of issues, such as customer insights and the dynamic exchange of product performance data through the IoT, to stimulate ideas for new products. The rapid sharing of data and ideas can speed up innovation, improve competitiveness and lead to increased economic growth.

6.3.4 Replication

Once identified, digital technologies make it easy to replicate and scale up innovations. Digital innovations are composed of bits, software, music and web pages that can be replicated many thousands of times, and this process of replication has disrupted many industries. Furthermore, business processes can also be replicated by digital technologies. For example, CVS pharmacy in the US implemented an improved business process for prescription drug ordering at one of its pharmacies, which led to improved customer satisfaction. This business process was embedded into an enterprise system and then replicated to 4,000 other CVS stores within a year.

Each of these drivers of innovation is mutually reinforcing. Improved *measurement* increases the value of *experimentation*, and value can be further enhanced when the results are *shared* with other business units across the firm. Where the outcomes are significant, there will be a further impetus to *scale* the outcomes across the firm.

> **Illustration 6.1 The Role of Digital Technologies in Incremental and Radical Innovation**
>
> The concept of incremental or radical innovation refers to the pace and scale of change involved. Each of these concepts is relevant to applying digital technologies, as explained below.
>
> *Incremental innovation.* This is more likely to involve modest technological changes and refines, building upon existing knowledge and firm capabilities. Incremental innovation tends to be favoured by established firms in a market, as they already have the required knowledge and expertise in the technology. Making incremental changes to their products allows them to increase sales in existing markets and create new market segments.
>
> Digital technologies can be employed to make incremental changes to products and services. For example, smartphone manufacturers such as Apple and Samsung continuously add new product functionality and software features to their devices in product upgrades. Firms can add additional functionality and features to their digital platforms in innovation efforts at the business model level. Such innovation emphasises continuity and builds upon the firm's existing resources and capabilities.
>
> *Radical innovation.* This refers to a significant technological advancement that involves new knowledge and resources, making existing products and services obsolete. In this case, the pace of change is rapid, and the scale of change is significant, leading to considerable market upheaval and the displacement of existing firms. Radical innovations also tend to require different capabilities than those of established players and are often launched by new entrants into the industry.
>
> Again, digital technologies can be an enabler of radical innovation. For example, firms have been able to add digital features to their products, which has led to radical change in their respective markets. For instance, digital technologies have allowed Airbnb to develop an innovative business model that has altered the nature of competition in the travel accommodation market.

6.4 How Digital Technologies Transform the Design Process

The traditional design process for products has been dominated by the staged model, where the process goes through a number of stages, including idea generation, development, testing and validation, and product launch.

Throughout these stages, managers assess the viability of developing a new product or improving a process, and several of these stages include decision points on business case development, resources and risks. The new product development team must undertake development work, obtain information and perform data integration and analysis at each stage. At the end of each stage, the team must decide whether to continue investing in or discontinue the project.

This process depends largely on human decision-making and is labour-intensive. Once the product goes to market, significant investment is required to redesign and improve the product, and this can necessitate a new design process to restart. Digital technologies can transform this process and remove these limitations for firms offering digital services. For example, digital twins have become powerful tools in the design process by allowing product design teams to create virtual replicas of physical products and then use data to mirror functionality whilst the product is in operation. Digital twins enable designers to design, build, test and optimise what-if scenarios and undertake predictive maintenance, thus extending the life of the product. The virtual aspect of digital twins facilitates real-time collaboration amongst designers, regardless of their location.

AI can also transform the design process by reducing the constraints of scale, scope and learning, as explained below [6]:

- *Scale*—design can be difficult to scale due to the labour-intensive nature of the process, and for many products, it is not possible to design a new, bespoke solution for each customer. AI can remove some of these limitations, as customisation of the product at scale can be performed by the algorithm. For example, Netflix employs AI to mine a rich, detailed stream of data on viewers to develop a specific viewer experience customised around the viewer's own data. Moreover, the larger the number of users and the more detailed the data, the better the understanding of user behaviour.
- *Scope*—products are often designed for a single market, and once released, they are difficult to adapt to another context. AI can reduce this constraint by allowing a design to be adapted post-product release. For example, Airbnb has employed AI to develop new services. Through analysing the behaviour of guests, it has expanded into the area of 'travel experiences', where guests are offered complementary services such as horse riding or hiring musicians.
- *Learning*—in traditional design, the learning that comes from when the product is in the market is only used to inform future developments of the

product. Through digital technologies, it is now possible to learn about the product whilst it is in use and re-design it in real time. For example, as users on Netflix and Airbnb access their services, these firms use data and AI algorithms to learn about user behaviour to re-design the service for each user in real time. Learning is based on real use by the user and is not dependent on testing or prototyping. The learning is iterative and continuous, as the user experience is not the same as when the service was first released and is being updated on a real-time basis.

Illustration 6.2 How Nike Uses Digital Technologies to Revolutionise Product Design

Nike is using a range of digital technologies to revolutionise the design of its running shoes and sportswear. Digital technologies such as AI, virtual reality and 3D printing are speeding up the design process through rapid prototyping and amplifying the creativity of Nike designers. For example, Nike has developed its own generative AI model to design products based on combining exclusive athlete data and other public data. Generative AI has been used to create prototype shoes based on the preferences of top athletes such as Kylian Mbappé. These prototypes have then been input into AI models to generate hundreds of designs, which are then refined through digital fabrication techniques.

Nike has used digital technologies to predict product reactions to physical forces in the design of its running shoes. Designers worked with athletes to develop a sole that contours to the runner's foot, enhancing springiness and energy through foam cushioning. It also employs 4D motion capture data and advanced body-mapping technology to personalise highly precise kits for national teams in soccer. Nike actively involves customers in the design process as well. For example, the 'Nike Maker Experience' allows customers to design their own personalised shoes using voice commands to select colours and graphics. The 'Nike By You' lifestyle programme extends customisation to design and offers customers limitless options for personalisation of products. This programme is promoted by its brand ambassadors and integrated into its social media channels to increase customer engagement and satisfaction.

Source: Mathews, A. (2024, Jul 3). How Nike is using AI to transform product design, customer experience, and operational efficiency, *AIM Research*. https://aimresearch.co/market-industry/how-nike-is-using-ai-to-transform-product-design-customer-experience-and-operational-efficiency

6.5 An Overview of Digital Innovation

The advent of digital technologies has led to the emergence of the concept of digital innovation. Digital innovation refers to the practices and processes involved in employing digital technologies to create new and improved products and services on an ongoing basis. Digital innovation can include a range of innovation outcomes, such as new products and services, as well as new customer experiences and other sources of value. Digital innovation is enabled by a range of digital technologies, including the IoT, AI technologies, cloud computing and data analytics tools. It involves continuously experimenting with new ideas and digital technologies to create value for customers.

Consider a kitchen manufacturer and how it uses digital technologies for digital innovation. The firm employs augmented reality and AI to enhance the customer experience during the kitchen design phase. The augmented reality app allows customers to virtually position life-sized 3D models of kitchen cabinet options in their homes. The app employs camera and AI algorithms for depth perception and light estimation to make the kitchen design options as realistic as possible within the space. This digital innovation improves the customer experience by visually positioning the kitchen options in their environment pre-purchase, whilst allowing the manufacturer to reduce quality problems and lower costs.

6.5.1 Digital Innovation Versus Digital Transformation

Digital innovation is about how digital technologies can create new products and services on a continuous basis. It allows firms to experiment with new ideas and digital technologies on a smaller scale, learning from the outcomes and gradually implementing successful innovations. In contrast, digital transformation involves employing digital technologies to transform processes, products and business models, and leads to a holistic change in the operations and structure of the firm.

6.6 How Data Drives Digital Innovation

Data have increasingly been playing a critical and more sophisticated role in the digital innovation process. Already, firms have been accessing and analysing a variety of data, such as online shopping purchases, social media and web-browsing behaviour, and employing it as a critical input into their innovation processes. For example, online product and service reviews can be analysed to better understand customer perceptions of product functionality and quality, and this analysis can then inform the development of new products or product upgrades.

6.6.1 Innovation from Data

This approach is referred to as *innovation from data* and involves a centralised and firm-led process where digital tools are employed to acquire, analyse and act upon consumer data to enhance innovation [7]. The consumer plays a largely passive role in the innovation process, and the analysis of data happens without their knowledge. Therefore, consumers are largely passive data providers rather than active players in the innovation process, as summarised in Table 6.1.

6.6.2 Innovation as Data

A further level of sophistication in the role of data in the innovation process is referred to as *innovation as data*. This involves a decentralised, consumer-led process where consumers use digital tools to acquire and generate data to create their own innovative products. For example, consumers can use 3D software to remix designs created by other consumers, and this remixing activity, in the form of data generation by consumers, results in a new digital

Table 6.1 Innovation from data versus innovation as data [8]

Key characteristic	Innovation from data	Innovation as data
Role of consumers	Consumer acts as passive data providers and buyers of new products	Consumers act as data generators and can be new product creators
Relevance of the firm	The firm is solely responsible for acquiring, analysing and acting upon consumer data, and therefore plays a key role	Consumers are actively involved in acquiring, analysing and acting upon data and thus limiting the relevance of the firm
Nature of product	Products are closed in design and hard to adapt as consumers have only access to the product physical form	Products are open format and easy to adapt as consumers have access to their digital form

offering that can then be created on a 3D printer [9]. Therefore, consumers play an active role in the new product development process, developing their own new products and often actively involved in further adapting products created by other consumers. This *innovation as data* approach is summarised in Table 6.1.

6.7 Challenges of Digital Innovation

Despite the potential opportunities that digital innovation offers, the benefits have tended to be modest, with the achievement of only incremental improvements and cost savings. There are a number of challenges for established firms in their pursuit of digital innovation [10].

- *Lack of awareness of the value of digital technologies*—employees involved in digital innovation tend to focus on the value of data in a context such as the manufacturing process and fail to consider the value of data throughout the lifetime of the product being used by the customer. This leads to insufficient attention being given to how digital technologies can improve the product experience for the customer.
- *Lack of strategic vision and expertise*—employees involved in digital innovation projects tend to focus on short-term objectives and well-established requirements, such as price and quality, which leads to a lack of understanding of potential future opportunities through the better use of data analytics. This tension can lead to a focus on optimising the physical product rather than exploring how digital technologies can drive innovative activities in both the physical product and the manufacturing process.
- *Benefits not clear and short-term financial focus*—the benefits and costs of digital innovation can be difficult to quantify, as it is often challenging to specify the digital requirements upfront. Where there is a strong focus on financial key performance indicators, this can harm digital innovation, as it is difficult to justify from a short-term financial perspective. Moreover, the complexity of digital innovation, along with this short-term focus, means firms concentrate on traditional development processes and methods, which, in turn, can hinder digital innovation efforts.
- *Lack of collaboration*—digital innovation often requires collaboration in the innovation process between internal departments, which are often not accustomed to working together, such as R&D and information

technology specialists. The pursuit of control by some functions can harm collaboration and result in some functions not being equal partners in the process. This can lead to digital innovation occurring in an isolated manner, fostering siloed thinking and a failure to consider both the complexities and potential benefits.
- *Employee resistance*—digital innovation can challenge established working practices and lead to managers and employees having to embrace new capabilities. For example, digital innovation may mean that managers have to approach innovation in an experimental manner rather than through a rigid, staged process.

6.8 A Framework for Understanding the Digital Innovation Process

Firms manufacturing products with digital capabilities are likely to require a different organising approach to digital innovation than with conventional innovation, as digital technologies are continuously evolving and changing. Where previously the innovation process was driven by discrete stages in a pre-determined product life cycle, now product services can be improved and customised digitally to meet the needs of customers whilst the product is in use. Pursuing digital innovation requires new capabilities to exploit the benefits of digital technologies, whilst at the same time not damaging existing practices around conventional innovation in the firm. The increasing prominence of products with digital capabilities means that many products must be both functionally and digitally world-leading.

This section presents a framework that provides an understanding of how firms manufacturing products with digital capabilities should manage the digital innovation process, as shown in Fig. 6.2. The framework is based on a process approach, where digital technologies such as the IoT, social media technologies and data analytics tools are inputs into the digital innovation process in the framework. The digital innovation process shows the stages involved in the process and how the innovation process is supported by a number of enablers, as shown in Fig. 6.2.

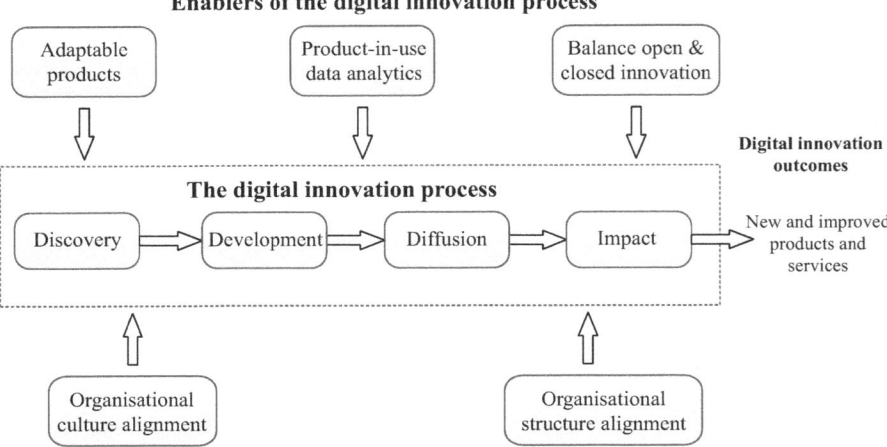

Fig. 6.2 A framework for understanding the digital innovation process

6.8.1 The Digital Innovation Process

The digital innovation process includes a number of iterative stages in the digital innovation process, as shown in Fig. 6.2. These stages are outlined below [11]:

- *Discovery*—this involves identifying ideas on how digital technologies can be developed into new products or services for customers. Ideas can be generated by gathering intelligence on new devices, digital channels and social media to identify opportunities for applying digital technologies. For example, IoT and data analytics technologies can be applied to gain more data and insights whilst the product is in use, allowing the firm to embed new services into the product. This stage can include invention, which involves creating something new through the internal creative process within a firm. Part of this analysis can involve assessing how the digital technology can address problems and opportunities for the customer. This stage also involves assessing and selecting a digital technology in the external environment to potentially develop or adopt.
- *Development*—this involves deploying the digital technology into a usable innovation for the customer. It involves developing and adapting the digital technology, augmenting it with current products and services to create an additional value proposition for the customer. The development stage also involves deciding which technology features will be used, how

the technology will be integrated with other systems in the firm, how firm structures and processes will be changed and the implications for data security.
- *Diffusion*—this involves diffusing the digital innovation amongst a significant group of potential customers. Deployment is an important activity here, which involves allocating the necessary resources to encourage users to adopt the innovation. For example, for digital products and services, the firm has to demonstrate to potential users that they are easy to use and learn. This will involve clearly articulating the value proposition of the digital innovation and how it creates value for users [12].
- *Impact*—this stage involves assessing the impact that the digital innovation has on customers and the firm. A digital innovation can both have a positive impact on the cost position of the firm and allow the firm to differentiate its offerings from competitors. Consideration should be given to managing intellectual property issues associated with the innovation so that profits are protected from suppliers, customers and imitators. This also involves continuously refining and improving the digital innovation so that further value can be added for customers.

6.8.2 Enablers of the Digital Innovation Process

Enablers of the digital innovation process include adaptable products, product-in-use analytics, balancing open and closed innovation, organisational culture and organisational structure alignment, as outlined below.

Adaptable products. Developing adaptable products involves designing products that can be changed and updated during use. Adaptable products follow some of the logic of digital products, such as smartphones, where the operating system of the device and apps can be adapted and improved through software updates. Physical products, such as cars and industrial equipment, have been adopting some of the features of digital products, where software can be embedded in them, thus allowing changes in their functionality during product use. These adaptive features are an important enabler of the digital innovation process. There are four ways in which firms can build adaptable products [13]:

- *Configurable hardware*—some products can have hardware that can be adapted to the needs of customers. For example, wheelchairs with modular bases can extend, shrink or be reformatted as the medical needs of the users change.

- *Preconfigured software*—some products can learn from and adapt to the user to improve the experience for the user. For example, advanced wearable devices include software that gives users advice on how to improve performance.
- *Updatable hardware*—some products can allow repair and customisation. For example, security systems can allow new physical devices to be added, such as facial recognition cameras and motion sensors.
- *Updatable software*—products can have software that can be updated over time whilst the product is in use. For example, the software embedded in smart thermostats can be adjusted to improve heating and cooling efficiency.

Building these features into products allows firms to drive improvements whilst the product is in use and allows firms to constantly innovate. Innovation is more straightforward when the design of the physical product allows additional features to be added to the product without the need for physical changes to the product.

Consider the case of Tesla, which redefined its approach to the design of the car [14]. As the physical features of the car cannot be redesigned remotely during the product's lifetime, it eliminated all the physical interacting elements, such as buttons, to embed most of the controls into the digital user interface, such as the in-cabin driver touchscreen. Furthermore, the sensors in the car, including ultrasound equipment, GPS input, cameras and radar transmitters, allow Tesla to collect and analyse data to offer new services to customers over the lifetime of the car. This allows Tesla to update certain features of the car after it is sold, whilst at the same time employing digital technologies to offer the potential for new sources of revenue through improving the driver experience.

Product-in-use data analytics. A firm can employ data analytics tools to monitor the performance of the product whilst it is in use to drive digital innovation. This can also involve having mechanisms in place to allow the customer to provide feedback data on product performance. There are two features to this product-in-use data analytics enabler:

- *Data connectivity*—the firm should have infrastructure in place to connect the firm with its products whilst they are in use. Ideally, the transfer of data should happen without human intervention and be in real time from the user, the product and the user environment. Other data sources, such as social media channels, can also be useful for identifying areas for digital innovation. The presence of this connectivity and software can increase product functionality and allow for remote service.

- *Analytics capability*—this involves having the capability to analyse the product-in-use data, which should allow the firm to develop a detailed understanding of the needs of the customer. These insights can be used to generate ideas for digital innovation. For example, this can involve extracting insights and trends from data such as text, voice interactions, video and high-resolution 3D images to quickly develop complex new designs. Continuous monitoring and analysis of product-in-use data can also allow firms to identify and address design problems not detected during initial product design testing.

> **Illustration 6.3 How Deere and Company Employ Product-In-Use Data Analytics in Digital Innovation**
>
> Deere and Company, the US farm equipment manufacturer, employs product-in-use data analytics. It collects billions of data points on soil, crop and weather conditions from thousands of machines on over 325 million acres of land. These data are fed into its cloud-enabled system, where it is analysed and used to generate future improvements and innovations in its products. The product-in-use data analytics capability has allowed farmers to decrease their use of herbicide by more than two-thirds and increase productivity.
>
> Product-in-use data analytics also allows the firm to develop longer-term and deeper relationships with customers. Through integrating the physical and digital elements of the product, the firm can involve customers throughout the life cycle of the product and, at the same time, bring them into the product design process to generate insights for new products rather than only collecting feedback on existing products. These interactions can build stronger relationships, brand loyalty and value. Moreover, they even foster the growth of communities around a product, which take on the task of identifying ways to improve it.
>
> Source: Govindarajan, V., and Venkatraman, V. (2024). Heavy Machinery Meets AI. *Harvard Business Review*, 103(3–4), pp. 98–107.

Balance open and closed innovations. The nature of a product with digital capabilities means that firms must strike a balance between maintaining internal knowledge and capabilities required for designing the physical product, whilst at the same time increasingly relying on external knowledge and partners for the digital services embedded in the product.

Closed innovation. For many firms, the design of the components of physical products has tended to rely mainly on internal knowledge. These products have clearly defined functionality over the life cycle of the product, along with specified components and manufacturing processes. This approach to innovation is often referred to as *closed innovation*, where firms are keen to protect intellectual property and avoid competitors free-riding on their ideas. Know-how, technology, processes and intellectual property remain under the control of the firm, with little collaboration with external parties.

However, the nature of digital technologies, such as the digital elements that complement the physical product, requires a different approach from *closed innovation*. Digital technologies are constantly evolving, often over time offering more functionality at a lower cost, and it is not possible to define all the digital features of the product in advance due to rapidly changing and emerging digital technologies.

Open innovation. In the context of digital innovation, firms have to access much of the knowledge and technologies externally, as it is not possible to develop all the product requirements in-house. This is similar to the concept of *open innovation,* where a firm increasingly uses inflows and outflows of knowledge to speed up the internal innovation process and expand the markets for the external use of innovation [15]. Open innovation involves the deliberate import and export of knowledge by a firm to accelerate and enhance its innovation efforts. Exchanging ideas openly is seen as likely to produce better products more quickly.

In a digital innovation context, it is necessary for many firms manufacturing products to pursue a combination approach where open and closed innovations are aligned. Some technologies can be developed by integrating the activities of external parties, such as customers or suppliers, to complement the firm's own products. Alternatively, closed innovation can be employed to develop a new technology where the entire internal resource and knowledge requirements reside in-house. The combination approach is particularly relevant to digital innovation, where closed and open innovations can co-exist.

Illustration 6.4 Open and Closed Innovations at Volvo in Digital Innovation

Volvo refreshed its innovation capability to compete in an increasingly digital environment, despite the reservations of many managers who viewed Volvo as a car company and not a digital business. Volvo developed a vision where the digital features of the car could be updated after the car was sold to improve the customer driving experience and generate additional revenue. It viewed digital innovation as an organisational capability, which involved developing digital innovation capabilities and maintaining its current capabilities in car design and manufacture.

Volvo had to strike a balance between its existing design processes for the car, whilst at the same time integrating digital technologies. In contrast to the design of the car and associated components, which can be designed four years in advance, this approach was not feasible for digital technologies. Digital services could not be designed that far into the future and had to be generated through ongoing collaboration with car makers, external developers, end users and regulatory authorities.

Therefore, Volvo adapted the conventional product development cycle for the physical car and engaged with external players to align more closely with developments in digital technologies. This led to an open innovation approach being pursued for digital innovation, whilst still aligning with a largely closed innovation process for the design of the physical car.

Open innovation allowed Volvo to jointly develop and add new digital services to its cars. This involved implementing a cloud-based platform, which created opportunities for collaboration with external players without impacting current internal design practices around the car. This approach allowed the functionality in the car, related to digital services, to be enabled, updated or replaced over the lifetime of the car without impacting the configuration of the car.

Open innovation for Volvo required a new approach to contracting with external players, such as digital service providers. Traditional supplier contracts for car components, which involved financial transactions, were often not appropriate. In its collaboration with Spotify, Volvo did not write complex contracts or payment terms. It recognised the need to establish relationships with partners for digital services that balanced control with sufficient flexibility to co-create value. Therefore, it developed a new form of contract that emphasised joint liability and cost neutrality.

Volvo also adopted an approach to digital platforms that would allow new digital services to be easily added in the future. This involved developing generic digital resources that could act as digital building blocks, which, in turn, could be used, combined and built upon to resolve new innovation problems in the future. This allowed Volvo to shift the focus from product platforms for efficiency-driven, predefined products to digital platforms that enabled the addition of new digital services.

Source: Svahn, F., Mathiassen, L., and Lindgren, R., 2017. Embracing Digital Innovation in Incumbent Firms: How Volvo Cars Managed Competing Concerns. *MIS Quarterly*, 41(1), pp. 239–253.

Organisational culture alignment. Organisational culture can have a significant impact on the digital innovation process through the value it places on issues such as challenging current ideas and practices, willingness to take risks and the stigma associated with failure. Culture reflects the way in which innovation activity is perceived and implemented in a firm. Firms with a strong innovation culture normally promote the following six practices [16]:

- *Outward-looking orientation*—this strongly links with external parties such as customers, competitors and industry bodies. The culture should allow the firm to respond to signals or actions by these parties, and this contrasts with inward-looking firms that emphasise the 'not-invented-here' attitude.
- *Promotes communication*—communication should be straightforward and frequent across the firm, thus allowing employees with different perspectives to share knowledge.
- *Open to new ideas*—this involves allowing employees to experiment, putting forward new ideas and ensuring that both employees and managers are receptive to such ideas.
- *Challenging established ideas*—this involves a willingness to question the status quo. This approach should allow assumptions and established norms to be examined, while seeking new and better ways of doing things.
- *Acceptance of failure*—as innovations do not always succeed, a culture of accepting failure is necessary to drive innovation. It is also important that lessons are learned from failure.
- *Evaluation and reflection*—there should be an emphasis on reflection and not jumping to unreasonable judgements based on incomplete information.

These six practices that promote innovation are relevant to promoting digital innovation. In particular, culture change has to occur in established firms to drive digital innovation. For example, as manufacturers increasingly pursue digital innovation as a means of generating aftermarket sales throughout the product's lifetime, employees must move away from a culture of viewing innovation as solely focused on the initial design of the physical product.

Important mechanisms for building a culture of digital innovation include the following:

- There should be a lower aversion to risk, with a willingness amongst employees to take risks and experiment with applying digital technologies to improve business processes and products.
- Firms should encourage learning by implementing small, incremental and iterative changes through experimentation. A culture of learning should be supported and promoted throughout the firm. Digital innovation involves continuous learning, whereby new digital technologies are explored to create an understanding of their unique attributes and potential for application.

- A culture of collaboration is necessary for bringing disparate functions together [17]. This involves developing shared norms, beliefs and values within a firm that enable successful innovation in a digital context.

Organisational structure alignment. Embedding digital features into physical products requires a different organising logic for firms, as the technologies are rapidly changing, and it is often not possible to specify upfront the digital requirements or predict the functionality and cost of digital technologies required over the lifetime of the product. Product designers and engineers are used to working in an environment where the product technologies are relatively stable and operate over a defined life cycle. Firms must ensure that their approach to innovation for the physical product and the digital features co-exist and complement one another.

Digital innovation often requires changes in organisational structures. For example, there is a recognition that the organisational form associated with traditional manufacturing, characterised by hierarchy and centralised, top-down decision-making, is not fit for purpose in the pursuit of digital innovation. Firms must embrace organisational forms that are characterised by a high degree of openness and facilitate flexible collaboration and coordination with innovation networks, as evidenced by the following developments:

- *Leadership*—structures must be developed that combine dominant and consensus-seeking leadership during digital innovation projects to nurture collaboration amongst employees from different functions and skill backgrounds [18]. For example, digital innovation requires a more prominent role for information technology specialists in new product design programmes. This can also extend outside the firm to include collaboration between internal and external stakeholders. For example, involving customers to generate ideas for new products and services is an important source of digital innovation.
- *Governance*—there is an onus on top management to ensure that it has the governance structures in place to ensure coordination and that projects are not carried out in isolation from one another. Often, in established firms, there is a strong silo and departmental culture and a lack of collaboration between the information technology function and other functions.
- *Skills development*—management has to assess the status of employee skills, ensuring that they can be effectively assembled into digital innovation teams with the right combination of skills. This will require ongoing investments in both digital and management skills through recruitment

and retraining. Essentially, a firm should have human resources practices in place that encourage talent development amongst internal staff, whilst at the same time scanning the labour market for new recruits that can augment and refresh the existing innovation knowledge base within the firm. Firms also need to carefully consider the balance between carrying out digital innovation projects in-house and engaging specialist external consultants. Therefore, firms often need to redefine the role of middle managers to react to the demands of digital innovation.

> **Discussion Questions**
>
> 1. Referring to Sect. 6.3, select an organisation with which you are familiar and analyse how it employs digital technologies to drive innovation at the *measurement, experimentation, sharing* and *replication* levels.
> 2. Referring to Sect. 6.4, research the role of digital technologies in the design process for a product and analyse how digital technologies can reduce the constraints of scale, scope and learning.
> 3. Referring to the adaptable product enabler in Sect. 6.8.2, highlight how some firms are embracing this concept and provide examples from these firms to illustrate your analysis.
> 4. Referring to the product-in-use data analytics enabler in Sect. 6.8.2, identify three firms that are adopting this concept. Highlight the benefits and challenges involved for these firms.
> 5. Referring to the 'Organisational culture alignment' section, select a firm with which you are familiar and analyse how it promotes the six practices required for a strong innovation culture.

References

1. Slack, N., Brandon-Jones, A., & Burgess, N. (2022). *Operations Management* (10th ed.). Pearson.
2. Adapted from Slack et al. (2022) in Reference 1 Above.
3. Hopkins, M. S. (2010). The four ways IT is revolutionizing innovation. *MIT Sloan Management Review, 51*(3), 51.
4. Cuofano, W. I. G., & Cuofano, G. (2024) How does spotify make money? Spotify freemium business model analysis 8 February. https://fourweekmba.com/spotify-business-model/. Accessed: 09/05/24
5. Barthle, C. (2023) *Humans + Machines: A look behind the playlists powered by Spotify's algotorial technology - Spotify Engineering.* https://engineering.atspotify.com/2023/04/humans-machines-a-look-behind-spotifys-algotorial-playlists/. Accessed: 09/05/24

6. Verganti, R., Vendraminelli, L., & Iansiti, M. (2020). Innovation and design in the age of artificial intelligence. *Journal of Product Innovation Management*, *37*(3), 212–227.
7. Rindfleisch, A., O'Hern, M., & Sachdev, V. (2017). The digital revolution, 3D printing, and innovation as data. *Journal of Product Innovation Management*, *34*(5), 681–690.
8. Adapted from Rindfleisch et al. (2017) in reference 7 above.
9. Adapted from Rindfleisch et al. (2017) in reference 7 above.
10. Moschko, L., Blazevic, V., & Piller, F. T. (2023). Paradoxes of implementing digital manufacturing systems: A longitudinal study of digital innovation projects for disruptive change. *Journal of Product Innovation Management*, *40*(4), 506–529.
11. Some of the logic of these stages is related to the digital innovation model in, Fichman, R. G., Dos Santos, B. L., & Zheng, Z. E. (2014). Digital innovation as a fundamental and powerful concept in the information systems curriculum. *MIS Quarterly*, *38*(2), 329–A15.
12. Nylén, D., & Holmström, J. (2015). Digital innovation strategy: A framework for diagnosing and improving digital product and service innovation. *Business Horizons*, *58*(1), 57–67.
13. Govindarajan, V., Eapen, T., & Finkenstadt, D. J. (2024). Design products that won't become obsolete. *Harvard Business Review*, *102*(6), 96–103.
14. See Verganti et al. (2020) in reference 6 above.
15. Chesbrough, H. (2003). *Open Innovation: The New Imperative for Creating and Profiting From Technology*, Harvard Business School Press.
16. Smith, D. (2025). *Exploring Innovation* (4th ed.). McGraw-Hill.
17. Hund, A., Wagner, H. T., Beimborn, D., & Weitzel, T. (2021). Digital innovation: Review and novel perspective. *The Journal of Strategic Information Systems*, *30*(4), 101695.
18. Reypens, C., Lievens, A., & Blazevic, V. (2021). Hybrid orchestration in multi-stakeholder innovation networks: Practices of mobilizing multiple, diverse stakeholders across organizational boundaries. *Organization Studies*, *42*(1), 61–83.

7

Business Model Innovation

7.1 Introduction

Digital transformation can involve considerable change both inside the firm and in relationships with customers and suppliers. It can involve changes in the traditional way the firm does business and lead to the introduction of new processes and practices. Digital transformation is often a response to disruption in the business environment in the form of the emergence of new start-ups and competitors.

The business model concept is a useful approach for understanding and modelling the changes associated with digital transformation. A business model can explain how a firm creates value for customers, for example, in the form of superior service, and captures value for the firm, for example, through having a better cost structure than competitors. The business model can reflect issues such as the architecture of the firm's value proposition, market segments, revenue model and cost structure. It can be employed both to create a business model for a new start-up and to allow an established firm to redesign its existing business model.

Business model innovation has evolved from the business model concept to consider how firms can both innovate in and reconfigure their business models during the digital transformation journey. At the same time, digital technologies have increasingly played an important role in business model innovation efforts. For example, firms have been adapting their business models via digital technologies to transition from product ownership models to customer pay-per-use

---

The original version of the chapter has been revised. A correction to this chapter can be found at https://doi.org/10.1007/978-3-031-99258-2_11

business models. This chapter highlights tools that firms can employ to design and redesign their business models in response to advances in digital technologies and the pursuit of digital transformation.

> **Learning Outcomes**
> - Understand the business model concept.
> - Understand disruptive innovation and its impact on business models.
> - Understand business model innovation.
> - Understand how digital technologies drive business model innovation.
> - Understand the barriers to employing digital technologies in business model innovation.
> - Understand how the business model canvas can be used in business model innovation.
> - Understand how design thinking can be used in business model innovation.

7.2 The Business Model Concept

A business model outlines how a firm creates and captures value and involves *choices* and *consequences*. Senior management has to make *choices* around how the firm should operate, including choices on employment contracts, procurement practices, facility location, extent of outsourcing and service levels [1]. These managerial choices have *consequences*. For example, pricing policies impact the volume of sales, which in turn affects economies of scale and bargaining power over suppliers.

Ryanair, the low-cost Irish airline, provides an illustration of the *choices* and *consequences* of a business model in action. Ryanair, in the 1990s, became a low-cost airline by pursuing a no-frills customer service approach, reducing costs and cutting prices relative to its competitors. Key *choices* the company made included offering low fares, flying in and out of secondary airports, charging for any supplementary products or services, focusing on the short-haul flight market, offering generous incentives to employees and using a standardised fleet of Boeing 737s. The *consequences* of these *choices* meant that Ryanair could achieve high volumes, low fixed and variable costs, and a strong reputation for the lowest fares in the industry.

A business model has a number of components, including defining the customer value proposition and the pricing structure, how the company will organise itself and partner with others to create value and how its supply chain is structured [2]. These components can be summarised in a digital context as follows [3]:

- *Value creation* refers to the value that is offered to the customer and includes the type of digital product or service. It can involve other ecosystem players with digital capabilities, such as new digital start-ups and cloud providers. These players can offer skills to develop innovative applications that create additional value and provide more advanced digital offerings for existing firms in the ecosystem.
- *Value delivery* refers to how processes are employed to deliver value to customers, and this can involve delivery and logistics resources and capabilities. Digital technologies can facilitate the addition of new players to the ecosystem, offering digital applications in areas such as predictive maintenance and route optimisation for logistics providers. This can also involve changes in the roles and capabilities of existing logistics firms to further exploit the potential of digital technologies.
- *Value capture* refers to how firms will generate a margin and, therefore, plots the balance between revenue and costs. The emergence of digital players and digital infrastructure can alter cost structures and revenue models in areas such as subscription and pay-per-use, leading to greater sharing of revenues and risks between players in the ecosystem.

> **Illustration 7.1 How Digital Technologies Drive AirBnB's Business Model**
>
> Airbnb disrupted the hotel industry by creating an innovative business model driven by digital technologies. Airbnb recognised that digital technologies allowed it to create a new business model that would disrupt the traditional economics of the industry. It does not own or manage any physical property and allows its users to rent any habitable space on a digital platform, which contrasts with the established business model of hotels. The key components of Airbnb's business model are as follows:
>
> - *Value creation*—it creates value for hosts by allowing them to generate income on the platform through renting their accommodation, giving them control over bookings, and providing insurance against damage or accidents. Airbnb creates value for guests through lower rental costs relative to hotels, booking convenience, transparent ratings of accommodation and payment security. It has redefined the customer value proposition by providing a lower-cost and more personalised service.
> - *Value delivery*—Airbnb delivers value by providing a platform that matches renters of accommodation with those seeking accommodation and takes a percentage of the rent. It has a number of channels to reach hosts and guests, including the website, smartphone app, social media, digital marketing and the affiliate model. It builds trust with hosts and guests through strong communication on the platform, protection of data, personalised recommendations and 24/7 customer service support.

> - *Value capture*—Airbnb generates revenue from host fees, ranging from 3 to 5%, and from guest fees, ranging from 0 to 20%. Airbnb's costs are considerably lower than hotels, as hosts are managing and maintaining the property and services on offer. Moreover, Airbnb can scale up more quickly than hotels by not owning physical assets, which also allows it to charge lower prices.

7.3 Disruptive Innovation

Clayton Christensen developed the theory of disruptive innovation to explain the threat posed by a significant new technology to the existing business models of established firms in an industry [4]. Disruptive innovation occurs when a product or service is targeted at an overlooked market or customers by established firms within an industry. Over time, the product or service begins to attract the attention of more profitable customers in higher-end segments.

Christensen's primary interest was in analysing the failure of successful companies and the influence of new disruptive technologies. Critically, his analysis revealed that successful firms failed specifically because, when faced with disruptive technologies, they continued to make decisions and choices that had made them successful in the past rather than adapting to the new business environment [5].

Christiansen's theory of disruptive innovation had a significant impact as it challenged much of the contemporary thinking around business strategy and competition, which was dominated by the work of Michael Porter [6]. Porter employed the concept of generic strategies to explain how firms could compete through either cost leadership at the low-priced end of the market, differentiation at the higher-priced end of the market or focusing on serving a specific niche market. Christiansen's theory challenged this view by highlighting how competitors could enter at the low end of the market, where profit margins are low, customers are price-conscious, and, critically, this part of the market is not defended by existing players [7].

A disruptive technology normally has the following two characteristics:

- Firstly, it initially underperforms compared to the products of incumbent firms in serving customer needs in the market. When first introduced to the market, the technology appeals to customers at the lower end of the market, thus limiting the profit potential and market attractiveness for

incumbents. Although the technology may be attractive to a segment of customers not currently served by the incumbent, this can provide a market opportunity for the new entrant. The new entrant can then develop their capabilities to start serving the needs of existing customers in the market, whilst at the same time bringing new customers into the market.
- Secondly, the disruptive technology's products can become a threat by improving rapidly along features that mainstream customers of the incumbent are not interested in. The disruptive technology initially underperforms the incumbent on features demanded by mainstream customers, but with steady improvements, it starts to meet or outstrip those demands. The incumbent also fails to recognise that their existing customers are unwilling to pay more for product features that were important in the past. The disruptive technology starts to become more aligned with the needs of the customers, which threatens the existence of the incumbent.

The reaction of the incumbent to the disruptive technology further exacerbates the problem for the following reasons:

- Investing in disruptive technologies is not a rational financial decision for senior management in the incumbent, as the technology is only of interest to the least profitable customers in the market.
- Successful firms tend to have systems in place for eliminating ideas customers do not ask for, thus making it difficult for them to invest in new, disruptive technologies.
- Decisions around resource allocation that have made established firms successful often lead them to reject disruptive technologies. Performance management approaches and incentive structures often reinforce this practice and discourage investment in new technologies.
- The reason the incumbent firm has failed to adapt to disruptive technologies is that it has practiced principles of good management. For example, successful firms are often displaced, even though they followed the basic rules of strategy and marketing that proposed they should listen to their most profitable customers.

> **Illustration 7.2 Kodak and Disruptive Innovation**
>
> Kodak is often cited as an example of a company that failed to adapt to the challenge of disruptive innovation in the form of digital photography. Kodak filed for bankruptcy in 2012 due to increased competition, the shift from analog film to digital photography and increasing debt. This is all the more interesting as Kodak invented the first digital camera in 1975 and, in the mid-1970s, accounted for 95% of global film sales.
>
> Digital photography was a disruptive innovation, as it was initially inferior to traditional film, although it improved rapidly. It appealed to customers who wanted instant and convenient photos, which contrasted with the traditional film market. Digital photography then became of sufficient quality to act as a replacement for traditional film. As most of its profit came from selling chemicals used for developing film, Kodak was reluctant to invest in digital photography, as it posed a threat to its traditional film business.
>
> The culture of Kodak was dominated by an analog chemistry mindset and the sources of success in the past were an impediment to change, as the nature of competition had completely changed with digital photography gradually destroying the traditional film mass market. Kodak's knowledge of chemistry, film production and patents—core capabilities in the past—had almost become redundant as the shift towards digital photography happened.
>
> The history of the business was one of competing in a high-margin industry, and therefore, it struggled to move effectively into low-margin businesses. Kodak had a near-monopoly position in the analog business and, as a result, developed a mindset that was inappropriate for competing in the much more competitive digital business. For example, the mindset amongst middle managers involved focusing on more profitable customers, and they were resistant to embracing ideas on how to address the challenges brought about by digital photography. When firms become overly reliant on following what was successful in the past, they often fail to recognise changes or disruptions in the business environment and do not possess the capabilities required to react.
>
> Source: Shih, W. (2016). The real lessons from Kodak's decline. *MIT Sloan Management Review*, 57(4), pp. 11–13; and Lucas Jr., H.C., and Goh, J.M. (2009). Disruptive technology: How Kodak missed the digital photography revolution. *The Journal of Strategic Information Systems*, 18(1), pp. 46–55.

7.4 Business Model Innovation

Business model innovation involves reconfiguring how a firm operates, including strategic choices that owners and managers can make, as it involves defining how the firm interacts with other players and customers in its ecosystem [8]. It can bring previously unconnected players together and link current players in novel ways. Digital technologies can facilitate the introduction of new digitally supported processes and players, whilst at the same time eliminating redundant ones.

In contrast to innovation at either the product or process levels, innovating at the business model level has the potential to provide a more sustainable advantage, as it is more difficult to replicate [9]. For example, competitors might find it more challenging to replicate an entire novel activity system than to copy a distinct product or process. Thus, the returns from product or process innovation can be eroded, whereas innovation at the business model level can sometimes provide a sustainable advantage. The imperative for business model innovation has become more significant in a digital context, as competitive threats can rapidly emerge from outside traditional market boundaries. Business model innovation can be achieved in the following ways [10]:

- *Content of the ecosystem* refers to the selection of activities involved in the system, which can include adding or removing activities. For example, in the early 1990s, IBM transitioned from being a hardware manufacturer to becoming a provider of business services, including consulting, IT maintenance and other business services.
- *New activity ecosystem structure* refers to how activities are linked and in what order in the system. Priceline, the online travel agency, established links with airline companies, credit card companies and others to create a reverse market in which customers can post desired prices for the acceptance of sellers. This has fundamentally changed the way in which these players interact and how airline tickets are sold.
- *New ecosystem governance structure* refers to who performs the activities in the system. Next Issue Media, acquired by Apple in 2018, is an example of a firm in the magazine market pursuing business model innovation in response to changes brought about by digital technologies. A consortium of magazine publishers, including Time and Hearst, established an online magazine newsstand using multiple digital formats. Initially, the online platform was jointly owned by industry competitors to address declining print circulation and advertising revenue.

The value drivers of novelty, lock-in, complementarities and efficiency provide a useful basis for assessing the strength of a firm's business model and analysing changes made in the current and redesigned business model, as outlined below [11]:

- *Novelty* refers to the level of innovation encapsulated in the business model. For example, when first established, Uber developed a novel business model with an app that allowed passengers to hail a taxi and drivers to charge fares and get paid, whilst hiring drivers as independent contractors.
- *Lock-in* refers to aspects of the business model that build switching costs and/or incentives for business model participants to stay and transact

within the activity system. For example, Apple has services such as iTunes, AppleTV +, Apple Fitness + and iCloud that generate income, which at the same time builds loyalty amongst customers when buying hardware devices such as iPads, iPhones and iMacs. Such an arrangement discourages customers from moving to other platforms, such as Android, because of the practical difficulties of switching.

- *Complementarities* refer to how interdependencies between business model elements create additional value, and bundling elements together in the business model adds more value than running them separately. In commercial banking, deposit banking acts as a key source of funding that complements the lending activity of a bank.
- *Efficiency* refers to how a firm manages its business model to achieve greater efficiency by reducing transaction costs. It should deliver cost savings through the linkages in the business model. Aldi, the German grocery discount retailer, has designed a business model that supports its low-cost strategy. This is based on focusing on high-volume products, having a limited variety of each product, bare-bones stores and private-label brands. These features allow Aldi to have significant bargaining power over suppliers and a less complex—and consequently lower-cost—supply chain than its competitors. This business model allows Aldi to have a cost advantage over competitors, thus giving it an important competitive advantage.

Illustration 7.3 Diagnosing Disruption Threats to Business Models

Research has been undertaken to understand the threat of disruption amongst professional services firms, including McKinsey, Boston Consulting Group, Accenture and PwC. The authors of this research have developed a useful framework for diagnosing the threat of disruption by analysing the experiences of professional service firms (PSFs) and their strategic responses. This framework is based on considering the level of disruption from both the supply and demand sides, as shown in Fig. 7.1. Supply-side disruption increases when the capabilities of the incumbent decrease in value to the customer, whilst demand-side disruption grows when the incumbent has blind spots about what customers want.

Employing the framework involves addressing issues on the supply and demand sides and then positioning the technology or competitor on Fig. 7.1.

Supply Side
The extent of disruption caused by the new technology on the supply side should be considered:

- How the new technology matches the capabilities of incumbents in terms of quality and efficiency.
- How the new technology or competitor makes existing capabilities in creating the product or coming up with solutions obsolete.

- How the incumbent is struggling to access the people and capabilities required to compete with this new technology or competitor.

Demand Side
The extent of disruption caused by a new technology on the demand side should be considered:

- How clients or end users are changing their behaviour due to the new technology or competitors?
- How does the new technology or competitor make existing capabilities in distribution, sales and marketing obsolete?
- How the new technology or competitor can generate a first-mover advantage that will be difficult to replicate?

Zone A—Minimal Disruption
Although there may be new competitors or technologies on the supply or demand side, they are having limited impact on the market. For example, in a PSF context, new start-ups may enter the market and focus on a niche market, and therefore not pose a threat to the dominant players in the market. However, these firms should monitor these competitors as well as technologies and be alert to any competitive threats.

Zone B—Supply-side Disruption
In this zone, the technology or competitor is beginning to replace the product or service capabilities and challenge the incumbent's current business model. For example, generative AI has disrupted established PSFs by taking over many aspects of their work. New start-up firms have employed AI to detect fraud and use machine learning to solve problems for both public and private sector clients. Established PSFs have responded by developing in-house AI capabilities, acquiring new AI start-ups, or partnering with other firms.

Zone C—Demand-side Disruption
In this zone, customers start to take control of their own problems and solve some of them in-house, employing low-cost specialist vendors. For example, rather than sourcing a complete service from a large PSF, clients have unbundled these service tasks and used in-house or external service delivery models. This approach has allowed them to build internal capabilities and have more control over the service. The emergence of alternative legal service providers, offering a range of legal services such as contract management at lower costs, has driven this trend. Established PSFs have worked with clients to better understand their needs and further build their brands.

Zone D—Full-on Disruption
In this zone, there is significant disruption on both the supply and demand sides. The case of Kodak is an example where digital photography changed how images were both produced and consumed by customers. In this instance, there is a high degree of urgency to act, and this could involve seeking out an acquisition, setting up a separate business or moving into an adjacent market.

Source: Birkinshaw, J., and Lancefield, D. (2023). 'How Professional Service Firms Dodged Disruption'. *Sloan Management Review*, Summer, 34–39.

High	**Zone B** *Supply-side disruption:* E.g. AI replacing large parts of traditional PSF's offering, and disrupting existing business model. *Potential response:* Develop or acquire capabilities or partner with other firms.	**Zone D** *Full-on disruption:* E.g. New competitors on supply and demand side with new value proposition. *Potential response:* High level of urgency to act. Acquire another firm or establish a separate business.
Supply-side disruption		
Low	**Zone A** *Minimal disruption:* E.g. New competitors targeting niche markets or specific segments. *Potential response:* Monitor technology or competitor and be ready to respond.	**Zone C** *Demand-side disruption:* E.g. Some PSF's clients solving some problems in-house and using low cost service providers. *Potential response:* Work with clients to better understand their needs and build firm brand.
	Low	High
	Demand-side disruption	

Fig. 7.1 Diagnosing disruption threats to business models

7.5 How Digital Technologies Drive Business Model Innovation

Digital technologies can play an important role in driving business model innovation. Data analytics, cloud computing and AI technologies allow firms to store and manipulate large amounts of unstructured data into rules and decisions. Firms can use IoT and sensor technologies to capture and analyse data to optimise production and logistics operations. The effective deployment of digital technologies also means that they should be aligned with meeting the needs of the market. Digital technologies can be used in business model innovation in the areas outlined below [12].

Product or service personalisation. New business models, enabled by digital technologies, can provide products or services that are better customised to the individual needs of customers and, in some cases, provide solutions to customer problems. Digital technologies, such as online tracking tools, allow firms to monitor and analyse customer interaction patterns across websites and apps, which enables them to offer customised product suggestions. In a business-to-business context, providers of healthcare equipment can employ the IoT to access real-time information on equipment when in use, and this allows them to monitor usage patterns and respond to faults more quickly.

Customer co-creation. Digital technologies allow firms to eliminate intermediaries and build direct relationships with customers. For example, in a retail context, firms can quickly experiment and customise products and services for customers through a direct relationship rather than having to deal with a powerful retailer. This allows the firm to create a more interactive retail experience where, for example, clothing and footwear manufacturers can offer customised product designs through their online digital channels [13].

Asset sharing. Digital technologies can allow firms to share expensive assets and provide significant value to customers. This business model contrasts with many firms that have used the ownership and protection of assets as both a source of competitive differentiation and an entry barrier to the industry. Consider the hotel industry prior to the entry of Airbnb into the accommodation market. Many hotel groups owned and operated global networks of hotels and encouraged customer loyalty through incentive schemes, which made it difficult for new entrants to compete. However, Airbnb entered the industry through a sharing business model that allowed homeowners to share rooms with travellers. These types of asset-sharing models are emerging in other areas, such as firms allowing homeowners with excess rooms to connect with other people who need storage space.

Usage-based business models. Digital technologies allow firms to create business models that charge customers for when they use the product or services, meaning that the customer does not have to purchase the entire product. Digital technologies can measure product usage, and customers can pay on a pay-per-use or subscription basis. Although this model started off in software services via the software-as–a-service model, it has now been extended into a range of business areas, including cars, bicycles and furniture. Customers benefit by only paying for the product or service they use, and the firm benefits as the number of customers is likely to grow.

> **Illustration 7.4 How Digital Technologies Drive Business Model Innovation at Uber**
>
> Uber, the taxi service company, provides an interesting illustration of some of the ways in which digital technologies can drive business model innovation. Uber's business model is built on *asset sharing*, as drivers own their own cars. The digital platform can respond to market demand in real time, which allows Uber to employ *usage-based pricing* and direct drivers to areas where there is high demand for taxis. Uber's platform allows customers to rate drivers, and this enables customers to find both the closest drivers and their ratings. This rating system also encourages drivers to offer clean cars and quality service.
>
> *Personalisation* is evident as customers can decide between the nearest car and the one with the highest rating on service, even though it may be further away. These features can be considered in the context of existing players or new entrants into a market. Firms can compare themselves with competitors along each of the features and assess where they have significant strengths. Where a firm has performance advantages over a number of these features, it is in a strong position to succeed in the market.
>
> Source: Kavadias, S., Ladas, K., and Loch, C., 2016. The Transformative Business Model. *Harvard Business Review*, *94*(10), pp. 91–98.

7.6 Barriers to Employing Digital Technologies in Business Model Innovation

There are a number of barriers in established firms to digitising ecosystems that are also closely related to business model innovation barriers [14].

Digital value myopia. This refers to the failure of firms to look beyond their established physical product design approach. In this case, digital technologies have been focused mainly on enhancing the functionality of the product rather than creating new digital value in conjunction with other players in the ecosystem. Moreover, firms often lack the foresight to view the scope and value that digital technologies can bring to innovating their current business models. An internally focussed culture can lead to resistance and uncertainty when collaborating with external players to create new value in digital partnerships.

Traditional value chain inertia. This refers to the absence of digital skills amongst other players in the activity system, thus hindering how digital technologies can be employed for business model innovation. It also includes resistance to change in the established positions of players in the activity system and a lack of awareness of the potential value that digital technologies can offer in the overall activity system. For example, many manufacturing supply chains are built around product sales and after-sales services, characterised by long-established relationships between customers and suppliers. Implementing digital solutions such as predictive maintenance and route optimisation can require changes in roles and capabilities, which can lead to resistance amongst certain members of the supply chain. Although the IoT can lead to improved product features and offer significant value in performance monitoring, issues around responsibility and ownership of data can lead to resistance and impede implementation amongst some supply chain members.

Firm-centric value capture. This refers to the traditional revenue model used to profit from selling physical products and services, which conflicts with attaining a profit for the digital service within the ecosystem. For example, employing digital technologies to optimise product usage and reduce maintenance can conflict with the revenue models of distributors, thus making them reluctant to buy into new digital solutions. The lack of an appropriate revenue-sharing model for digital solutions leads to the risk of manufacturers imposing their existing business models rather than sharing revenues fairly with current and new players in the ecosystem.

7.7 How the Business Model Canvas Can be Employed in Business Model Innovation

The business model canvas can be used by firms to map out and redesign business models [15]. It is also a powerful framework for understanding business model innovation and how digital technologies can reshape key aspects of a firm's business model. Figure 7.2 highlights the nine elements of the business model canvas and the key issues that must be addressed in each element. It also shows examples of how digital technologies can impact each of the nine elements.

The *value propositions* refer to the products and value-added services offered by the firm to meet customer needs, as well as the value provided by the firm. The *customer segments* refer to the types of customers that the firm intends to focus on by offering the intended value propositions. The *channels* outline how a firm interacts with its customers and how it delivers the value propositions.

The *revenue streams* refer to the income streams for the firm through offering the value propositions. It also describes the activities and pricing

Key partners	Key activities	Value propositions	Customer relationships	Customer segments
- Key partners - Key suppliers - Key resources acquired from customers - Key activities partners perform *Digital technology impact:* Partner with digital platforms such as eBay to reach new customers	- Key activities required for value proposition - Distribution channels - Customer relationships - Revenue streams *Digital technology impact:* AI automation of some design and marketing activities	- What is being delivered to customer - Customer problems being solved - Bundles of products and services offered to each customer segment - Customer needs being satisfied *Digital technology impact:* Offer customers more convenience via mobile apps and social media channels	- Type of customer relationship each customer segment expects - Integration with business model - Cost of serving each segment *Digital technology impact:* Greater personalisation via online referral and loyalty mechanisms	- Who value is created for - Who the most important customers are *Digital technology impact:* Reach new global markets or personalise offerings for market segments
	Key resources		**Channels**	
	- Key resources value proposition requires - Distribution channels - Customer relationships - Revenue streams *Digital technology impact:* Data becomes a strategic resource via analytics tools		- How customer segments are reached - How channels are integrated - Which channels are in use - Which channel is best *Digital technology impact:* Create new digital touchpoints and integrate digital and physical channels	
Cost structure			**Revenue streams**	
- Most significant costs in the business model - Key resources that are most expensive - Key activities that are most expensive *Digital technology impact:* Investing in cloud services can drive a more scaleable business			- The value that customers are willing to pay - What they are currently paying for - How they are currently paying - How they would prefer to pay - How much each revenue stream contributes to overall revenue *Digital technology impact:* Usage-based or sharing business models	

Fig. 7.2 The business model canvas and the impact of digital technologies

of the values that allow the firm to increase its revenue. The *key resources* are the resources and capabilities that a firm has to deliver the value propositions to its customers. The *key activities* refer to the processes that a firm must undertake to create, market and deliver the value propositions to customers and return a profit.

Key partners describe the collaborative ties of the firm with other firms that allow it to undertake activities related to the value propositions. The *cost structure* refers to the costs involved in delivering the value propositions to customers and performing other business activities, such as building

Key partners	Key activities	Value propositions	Customer relationships	Customer segments
- Web site owners - Advertising partners - Device manufacturers - University and research partners - Cloud and enterprise solution partners	- Search and data organisation - Data capture - Search and match - Research and innovation	- Targeted advertising via AdWords - Better advertising return on investment - Google search: find and access information and solutions - Low search costs - Well match traffic for web sites - Etc.	- Personalised advertising relationships - Self service and automated interactions - Dedicated sales for corporate clients	*Advertisers:* - Ad agencies - Large and small firms - Entrepreneurs - Etc. *Search users:* - Shopping - Entertainment - Knowledge - Etc.
	Key resources		**Channels**	
	- Technology infrastructure - Intellectual property and algorithms - User data - Google brand		- Digital platform - Hardware devices - Partner networks - Mobile ecosystem	*Web sites:* - Content creators - Bloggers - Web sites - Etc.
Cost structure			**Revenue streams**	
- Infrastructure and data centre operations - Traffic acquisition costs - Marketing costs - R&D costs - Etc.			- Google advertising - Google cloud services - Google Play - Other services - Etc.	

Fig. 7.3 The business model canvas for Google

relationships with other players in the business model. Figure 7.3 presents an illustration of Google on the business model canvas.

The business model canvas is useful for analysing the impact of digital technologies on business models for the following reasons:

- *A holistic view*—it can provide a holistic view of how digital technologies impact the firm's business model and allow a firm to prioritise the allocation of resources to areas where digital technologies can make a significant impact and be aligned with the overall firm strategy. Furthermore, the nine elements can be analysed to determine how digital technologies can reduce costs, create value or disrupt established business models.
- *An understanding of the linkages*—it serves as a framework for understanding all the elements of the business models and how they are interlinked [16]. The business model canvas allows an analysis of how a change in one element affects other elements of the business model. For example, changes to both key activities and key resources are likely to affect the cost structure and the perceived customer value proposition elements.
- *Experimentation*—it allows a firm to experiment with different configurations of the business model elements, and a firm can refine various

elements of the business model and test the impacts with certain customers. For example, using different web page layouts for market segments means a firm can dynamically analyse the impact on the customer value proposition through focus groups with the affected customers. The business model canvas can allow a firm to identify elements where digital capabilities are lacking and how digital technologies and capabilities can help address capability deficits.

- *Stakeholder engagement*—changes to the canvas elements can be analysed through seeking feedback from key stakeholders and obtaining insights into changes that can improve the business model. In a digital context, this allows the firm to analyse how the technology and business dimensions are aligned with the reconfigured business model. The canvas can also be adapted on an ongoing basis as the firm reacts to changes in the business environment, such as changes in technology and customer needs.

7.8 How Design Thinking Can be Employed in Business Model Innovation

Design thinking has attracted increasing attention as a widely adopted practice in the areas of product and service innovation. It is a creative approach to innovation that focuses on users and has been employed across a range of areas, ranging from consumer products such as smartphones and tablets to digital systems such as websites and apps. More recently, it has been employed at the strategic level as a tool in the business model innovation process [17]. In contrast to traditional strategy approaches, design thinking is more focused on engaging with employees and ensuring they participate and contribute to the outcome.

Design thinking differs from other innovation processes as it is solution-focused and user-centric rather than being problem-based. It is a powerful approach for quickly testing whether an idea or solution can deliver real value to users. The creative and experimental nature of the approach allows firms to better understand how to create solutions that are valuable to users. Design thinking is based on the following two key aspects [18]:

- *Building empathy with the user*—the user-centric focus involves understanding the person affected by the problem and, therefore, being able to develop a viable solution. Every decision in design thinking should be

based on an in-depth awareness and understanding of the user profile and behaviour. In the context of business model innovation, this may involve asking questions such as what problems customers face and how the firm can create value differently.
- *Observing product–user interaction*—this involves observing the user interacting with the product or service, drawing conclusions from research and analysis, and ensuring the focus remains on the needs of the user throughout implementation.

Common tools and methods employed in design thinking include journey maps, brainstorming, mind maps, visualisation tools, prototypes and field experiments. Design thinking can also be employed along with the business model canvas to map out, iterate and communicate potential business models. Although there are different design-thinking frameworks, many are based on the following key iterative stages:

- *Exploration*—design thinking normally starts with a process of exploration, with the objective being to understand the problem in order to come up with the optimal solution. This can involve collecting and analysing data through observation and interviews to empathise with users and understand their priorities, asking questions about their pain points, and using, for example, mapping tools such as customer journey maps [19]. The findings from this analysis should allow a clear framing of the problem and be free from any preconceived assumptions or biased expectations.
- *Ideation*—this stage involves generating potential alternative solutions to the problem identified. The goal is to devise innovative ideas that address the problem and focus on meeting the needs of the user. Brainstorming is widely used in this stage, which can involve iterating between divergent and convergent thinking. Divergent thinking can be used to come up with all the potential ideas, no matter how difficult or unconventional, whilst convergent thinking involves working through these proposed ideas and selecting the optimal solutions.
- *Development*—this stage involves developing potential solutions from the ideas generated and then testing and experimenting with them to determine their suitability. A digital prototype can be developed to allow the design team to interact with the potential solutions. A visual representation using story boards with user scenarios, experience journeys and business model illustrations can be used in this stage.

- *Implementation*—this involves implementing the solution, testing and reflecting on the results, and, where necessary, iterating between the earlier stages in the process to improve the solution. The learning from the process should be shared with all the stakeholders involved in the design-thinking process.

Applying design thinking in business model innovation can deliver the following benefits:

- Managers can engage in significant experimentation and learning, as design thinking involves discovering and exploiting new business models. Therefore, it provides managers with a discovery-driven approach to business model innovation [20].
- Design thinking involves engaging with multiple stakeholders who can provide various perspectives on value creation and capture, and at the same time, allow them to contribute their knowledge, skills and resources to identify ideas for business model innovation.
- Digital technologies can also play a part in design thinking and business model innovation. For example, data analytics tools can be employed to support the ideation stage by collecting and analysing customer data, identifying target markets, conducting competitor analysis and exploring areas for revenue growth.
- Design thinking can be employed as a structured process for understanding how business models can be changed and how individuals and teams can be empowered to drive this change. Effective application of design thinking is highly dependent on the culture of the firm and the level of change readiness. Resistance to change amongst affected stakeholders, caused by the outcomes of design thinking, can negate any potential benefits. However, when effectively implemented, collaborative practices in design thinking can help secure buy-in from stakeholders to support any change.

Illustration 7.5 UberEats and Design Thinking

UberEats, the go–to food delivery service app, provides insights into the value of design thinking for problem-solving and empathising with customers. Their approach to design thinking focuses on the following key elements.

Empathises with users

UberEats continuously conducts interviews and prototypes with the people who use the product, including restaurant workers, delivery drivers and customers. For example, through fireside chats, they engage with delivery partners, restaurant workers and customers to gain feedback on their app. They use order-shadowing to test prototypes by observing how customers experience the prototype in a practical context.

Observes the design in use

UberEats places considerable emphasis on receiving feedback from users directly. For example, their Walkabout programme involves designers observing cities in which the firm operates and studying food culture, infrastructure, delivery processes and transportation. This programme has led to the development of the driver app, which focuses on the pain points of delivery drivers parking in densely populated areas and provides step-by-step directions from restaurant to customer to smooth the delivery process. Understanding that pain points vary between geographic locations helps UberEats implement service upgrades to solve problems in specific locations.

Iterate quickly and innovate constantly

UberEats employs design thinking to create new solutions to the problems and opportunities their products can address. For example, rapid field testing is used by designers to take prototypes into restaurants, delivery vehicles and the homes of customers to test them in the places where they are used. They often test and experiment with new designs in a single city to assess interest. An early version of the 'Most Popular Items' category in UberEats menus started as an operations team experiment in Toronto before being released to users in all cities. They also developed a restaurant sales dashboard for chefs to monitor the demand for individual dishes and adapt recipes to improve their menus, and they created the 'Under 30 Minutes' menu for customers who wanted to get food quickly.

Sources: Anonymous. (2022, May 9). Four inspiring design thinking examples and the valuable lessons they teach. Retrieved from https://www.hotjar.com/design-thinking/examples/; and Han, E. (2022). Five examples of design thinking. *Harvard Business School Online, Business Insights*. Retrieved from https://online.hbs.edu/blog/post/design-thinking-examples

Discussion Questions

1. Select a firm you are familiar with and analyse how it employs digital technologies to enhance the value creation, value capture and value delivery elements of its business model. Highlight areas where it can further improve its business model using digital technologies.
2. Identify a firm that has faced a disruptive innovation and analyse the disruptive threat posed to its business model. Critically assess the strategy the firm has taken in response to the disruptive innovation.
3. Drawing on the framework in Fig. 7.1, select a business sector of your choice and critically analyse the level of disruption on the supply and demand sides for firms in this sector. Highlight potential changes that established firms in this business sector can make in response to these disruptive threats.

4. For an organisation of your choice, undertake the following tasks: (i) map the organisation on to the business model canvas; and (ii) highlight the role of digital technologies in key elements of its business model.
5. For an organisation of your choice, employ key aspects of design thinking to highlight how it could improve its existing business model, giving particular attention to the role of digital technologies.

References

1. Casadesus, R., & Ricart, J. E. (2011). How to design a winning business model. *Harvard Business Review, 89*(1/2), 100–107.
2. Kavadias, S., Ladas, K., & Loch, C. (2016). The transformative business model. *Harvard Business Review, 94*(10), 91–98.
3. Sjödin, D., Parida, V., & Visnjic, I. (2022). How can large manufacturers digitalize their business models? A framework for orchestrating industrial ecosystems. *California Management Review, 64*(3), 49–77.
4. Christensen, C. (1997). *The innovator's dilemma: When new technologies cause great firms to fail*. Harvard Business School Press.
5. Gans, J. S. (2016). Keep calm and manage disruption. *MIT Sloan Management Review, 57*(3), 83.
6. Porter, M. (1985). *Competitive Advantage*. The Free Press.
7. McGrath, R. G. (2020). The new disrupters, in Special Issue on Disruption 2020. *MIT Sloan Management Review*, Spring 8–13.
8. Zott, C., & Amit, R. (2017). Business model innovation: How to create value in a digital world. *Business Model Innovation, 9*(1), 19–23.
9. Amit, R., & Zott, C. (2012). Creating value through business model innovation. *MIT Sloan Management Review, 53*(3), 41–49.
10. See Amit and Zott (2012) in reference 9 above.
11. See Zott and Amit (2017) in reference 8 above.
12. See McGrath (2020) in reference 7 above and Kavadias et al. (2016) in reference 2 above.
13. See McGrath (2020) in reference 7 above.
14. See Sjödin et al. (2022) in reference 3 above.
15. Osterwalder et al. (2005). Clarifying business models: Origins, present and future of the concept. *Communications of the Association for Information Systems, 16*(1).
16. Mueller, B. (2022). How to Map Out Your Digital Transformation. *Harvard Business Review*

17. Santa-Maria, T., Vermeulen, W. J., & Baumgartner, R. J. (2022). The Circular Sprint: Circular business model innovation through design thinking. *Journal of Cleaner Production, 362*, 132323. You, X., 2022. Applying design thinking for business model innovation. *Journal of Innovation and Entrepreneurship, 11*(1), p.59
18. Han, E. (2022). What is design thinking and why is it important? Harvard business school online, business insights, https://online.hbs.edu/blog/post/what-is-design-thinking
19. Vendraminelli, L., Macchion, L., Nosella, A., & Vinelli, A. (2023). Design thinking: Strategy for digital transformation. *Journal of Business Strategy, 44*(4), 200–210.
20. See You (2022) in reference 17 above.

8

Digital Transformation Strategy

8.1 Introduction

Digital transformation for established firms involves rethinking existing business strategies and the key drivers of success. Although firms have always had to respond to changes in the business environment, the changes associated with transitioning from a physical world to a primarily digital one have been beyond the capabilities of many firms. There are many diverse perspectives on digital transformation, which have created misunderstandings amongst managers around the selection of the most appropriate digital transformation option for their business. Managers have failed to understand important aspects of change management and have underestimated the resistance from employees to new ways of working associated with digital transformation. Some have argued that digital transformation failure has largely been due to a disconnect between strategy formulation and strategy implementation [1].

This chapter provides an understanding of digital transformation strategy and considers a number of key issues, including the link with business strategy, the influence of digital technologies on disruption in the business environment and the importance of digital resources and capabilities. A digital transformation strategy framework is outlined, which presents a typology of digital transformation strategies based on the level of disruption in the business environment and the strength of a firm's digital resources and capabilities. The framework reduces the complexity of issues involved and, at the same time, offers managers a practical framework for identifying, analysing and implementing an appropriate digital transformation strategy option.

The framework highlights, in some cases, how digital transformation can involve radical change in a firm's business model and internal business processes. However, the framework also presents options that do not require radical upheaval of a firm's core business but involve employing digital technologies to further strengthen the competitive position of the firm in its current markets. Although the needs of customers may not radically change, digital technologies can be deployed to better serve their needs and, at the same time, deliver cost efficiencies.

> **Learning Outcomes**
> - Understand why digital transformation should be linked to business strategy.
> - Understand why the deliberate and emergent strategy perspectives should be aligned in the digital transformation strategy process.
> - Understand how digital technologies drive disruption in the business environment.
> - Be able to analyse the resources and capabilities required for digital transformation, and understand the link with competitive advantage.
> - Understand how the level of disruption in the business environment, as well as digital resources and capabilities, influence the choice of digital transformation strategy option.
> - Understand the issues involved in implementing a digital transformation strategy.

8.2 Why Digital Transformation Should be Linked with Business Strategy

Business strategy is concerned with defining the direction and scope of an organisation over the long term, achieving advantage through the configuration of resources within a changing environment to meet the needs of customers [2]. Key concepts in strategy include new market entry decisions, understanding firm capability and performance, the scope of firm activities, the link between industry structure forces such as buyer and supplier power and profitability, and the pursuit of competitive advantage.

The disruption brought about by digital technologies across many industries has had a significant impact on the business strategies of firms. For example, in a retail context, firms often erected entry barriers by creating a large presence on the high street to prevent new competitors from entering their markets and reduced the power of key suppliers through volume buying to increase profitability. However, digital technologies have allowed retailers such as Amazon and Alibaba to use online channels to compete across a whole range of markets, making it difficult for established players to compete. Banks such as ING consider Amazon a potential competitor, whilst one of the largest global shipping and logistics companies, Hapag-Lloyd, is facing potential competition from Alibaba.

These disruptions have challenged the value of strategy frameworks, such as the capability-based and industry-positioning approaches [3]. The rapid development of digital technologies has created challenges in the strategy process by introducing changes to how strategy is formulated and organisational change is implemented. Despite being confronted with these challenges, firms still have to formulate and execute a strategic response, and strategy concepts such as environment and competitor analysis, as well as internal capability analysis, can explain some of the realities of digital transformation.

8.3 Digital Transformation and the Strategy Process

There are two views on the strategy process, namely *deliberate* and *emergent*, which are particularly pertinent to formulating a digital transformation strategy.

- *Deliberate* involves a rational, analytical approach that identifies the optimal strategy prior to strategy implementation. Strategy is often driven by objective analysis, planned in advance, and then executed by a firm according to a defined plan. Making choices around the business model and strategic positioning suggests a deliberate process, with decisions made to organise the firm's resources to exploit opportunities and counteract threats in the external environment.
- *Emergent* refers to a strategy that emerges from a process of experimentation, learning and adaptation during implementation. Many strategies evolve in response to ad-hoc problem-solving, removing bottlenecks and addressing competitive threats. As in a military context, success comes from flexibility in planning rather than being locked into a single plan.

Why the deliberate and emergent views are complementary in digital transformation strategy

The deliberate and emergent views are complementary in the context of digital transformation strategy for the following reasons:

- Flexibility is required in the strategy process to allow for rapid changes in digital technologies. Existing strategy practices, developed when the pace of change was slower and changes were far less disruptive, are likely to be ineffective.
- Established processes for formulating yearly and multi-year strategic plans are less relevant in a digital context, as many of the assumptions associated with digital technologies can change in a matter of months, often in unforeseen ways [4].
- Digital transformation strategy requires a more adaptive process, where a firm has established an overall vision and direction, whilst at the same time allowing for assumptions and principles to be continually reassessed during the implementation of the strategy.
- Senior executives have to be aware of novel digital technologies to drive the required change and effectively communicate with employees at lower levels in the firm. In effect, digital technologies change the traditional role of senior managers from makers of the digital strategy to coordinators of the strategy process [5].

8.4 A Framework for Understanding Digital Transformation Strategy

This section presents a framework with four stages for understanding digital transformation strategy, as shown in Fig. 8.1. Digital disruption and digital capability analysis in Stages 1 and 2 will yield potential digital transformation strategy options, as shown in the matrix in Stage 3 of the framework. Stage 4 involves implementing the strategy selected in Stage 3. Although the framework is sequential in nature, there is likely to be a high degree of iteration between the stages to reflect changes in the business environment, such as the emergence of new digital technologies or competitor actions. The logic of each of the stages in the framework is now outlined.

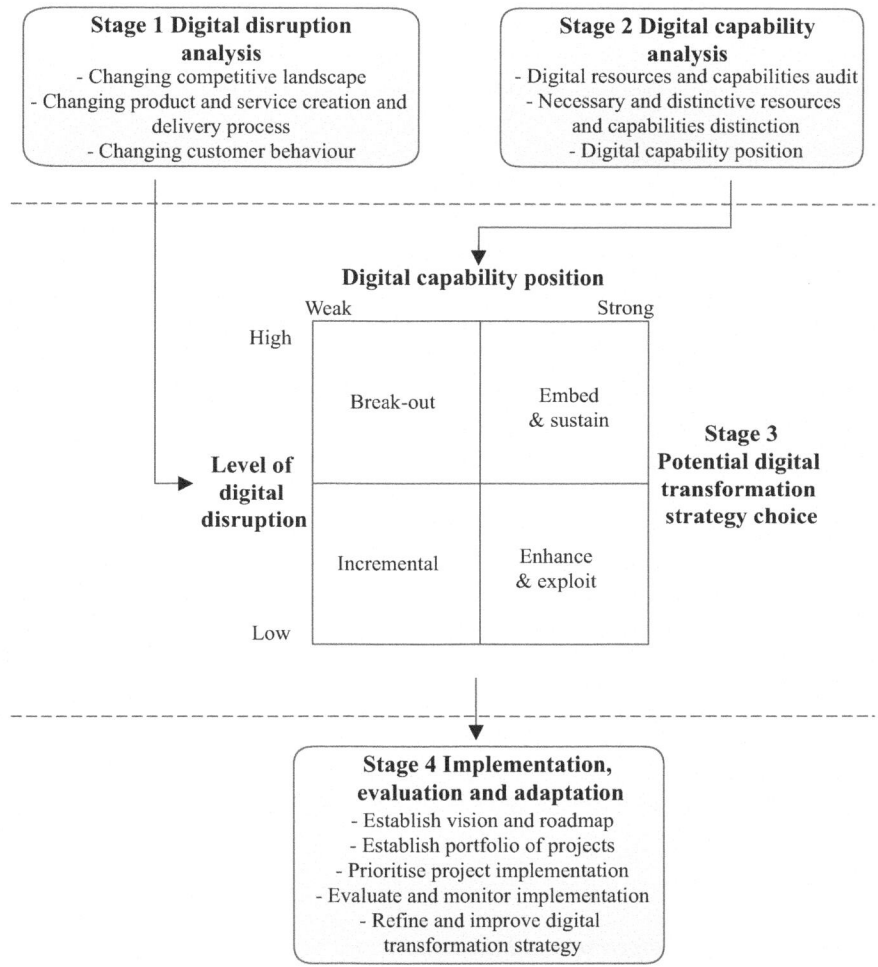

Fig. 8.1 A framework for understanding digital transformation strategy

8.5 Stage 1 Digital Disruption Analysis

The diffusion of digital technologies across many business sectors has led to extensive changes in the form of new competitors, an increasing digitisation of product and service offerings, and changing customer buyer behaviour. There can be a trigger that leads to extensive industry disruption, resulting in a significantly different way of doing business, which, in turn, has a major impact on how companies create value for customers. This stage involves understanding how digital technologies are driving disruption in the business environment. The disruptive impact of digital technologies can typically be grouped into the following drivers.

8.5.1 Changing Competitive Landscape

The emergence of new digital technologies is altering the nature and dynamics of competition across a range of sectors. Competition has become more global and intense as large digital firms from the United States and China, such as Amazon, Facebook and Alibaba, have been dominating many industries globally. Digital technologies are driving change in the competitive landscape in a number of ways, as outlined below [6].

Increasing interdependence across firms

- *Increasing collaboration and alliances*—companies from different industries can readily combine their resources and capabilities to achieve mutual benefits. For example, Uber and Spotify have collaborated to allow Uber users to connect their Spotify accounts to car entertainment systems, which has facilitated better personalisation of services for both companies.
- *Co-opetition*—this has become more common as competitors can co-create value if they have compatible objectives. In response to competition from online travel agencies, Airbnb has attempted to establish partnerships with hotel groups to diversify and augment its service offerings. Previously, these hotel groups would have been considered competitors of Airbnb.

Emergence of new competitors and start-up firms

- *Competition from adjacent markets*—firms have started to compete across a range of adjacent markets. For example, Uber has entered the food delivery service market, whilst, at the same time, Google has entered the smartphone market.
- *Rapid emergence of start-up firms*—digital technologies have led to the rise of born-digital firms that can enter markets and disrupt the nature of competition. For example, digital technologies have transformed the competitive landscape in many retailing contexts and facilitated the emergence of new digital start-up firms such as Boohoo and ASOS.
- *Industry convergence*—it refers to the blurring of boundaries between traditionally distinct industries, often driven by changes in technology,

innovation or shifts in market demands. For example, automakers have increasingly become important players in the semiconductor industry, as cars now feature ever greater computing power and digital services.

8.5.2 Changing Product and Service Creation and Delivery Process

Digital technologies have had a significant impact on how products and services are *created* and *delivered* across many business environments through the automation and digitisation of many tasks. For example, AI technologies have transformed the way in which many software applications are *created* through the automation of tasks such as coding. At the same time, software applications can be *delivered* digitally to customers without the need for human intervention.

Firms have to consider how developments in digital technologies, such as AI, the IoT and robotics, are impacting the product and service creation and delivery process, as this will be a reliable indicator of the extent of disruption in the business environment. For example, the music industry has been significantly disrupted by the move towards the full digitisation of the distribution and listening experience, which has led to the entry of new, powerful players into the music industry, such as Spotify. In contrast, digitisation has not had a significant impact on industries such as construction due to the physical nature of the core construction processes and, in many cases, the need for extensive customisation for each project.

8.5.3 Changing Customer Behaviour

Digital technologies have had a significant impact on customer behaviour in the following areas:

- *More demanding and knowledgeable*—the availability of online search and social media tools has allowed customers to readily access information on a whole range of product and service attributes. Customers have become more demanding and knowledgeable about issues such as price, reliability and availability.
- *Greater mobility*—customers have become more mobile in terms of ease of access to alternative sources of supply due to the increasing prominence of digital technologies. With global access through digital technologies to

more products and services than ever before, and with instant communications, typical constraints for customers, such as time and distance, have increasingly disappeared.
- *Diminishing loyalty*—the loyalty of customers has diminished due to greater choice and mobility driven by digital technologies. Firms are now being forced to be more responsive to customer needs through the greater use of digital technologies. For example, firms such as Nike have used digital technologies to allow consumers to create value through the joint development and customisation of products. The use of mobile technologies has also become an important aspect of customer behaviour and has facilitated practices such as viewing a product in a physical store and then purchasing it online.

Digital technologies have radically changed customer behaviour and led to significant disruption in many product and service markets. Therefore, firms across many markets have had to respond or face being replaced by firms with superior digital capabilities [7].

Once the *competitive landscape, product and service creation and delivery process,* and *customer behaviour* drivers of disruption have been analysed, the following issues should be considered:

- *Level of disruption*—the level of disruption the drivers are causing to the position of firms and the general business environment should be assessed. It is important to prioritise the drivers that are having the most significant impact on disruption. Disruption driven by digital technologies is likely to vary across different sectors and industries. For example, industries such as retail have been significantly disrupted by digital technologies through the entry of new start-ups, a greater trend towards purchasing online, and the entry of powerful global online competitors.
- *Time dimension*—in addition to assessing the current drivers of disruption, it is also necessary to consider factors that are likely to have a disruptive impact in the future. Where possible, data should be introduced to support this analysis, and trends in areas such as technology adoption levels should be considered using up–to-date information.
- *Strategies for dealing with disruption*—the ability of firms to deal with disruption is likely to have a significant impact on the success or failure of a digital transformation strategy. Drivers of disruption can often present positive opportunities rather than being viewed as threats. Managers can use their creativity and judgement to influence disruption to strengthen their competitive position by investing in and deploying new digital

technologies to shape customer buying behaviour. This analysis is further considered in Stage 3 of the framework, as shown in Fig. 8.1.

8.6 Stage 2 Digital Capability Analysis

This stage involves analysing the current digital capability of the firm and considers how well it deploys digital technologies in its operations. The analysis in this stage will have a significant impact on the ability of the firm to develop an effective digital transformation strategy, as well as act as an important influence on how sophisticated and ambitious the strategy can be.

The analysis of the current digital capability position of the firm can be linked to competitive advantage. The capability-based view can explain how digital resources and capabilities can be employed as part of formulating a digital transformation strategy. The capabilities view asserts that the competitive advantage and superior performance of a firm are explained by the distinctiveness of its capabilities, and there are a number of indicators of the strength of a resource or capability [8]:

- *Value* refers to the way in which a resource or capability creates value in the products and services of a firm, and how it leads to differentiation from competitors.
- *Rarity* refers to how difficult it is to obtain a resource or capability. Where a resource is rare and competitors do not possess it, it is likely to give the firm a competitive advantage.
- *Imitability* refers to the difficulty of replicating a resource or capability. Where a resource is difficult to replicate, it can be a source of advantage for a firm.

> **Illustration 8.1 Resources and Capabilities in Practice**
>
> As an illustration of the indicators of the strength of a resource or capability, consider BMW's manufacturing quality, Google's search algorithms or Apple's innovation and user-experience expertise. Customers *value* the resources and capabilities that lie behind the superior products and services of these companies. BMW manufactures high-quality, reliable cars and is a global market leader. Customers value Toyota cars and are willing to pay a price premium for them. The capabilities are also *rare* and *difficult to imitate*. Bing and Yahoo! have failed to displace Google as the leading

search engine or replicate its revenue model. The rewards for these capabilities have been captured by these companies, allowing them to generate strong financial returns. Apple has become one of the most valuable companies in the world, reflecting its control over its own intellectual property *resources*, as well as the broader ecosystem it has created through its iTunes platform.

8.6.1 The Digital Resources and Capabilities Matrix

The logic of the capabilities view can be employed to assess digital capabilities as part of a digital transformation strategy, as shown in Fig. 8.2. This involves auditing and making a distinction between digital resources and digital capabilities, which is explained below.

	Necessary digital resources	Distinctive digital resources
Digital resources	*Value* – not a source of competitive differentiation. *Rarity* – widely available and straightforward to access. *Imitation* – straightforward to imitate. *Examples* include digital sensors, cloud computing technologies, servers etc.	*Value* – source of competitive differentiation. *Rarity* – difficult to access in the supply market. *Imitation* – difficult to imitate. *Examples* include an inspirational leader, scalable digital infrastructure etc.
	Necessary digital capabilities	**Distinctive digital capabilities**
Digital capabilities	*Value* – not a source of competitive differentiation. *Rarity* – widely available and straightforward to access. *Imitation* – straightforward to imitate. *Examples* include reservation systems in hospitality settings etc.	*Value* – source of competitive differentiation. *Rarity* – difficult to access in the supply market. *Imitation* – difficult for competitors to imitate. *Examples* include the capability to deploy data analytics to gain customers insights in a stronger way than competitors etc.
	Same as competitors	Better than competitors

Fig. 8.2 The digital resources and capabilities matrix

Digital Resources

These refer to the digital assets that a firm has access to, both internally and externally, from the supply market or from external partners. Digital resources can be categorised into the following:

- *Technical resources*—these refer to the systems and applications that can be employed to perform business processes. These can include hardware (such as smartphones, tablets, servers, sensors) and software applications (such as operating systems, algorithms, apps); networking (Wi–Fi, cloud computing); and digital technologies (AI, the IoT, augmented reality). For example, the transition to digital transformation requires a stable and flexible technology platform on which digital products and services can be delivered [9]. Analysing digital resources can include assessing the scalability of the existing technology infrastructure and the level of functional and process integration across traditionally isolated silos in the firm [10].
- *Human resources*—these include the human resources that can be employed to perform business processes. Examples of these resources include technical specialists and line managers. The current skill levels, experience and the availability of these resources in the labour market should also be considered. Digital skills not only involve technical skills but also the ability to adapt to new technologies, understand digital trends and collaborate effectively in a digital environment.
- *Financial resources*—digital transformation often requires a significant commitment in terms of financial resources. In particular, the current financial position of the firm is likely to influence the ease with which it can fund the strategy. Where the core business of the firm is still strong and generating significant profits, the strategy should be more straightforward to fund, and senior management may be more willing to take the risks. However, some firms, such as high-street retailers, have been too slow to react to the changes brought about by digital technologies and have lacked the required investment to digitally transform their business models, largely due to declines in their core business and a lack of finances to support their strategy. Where a firm is already struggling financially, the options for financing digital transformation will be severely constrained [11].

Digital Capabilities

These refer to the ways in which digital resources are deployed to effectively perform business processes. Digital capabilities include the digital technologies, skills and knowledge that the firm possesses to effectively employ digital technologies. Examples of digital capabilities include the following:

- A culture of digital innovation is an example of a digital capability. This refers to the presence of management practices that encourage innovation, including a mindset for digital technology adoption, incentives for innovation and how failure is viewed within the firm. This also involves considering the firm's ability to innovate and experiment with new digital technologies.
- Another example of a digital capability involves a care provider developing digital channels to enhance patient interaction with carers through the provision of access to patient healthcare data and digital communication between patients and carers.
- A further digital capability in the medical area involves using data analytics to develop more personalised medical plans for patients by tracking and analysing patient compliance with medication and prescribed treatments [12].

Distinguishing Between Necessary and Distinctive Resources and Capabilities

Clearly, certain resources and capabilities will have a higher level of importance than others. The following three indicators can be used to assess the relative importance of a digital resource or a capability:

- *Value*—the digital resource or capability provides superior value to customers and can be a source of differentiation in the marketplace.
- *Rarity*—digital resources or capabilities possessed uniquely by one firm or only a few others. For example, a company may have a strong customer service capability that is based on employing the IoT, as well as highly skilled and motivated employees, in a way that is superior to competitors.
- *Imitability*—resources and capabilities that competitors find difficult to replicate or obtain. For example, competitive advantage can be built on unique resources such as a key individual or proprietary digital

technology. However, these may not be sustainable, as key people may leave or other firms may acquire the same digital technology.

Figure 8.2 outlines categories of resources and capabilities based on their relative importance and performance, and each of these categories is now explained.

Necessary Digital Resources

These digital resources include generic digital resources that can be readily sourced from the supply market. Typically, these include digital sensors, cloud computing technologies, smartphones and servers. These technologies are generic as they can be sourced from multiple suppliers and do not have to be customised to the needs of the firm. Necessary digital resources also include employees who are straightforward to redeploy from inside the firm or people who can be easily recruited from the external labour market. As both digital technology and human resources are also accessible to competitors, they are unlikely to be a source of superior performance and/or competitive differentiation.

Necessary Digital Capabilities

Necessary digital capabilities include those that must be performed at a high standard but do not provide the firm with a performance advantage over its competitors. For example, hotels must have an online reservation system as a minimum requirement for participation in the market. Customers view these capabilities as standard and not as a source of differentiation in the marketplace. Moreover, these capabilities are straightforward to replicate and, in many cases, can be bought off the shelf from suppliers.

Distinctive Digital Resources

Distinctive digital resources allow the firm to achieve superior performance over competitors. In this instance, the firm possesses a resource that is valued by customers, is unique and is difficult for competitors to replicate. Examples of distinctive digital resources include an inspirational leader in digital technologies or a high-performing team in a specific digital technologies field, such as data analytics. Moreover, the development and control of proprietary digital technology applications can also be a distinctive digital resource. E-bay's large digital platform of a community of buyers and sellers in the online auction market is an example of a distinctive digital resource.

Distinctive Digital Capabilities

Distinctive digital capabilities are ways in which processes are performed that are unique to a firm and deliver superior performance to customers, which competitors find difficult to replicate. In the context of digital transformation, firms can progress from building necessary digital capabilities, such as a basic digital infrastructure, to more advanced capabilities that enable them to harness the full potential of digital technologies. An example of a potential distinctive capability for a firm is a data analytics capability that employs data analytics and machine-learning tools to develop customer behaviour insights to inform ideas for new products in a better way than competitors.

The analysis here has emphasised the importance of analysing digital resources and capabilities for digital transformation. It is also important to stress that the competitive strength of a firm can come from integrating digital resources and capabilities with existing firm resources and capabilities, as illustrated in the following related areas:

- *Combining digital technologies with existing resources and capabilities*—it is possible to combine digital technologies with other firm resources and capabilities, such as physical and human assets, to create a competitive advantage or further strengthen the competitive position of the firm. For example, large retailers such as Best Buy and Tesco have employed digital technologies to integrate their physical store networks with their digital channels, which further supports their scale economy advantage. These retailers strengthen their advantage by combining their digital resources and capabilities with their physical store networks.
- *The importance of managerial knowledge and digital technologies*—achieving a performance advantage from digital technologies is often based on how these resources are deployed to meet the specific needs of a firm. This has sometimes been referred to as managerial IT knowledge and requires a firm to develop unique insights about how digital technologies can be employed to improve different processes across the firm [13]. This knowledge is developed over a long period of time. Trust and firm-specific knowledge are developed through interpersonal relationships amongst digital technology specialists and other functional managers, which

allow them to effectively work together to develop and implement innovative applications.
- *Digital capability advantage more enduring than a digital technology advantage*—a specific digital technology, such as a data analytics tool, may only provide a temporary competitive advantage as it can become a standardised offering in the supply market. However, digital capabilities that are developed through both interactions between digital technology specialists and functional managers, as well as by integrating digital technologies and other resources, are more likely to be difficult to replicate.

How to Employ the Digital Resources and Capabilities Matrix

The digital resources and capabilities matrix in Fig. 8.2 can be applied in the following ways:

- *Resource allocation decisions*—the matrix can serve as a valuable basis for prioritising the allocation of scarce internal resources to certain digital resources and capabilities. The investment of finance and digital-related resources should be allocated to distinctive resources and capabilities, as they have the potential to drive digital transformation.
- *In-house versus outsourced options*—the matrix should provide guidance on which digital resources and capabilities a firm should invest internally and which should be sourced from the supply market. It may be more prudent to source necessary digital resources and capabilities from external vendors and invest internally in distinctive resources and capabilities.
- *Sustainability of performance position*—the firm should consider how long it can maintain its performance advantage in the resource or capability. The nature of digital technologies and ever-constant change means it is possible for digital resources and capabilities to rapidly move from being distinctive to being standardised and accessible in the supply market from external suppliers. Therefore, it is important for a firm to prioritise investments in digital resources and technologies in which it is likely to have a sustained superior performance position.
- *Digital capability position*—although the digital resource and capability matrix highlights certain digital resources and capabilities and their relative strength, it should allow a firm to assess its overall digital capability position. This serves as an important influence on the choice of digital transformation strategy option selected in Stage 3 of the framework in Fig. 8.1.

8.7 Stage 3 Digital Transformation Strategy Choice

This stage highlights the potential digital transformation strategy options based on the level of disruption in the business environment and the digital capability position of the firm. Considering these two dimensions of analysis yields potential digital transformation strategy options, as shown in Stage 3 in Fig. 8.1. Actions are proposed for each strategy option along the dimensions of vision, link with business strategy, resource and capability implications, and culture and organisational structure implications, as summarised in Table 8.1. Each of these digital transformation strategies is now outlined.

8.7.1 Breakout Digital Transformation Strategy

In this case, the firm is faced with a high level of disruption in the business environment and has a weak digital capability position. Firms that fit into this category are often under significant pressure to transform in order to survive due to the extensive disruption brought about by digital technologies. Although senior management in the firm may understand the need to embrace digital transformation and change strategic direction, they often struggle to build momentum and embed the organisational changes required. The firm often lacks the knowledge or motivation to formulate and implement the digital transformation strategy. In this context, there is a high level of urgency to act, as there is a limited window for transformation, and the consequences of failure can threaten the survival of the firm.

The case of many established high-street retailers, such as Sears and Radio Shack in the United States, provides an illustration of firms in this situation. These firms faced considerable threats from internet-only start-ups and larger online retailers such as Amazon and Alibaba. Although established retailers may have some digital capabilities in the form of employing social media technologies and data analytics, these tend to be located in functional silos, and there tends to be a lack of coordination of digital transformation initiatives within the firm. However, significant disruption in the business environment requires an urgent move towards digital transformation.

Table 8.1 Key elements and strategic actions in each digital transformation strategy option

	Breakout	Embed and sustain	Incremental development	Enhance and exploit
Key features				
Level of digital disruption	Significant disruption in the form of, for example, new competitors, significant digitisation of the product or service, and changing customer behaviour	Significant disruption in the form of, for example, new competitors, significant digitisation of the product or service, and changing customer behaviour	Limited disruption with, for example, few new competitors, limited digitisation of product and services, and relatively stable customer behaviour	Limited disruption with, for example, few new competitors, limited digitisation of product and services, and relatively stable customer behaviour
Digital capability position	Weak digital capability position in the form of, for example, a poor digital infrastructure, a culture of resistance to digital technologies, poor employee digital skills knowledge, etc.	Strong digital capability position in the form of, for example, a well-developed digital infrastructure, a culture of embracing digital technologies, strong employee digital skills, knowledge, etc.	Weak digital capability position in the form of, for example, a poor digital infrastructure, a culture of resistance to digital technologies, poor employee digital skills and knowledge, etc.	Strong digital capability position in the form of, for example, a well-developed digital infrastructure, a culture of embracing digital technologies, strong employee digital skills and knowledge, etc.
Strategy actions				
Vision	Strong leadership required. Firm needs to establish a strategic vision with digital transformation at its heart	Firm already has a clear, well-established strategic vision for digital transformation	Digital transformation not central to the strategic vision of the firm	Digital transformation not central to the strategic vision of the firm

(*continued*)

Table 8.1 (continued)

	Breakout	Embed and sustain	Incremental development	Enhance and exploit
Link with business strategy	Digital transformation should be central to the overall business strategy	Digital transformation central to business strategy	Digital transformation efforts supporting core operations	Digital transformation efforts focused on supporting core operations
Resource and capability implications	Significant financial commitment required. An urgent need to develop digital capabilities via employee development or recruitment. Ally with other firms to access digital capabilities. Upgrade and overhaul technical infrastructure	Continue to commit significant financial resource to further develop digital capabilities in areas such as employee skills development, upgrading technical infrastructure, etc.	Continue to commit sufficient resource to develop digital capabilities to maintain competitive position, satisfy customer needs and improve internal operations	Continue to commit resource to further develop digital capabilities at the level for leadership in the industry
Culture and organisational change implications	Urgent need to break down any impediments to change which may mean changes in culture and more flexible organisational structures	Embed and sustain a culture of encouraging digital transformation, which should be used as a basis for generating ideas for further potential process, product and business model transformations	Create a culture where digital technologies are viewed as an opportunity rather than a threat	Further develop and nurture a culture where digital technologies are employed to better serve the needs of customers and educate customers on the benefits of moving towards digitised product and service delivery channels

The following actions can be taken as part of a breakout digital transformation strategy:

- A breakout digital transformation strategy will require strong leadership and a strategic vision for embracing digital transformation. This involves communicating a new vision and addressing potential employee resistance to the changes required to digitally transform the business. Digital transformation should now be central to the overall business strategy of the firm. The required finance should be secured from either internal or external sources to fund the digital transformation strategy. The rapid erosion of profit margins and shrinking markets due to a high level of disruption means the firm will have to act quickly.
- There should be employee development programmes in place to develop the digital skills of current employees and recruit new employees with the required digital skills. This will involve changing employee attitudes and the firm's culture, and moving away from a position where the firm is missing out on valuable opportunities to deploy digital technologies.
- Consideration should be given to accessing the capabilities of other firms to enhance existing digital capabilities. For example, established banks have struggled to exploit a wealth of data for analytics purposes as a result of disjointed legacy infrastructures and departmental silos. Some banks have had to partner with digital technology platforms to better exploit the data at their disposal.
- The firm could start its digital transformation efforts by upgrading its technical infrastructure to enable it to explore new digital opportunities, improve its core operations and, in turn, offer higher levels of customer service.

Illustration 8.2 Digital Transformation at Lego

Lego, the toymaker, embarked on a digital transformation journey to improve its operations and create safe, innovative play experiences for children. Lego's chief digital and technology officer explained how the company built its digital presence brick-by-brick along a number of dimensions.

Lego scaled up its IT team from 600 to 1800 people in an effort to have the required technical talent to drive its digital transformation. This involved changing how the IT function worked in the firm and transitioning from an

> outsourced, supporting role to a primarily in-house team of software engineers, designers, programme managers, and network and security specialists. Particular emphasis was placed on developing digital skills and sharing developer knowledge across different global locations. This allowed Lego to explore what each team was doing around digital technologies, share knowledge and develop curiosity and continuous learning as part of the Lego culture.
>
> Lego used digital technologies to manage its supply chain across five factories in Asia, Europe and South America. It improved supply chain efficiency by implementing new systems to track and move finished products across its network of manufacturers, distribution centres and retailers. Orders from stores, partners or customers online were automated, allowing the retail team to deliver the right product to the right location at the right time. The introduction of a single ID system across its website and other channels enabled more personalised interactions. Lego has used cloud technology to support scalability during peak times of the year, including Black Friday and Christmas.
>
> Although Lego is primarily a physical toy company, it recognises the importance of having a digital presence for children and has partnered with Epic Games to offer a safe and secure digital experience for children. This supports Lego's core mission of inspiring children to learn and play in a safe environment.
>
> Source: Delandes, N. Lego. (2024, Nov. 22). Building the foundation for digital transformation. *TechInformed*. Retrieved from https://techinformed.com/lego-building-the-foundation-for-digital-transformation/

8.7.2 Embed and Sustain the Digital Transformation Strategy

In this instance, the firm faces a high level of disruption in the business environment and has a strong digital capability position. Firms are likely to have well-developed capabilities necessary for digital transformation and continue to pursue opportunities for improving processes and products. Therefore, the firm should continue to embed and sustain digital transformation across the business.

This strategy is particularly appropriate in the case of a firm having established capabilities that can take advantage of digital opportunities. For example, a firm can employ digital technologies to further enhance its value proposition in current markets by changing the way value is created for customers and captured by the firm. Automakers have established relationships with their customers over the life of the vehicle by employing digital technologies that allow them to update software and features of the car whilst it is in use.

An embedding and sustaining digital transformation strategy can involve the following actions:

- Digital transformation should be central to the overall business strategy of the firm, with a strong overarching vision and clear strategic goals. The firm should continuously identify opportunities for employing digital technologies.
- Attention should be given to further developing the skills base of internal employees in current and emerging digital technologies.
- The presence of significant disruption in the business environment means that the firm should continue to invest in digital resources and capabilities to maintain its strong position.
- A culture of encouraging innovation with digital technologies should be nurtured and employed as a basis for generating ideas for further improvements in processes, products and its business model. This culture involves encouraging risk-taking, rewarding innovation, promoting new ways of thinking and seeking solutions from different functions of the firm.
- There should be an effective governance framework in place to ensure there is coordination of digital initiatives inside the firm, and this will include having robust performance measures in place to ensure the digital transformation strategy is meeting its goals.

Illustration 8.3 How Next Built Digital Capabilities for Advantage

Next was launched in the UK in 1982 as a clothing retailer to address a gap in the market between clothing lines for younger shoppers and wealthier, older shoppers. Next has become the largest clothing retailer in the UK and thrived where other retailers, such as Debenhams and Topshop, have disappeared. A significant part of Next's success has been driven by its investment in building its digital capabilities to allow it to compete with both established clothing retailers and online players, such as Boohoo and ASOS.

Next has invested significantly in its existing warehouses and built an automated warehouse. This has involved upgrading its existing technology infrastructure. Notably, it developed the software in-house for its website, inventory allocation and other core operations rather than outsourcing to external vendors. Next employs more employees in technology than in its product teams.

This investment has delivered a number of benefits. More than half of customer purchases are online, and greater automation has allowed it to reduce both delivery times and the percentage of late deliveries. Next offers other smaller

> retailers its software for warehousing, delivery, returns and other back-office operations. It has acquired retailers such as Cath Kidston, FatFace and Made.com and taken financial stakes in Gap and Reiss. The investments in digital technologies have allowed Next to sell the products of some of these companies through its website, which has enabled Next to transition from a retailer to a conglomerate.
> Source: Anonymous. (2024, March 23). Britain's retail superstar. *The Economist*, 450, 26–27. Retrieved from https://www.proquest.com/magazines/britain-s-retail-superstar/docview/2972795900/se-2

8.7.3 Incremental Development Digital Transformation Strategy

In this case, the firm faces a low level of disruption in the business environment and has a weak digital capability position. The low level of disruption means that there has been a lack of emphasis on deploying digital technologies across the business, whilst the nature of the product and service delivery and creation processes has not been significantly impacted by digital technologies.

Industries such as construction, oil exploration and mining would fit into this quadrant. Although there has been some digitisation of business processes in these industries, the product and service creation and delivery processes are still dominated by physical processes. Furthermore, these industries tend to be largely composed of well-established players. Firms in industries offering highly branded products with little need for digital features, such as watches, chocolate and jewellery, would also fit into this quadrant.

Firms in these industries have not had to embrace digital transformation or develop sophisticated strategies for dealing with its impacts. Therefore, senior management tends to be sceptical of the benefits of employing digital technologies, which is further compounded by the lack of contemporary skills in digital technologies. These firms have not placed much emphasis on developing digital capabilities and tend to have more basic digital capabilities in areas such as booking and reservation systems. However, such a position can be sustainable due to the low level of disruption in the business environment.

The following actions can be taken as part of an incremental development digital transformation strategy:

- Firms should identify internal processes for improvement by employing digital technologies without harming the core operations of the business.

This could involve using digital technologies to enhance internal business processes and create better information transparency in the supply chain through digital technologies.
- Firms should seek new ways in which digital technologies could be employed to enhance customer value. For example, this could involve fully integrating both the physical and digital channels to provide a seamless buying experience for customers and offer them greater personalisation of products and services, which is not possible via their physical channels alone. Firms with strong brands could use social media technologies to further strengthen their brand and build a stronger online profile. Rolex and Crockett & Jones have attempted to modernise their brands by blending their rich product heritage and tradition with modern lifestyles, narrating their stories via social media technologies to influence consumers' choices [14].
- A firm should develop the digital skills of its employees and enhance their knowledge of digital technologies. The lack of awareness of the potential of digital technologies means that firms may miss out on opportunities to reduce costs across their business. For example, firms in industries with a low level of disruption, such as construction and mining, may erroneously believe that their customers are not interested in social media or mobile technologies and are already effectively servicing customer needs through traditional collaboration technologies.
- Firms must continuously assess the level of disruption in the business environment, as new start-ups and competitors can alter the traditional value proposition offered to customers. A risk for firms in this quadrant is the potential lack of awareness of competitors' actions and customers' needs in a digital context.

8.7.4 Enhance and Exploit Digital Transformation Strategy

In this case, the firm faces a low level of disruption in the business environment and has a strong digital capability position. The low level of disruption is characterised by limited digitisation in the product and service creation process, and, in some cases, the presence of high barriers to entry. Although digital technologies have not had a significant impact on the business environment, it is still possible for a firm to possess digital capabilities as a means of enhancing its competitive position. The following actions can be taken as part of an enhance-and-exploit digital transformation strategy:

- Firms should continue to employ digital technologies to improve and reduce costs in internal processes and better use existing resources.
- The firm can employ digital technologies to better serve the needs of customers, which may involve convincing existing customers to embrace digital technologies.
- Customers should be educated by the firm on the benefits of moving toward digitised product and service delivery. This is the case in many healthcare settings, where digital technologies have had a more prominent role, even though many of the patient-care processes are still highly personalised, people-intensive processes.
- Where a firm has well-developed digital capabilities, it is possible to exploit these capabilities by selling them to other firms. For example, Ocado, an online supermarket in the UK, has developed a strong capability in warehousing, which has allowed it to offer delivery fulfilment services to the online customers of grocery retailers Morrisons in the UK and Kroger in the United States.

Illustration 8.4 Digital Transformation at Maersk

Maersk, the shipping company, provides a valuable illustration of an enhance-and-exploit digital transformation strategy. The shipping industry is dominated by a few large, well-established global players, and barriers to entry in the industry are high due to the large capital requirements involved. The costs of shipping are influenced by trade barriers, inefficiencies and bottlenecks in international supply chains. Although digital technologies have been playing an increasing role in streamlining business processes, they have not been disrupting the industry in terms of the emergence of new entrants or start-ups. However, Maersk used its existing capabilities to improve its existing operations and reduce costs. For example, it implemented blockchain technology to create rapid and secure access to end-to-end supply chain information from a single source. This allowed Maersk to receive real-time sensor data, reduce administrative expenses and better manage risk with global shipments. The use of these digital technologies further strengthened the value proposition of Maersk as being a provider of a fast, reliable and cost-efficient shipping service.

Source: Furr, N., and Shipilov, A., 2019. Digital doesn't have to be disruptive: the best results can come from adaptation rather than reinvention. *Harvard Business Review*, 97(4), pp. 94–104.

8.8 Stage 4 Implementation, Evaluation and Adaptation

This stage involves implementing, evaluating and adapting the digital transformation strategy option chosen.

8.8.1 Implementation

Implementation is a key driver for achieving the potential benefits of digital transformation. Effective implementation is often more critical for achieving these potential benefits than crafting a good strategy. Indeed, some firms incorrectly assume that once a digital transformation strategy is developed, effective implementation will automatically follow [15]. Implementation involves creating a plan and a set of actions, building flexibility into the process through evaluation and adaptation during implementation, and pursuing an organisational learning approach as outlined below.

Establish a Vision and Road Map

A vision for the strategy should be established, which should consider how the firm intends to employ digital technologies across the business. For example, in the context of an established retailer, the vision could involve fully integrating both the physical and digital channels to provide a seamless buying experience for customers. This could include offering customers greater personalisation of products and services not possible via its physical channels alone.

The vision should then be operationalised into a road map with a set of objectives and specific time periods outlining how the firm intends to implement each aspect of the digital transformation strategy. This will include both technology and employee implications. For example, referring to the retail example above, the technology aspect of the road map could include the development of a scalable digital infrastructure for adding social media channels with customers, along with a time frame for completion. The firm may define a new role, such as a Chief Digital Officer, and ensure that employees have the necessary skills and capabilities to exploit the potential business opportunities that digital technologies offer [16].

Establish a Portfolio of Projects

This phase involves converting the digital transformation road map into a portfolio of projects for implementation. Examples of projects at this level could include the following:

- Building a scalable digital platform to enable the development of future digital investments.
- Developing a digital platform to enable a retailer to configure its own online storefronts and build its own brands.
- Establishing a simple and easy-to-use app that provides helpdesk-related services to customers.

Project sponsors and experts should identify people, roles and functions that are important for implementing the projects. A facilitator could be selected, who can work with management in developing supporting arguments for each project and perform the role of an analyst in the project. Part of this effort will involve engaging with employees who are going to be impacted by each digital transformation project.

Prioritise Project Implementation

The firm will have to develop a schedule that involves prioritising the development of some of the projects. Certain projects may need to be prioritised due to technical considerations. For example, a scalable digital platform must be developed before a firm can add digital features and functions to improve customer service. Moreover, projects with the potential for quick results, either in terms of process improvements or enhanced customer service, may be prioritised. Such projects can create early buy-in from employees affected by the project and the overall digital transformation strategy. Mapping the resource requirements of each project and the associated impact on digital transformation provides a useful framework for structuring this analysis, as shown in Fig. 8.3.

Resource requirements include the finances, people and time for each project, whilst *digital transformation impact* includes the potential effect on improving performance. Each of the quadrants in Fig. 8.3 is explained below:

- *Quadrant 1—High resource requirements/high transformation impact—* these projects are challenging to implement due to the high resources

8 Digital Transformation Strategy

	Quadrant 2	Quadrant 1
High	- Challenging to implement - Limited benefits - Not a priority unless there is a change in the business environment	- Challenging to implement - High risk of failure - Needs considerable resource commitment to ensure success - Potential for significant benefits if successful
Resource requirements	Quadrant 3	Quadrant 4
Low	- Straightforward to implement - Not a priority - Can be used to generate quick wins to build employee engagement - Low risk of failure	- Potential opportunities for quick benefit realisation - Demonstrate benefits of digital transformation to employees - Low risk of failure - These projects should be prioritised
	Low Impact High	

Fig. 8.3 Digital transformation project resource requirements and impact matrix

required but offer significant benefits. Reengineering business processes and building a scalable digital platform are examples.

- *Quadrant 2—High resource requirements/low transformation impact*—these projects are challenging to implement and offer limited benefits. As these projects drain a lot of resources, they should not be considered a priority.
- *Quadrant 3—Low resource requirements/low transformation impact*—these projects are straightforward to implement with limited resource requirements but offer limited benefits. These projects should be implemented and used as a basis for generating some quick wins to create greater buy-in from employees affected by the change. The firm should be careful not to commit too many resources and prioritise resources for important projects with potentially high impact.
- *Quadrant 4—Low resource requirements/high transformation impact*—these projects are straightforward to implement with limited resource requirements and offer significant benefits. These projects should be prioritised and used as a basis for demonstrating the significant potential of digital transformation.

8.8.2 Evaluation and Adaptation

This involves evaluating the effectiveness of the digital transformation strategy during implementation and making any necessary adjustments in response to developments in the business environment and digital technologies during implementation. Figure 8.4 provides a useful guide on how the evaluation and adaptation stage should be undertaken.

Figure 8.4 reflects the importance of integrating the deliberate and emergent views into the process. The vision highlights the significance of the digital transformation strategy and its connection with the overall business strategy. The deliberate strategy aspect is based on the analysis of how digital technologies drive disruption in the business environment and digital resources and capability position of the firm and, in turn, how they influence the digital transformation strategy option selected.

During the implementation phase of the digital transformation strategy, the firm will gain important insights into the effectiveness of aspects of the digital transformation strategy selected, including customer responses to the use of digital technologies or employee reactions to new work structures. During this phase, changes in the business environment, such as competitor actions and the emergence of new technologies, will also have to be considered. Employees from lower levels in the firm should be brought into this process, as they are closer to the needs of customers and changes in the business environment.

Insights into implementation issues and changes in the business environment are likely to require adjustments to the digital transformation strategy option chosen. This is the emergent aspect of the digital transformation strategy process, which requires a more flexible approach that allows a firm to continuously evaluate and adjust aspects of the strategy during implementation.

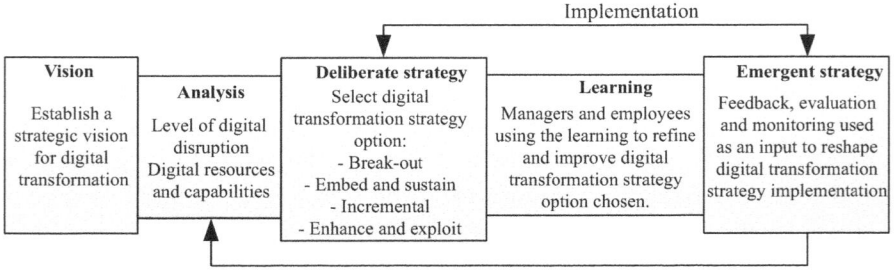

Fig. 8.4 Implementation, evaluation and adaptation in the digital transformation strategy process

The Importance of Organisational Learning

Organisational learning should be a key aspect of digital transformation strategy implementation, as success often depends on the ability of a firm to learn, adapt and evolve, as shown in Fig. 8.4. It involves acquiring and developing new knowledge and skills in response to individual and collective learning across the firm. Organisational learning plays an important role in the digital transformation strategy process in the following areas:

- Firstly, a firm has to take the learnings from strategy implementation and feed them back into refining initial assumptions in the original digital transformation strategy. For example, the unanticipated entry of new start-ups into the industry as a result of digital disruption may necessitate a change in approach.
- Secondly, as digital transformation occurs in the context of environmental change, there is a need for firms to adapt to the changes that may emerge during implementation. Consider Instagram's original strategy, which involved developing a private mobile phone app that would allow friends to check into locations, make plans, gain points for making friends, post pictures, etc. When Instagram implemented this strategy, it was rejected by users, and the founders had to revise their initial strategy. They quickly implemented their new strategy, which was developed as a result of analysing how users posted a lot of pictures and videos [17].
- Thirdly, a key aspect of digital transformation involves experimenting with new products or new processes facilitated by novel digital technologies. There should be a clear process in place to allow firms to effectively learn from these experiments. Where a firm develops a detailed understanding of the reasons for either success or failure with the experiment, it can use this learning to adjust the digital transformation strategy.

> **Discussion Questions**
>
> 1. Referring to Sect. 8.5.1, select a business sector and analyse how digital technologies have altered the competitive landscape along the dimensions of *increasing interdependence across firms* and the *emergence of new competitors and start-up firms*. Provide practical examples to illustrate your analysis.
> 2. Referring to Sect. 8.5.3, select a business sector and analyse how digital technologies have changed customer behaviour along the dimensions of *being more demanding and knowledgeable, having greater mobility* and *diminishing loyalty*. Provide practical examples to illustrate your analysis.

3. Referring to the digital resources and capabilities matrix in Fig. 8.2, select a business sector and highlight examples of necessary and distinctive digital resources and capabilities for firms in this sector. Using this analysis, identify digital resources and capabilities where firms in this sector should invest to create more value for customers.
4. Referring to Sect. 8.7.1, select a firm that has embarked upon a *breakout* digital transformation strategy. Critically assess the strategic actions the firm has taken to address the high level of digital disruption in the business environment.
5. Referring to Sect. 8.7.3, select a firm that has embarked upon an *incremental* digital transformation strategy. Critically assess the strategic actions the firm has taken in response to the emergence of digital technologies.

References

1. Correani, A., De Massis, A., Frattini, F., Petruzzelli, A. M., & Natalicchio, A. (2020). Implementing a digital strategy: Learning from the experience of three digital transformation projects. *California Management Review, 62*(4), 37–56.
2. Johnson, et al. (2017). Exploring Strategy: Text and Cases, Pearson, 11th Edition.
3. For an overview of the capabilities view refer to Barney, J, B. (1991). Firm Resources and Sustained Competitive Advantage, Journal of management, 17, 1, 99–120 and for an overview of the industry positioning approach refer to Porter, M.E. (1985). Competitive Advantage: Creating and Sustaining Superior Performance, New York: Free Press.
4. Volberda, H. W., Khanagha, S., Baden-Fuller, C., Mihalache, O. R., & Birkinshaw, J. (2021). Strategizing in a digital world: Overcoming cognitive barriers, reconfiguring routines and introducing new organizational forms. *Long Range Planning, 54*(5), 102110.
5. Hund, A., Wagner, H. T., Beimborn, D., & Weitzel, T. (2021). Digital innovation: Review and novel perspective. *Journal of Strategic Information Systems, 30*(4), 101695.
6. Li, T. C., Chan, Y. E., & Levallet, N. (2022). How Instacart Leveraged Digital Resources for Strategic Advantage. *MIS Quarterly Executive, 21*(3).
7. Verhoef, P. C., Broekhuizen, T., Bart, Y., Bhattacharya, A., Dong, J. Q., Fabian, N., & Haenlein, M. (2021). Digital transformation: A multidisciplinary reflection and research agenda. *Journal of Business Research, 122*, 889–901.
8. Barney, S. (1991) in reference 3 above.
9. Sia, S. K., Soh, C., & Weill, P. (2016). How DBS bank pursued a digital business strategy. *MIS Quarterly Executive, 15*(2), 105–121.

10. Weill, P., & Woerner, S. L. (2018). Is your company ready for a digital future? *MIT Sloan Management Review*, *59*(2), 21–25.
11. Hess, T., Matt, C., Benlian, A., & Wiesböck, F. (2016). Options for formulating a digital transformation strategy. *MIS Quarterly Executive*, *15*(2), 123–139.
12. Ross, J. W., Beath, C. M., & Sebastian, I. M. (2017). How to develop a great digital strategy. *MIT Sloan Management Review*, *58*(2), 7–9.
13. Ray, G., Barney, J. B., & Muhanna, W. A. (2004). Capabilities, business processes, and competitive advantage: Choosing the dependent variable in empirical tests of the resource-based view. *Strategic Management Journal*, *25*(1), 23–37.
14. Tekic, Z., & Koroteev, D. (2019). From disruptively digital to proudly analog: A holistic typology of digital transformation strategies. *Business Horizons*, *62*(6), 683–693.
15. Chanias, S., Myers, M. D., & Hess, T. (2019). Digital transformation strategy making in pre-digital organizations: The case of a financial services provider. *The Journal of Strategic Information Systems*, *28*(1), 17–33.
16. Correani, S., et al. (2020) in reference 1 above.
17. Collis, D. (2016). Lean strategy. *Harvard Business Review*, *94*(3), 62–68.

9

Building a Digital Core for Digital Transformation

9.1 Introduction

Many firms are increasingly aware of the productivity benefits that digital technologies can bring to their businesses. However, these same firms are often unable to achieve these potential benefits because their information technology (IT) infrastructures are highly inflexible, often cobbled together through a series of unrelated IT projects with little attempt made at systems integration. Such systems can lead to poor decision-making as managers do not have access to the full range of data required. These firms often lack a strategy for integrating their IT systems and are more likely to have fragmented systems that hinder performance and lead to poor customer service.

Consider the case of the National Health Service (NHS) in the UK. It has struggled to take advantage of advances in digital technologies, as its systems are often too slow and not user-friendly. It lags behind other sectors, such as banking and entertainment, in its use of data and technology [1]. Although digital technologies, such as AI and patient portals, provide enormous opportunities for increased productivity and quality of care, the lack of reliable, secure systems with connected data means that the NHS is not achieving the potential benefits on offer. Basic desktop clinical and office systems are slow and unreliable, whilst data are held in silos—hospital by hospital, general practitioner (GP) surgery by GP surgery—with little centrally held data available on mental health or community care.

Many other firms face similar problems to the NHS when seeking to take advantage of the benefits of digital technologies in digital transformation. Increasingly, firms have been developing a digital core that integrates processes, data and technical infrastructure to take advantage of digital technologies. A digital core allows firms to exploit the capabilities of digital technologies such as AI, the IoT and data analytics by providing the infrastructure needed to support these technologies and ensuring they are effectively integrated. It normally has a high level of data transparency, allowing access to data at any time from any location to perform analytics that lead to deeper insights for more informed decisions.

However, building a digital core can be complex, involving extensive planning and a clear strategy. It normally involves redesigning business processes, changing work practices, building new technical platforms and changing the firm's culture through change management. This chapter focuses on the key aspects of building a digital core to exploit the opportunities of digital technologies and achieve the productivity gains of digital transformation.

> **Learning Outcomes**
>
> - Understand the common causes of poor IT performance.
> - Outline the concept of the digital core in digital transformation.
> - Understand digital maturity frameworks and the transition to the digital core.
> - Highlight the increasing importance of modular architectures in the digital core.
> - Understand key practices for building a digital core, including process improvement, organisation redesign, sourcing strategy, customer experience, operational efficiency pathway choice, and cybersecurity and resilience management.

9.2 Common Causes of Poor IT Performance

There are a number of reasons why firms have struggled to achieve the benefits of digital technologies, and these are linked to the following causes of poor IT performance in established firms.

9.2.1 Presence of Silos

Silos include fragmented systems and functions where there is a lack of data sharing and communication across the firm. This is common in firms that have developed systems over many years, with a lack of strategy in place for systems integration. In many cases, IT systems were developed to address the needs of a single function, with little attempt made to integrate or standardise them across the firm with existing or future applications. Silos typically create inefficiencies and duplication of work, as different functions have redundant or incomplete information.

9.2.2 Tightly Coupled, Inflexible Systems

A firm's IT systems can be tightly coupled and, therefore, are inflexible and difficult to change. In many firms, the IT application driving the business process is highly customised and tightly integrated with the firm's IT infrastructure, including the operating systems and hardware [2]. Over time, the firm often develops tightly coupled solutions that integrate processes across multiple and disparate IT systems and business units. Standardising processes with links to tightly coupled systems can be time-consuming and expensive.

9.2.3 Outdated Legacy Systems

Legacy systems built on outdated technologies in firms create further difficulties, and they can be difficult to integrate with more contemporary systems. Although developments in areas such as enterprise systems have led to standardised processes, many firms are still relying on legacy applications with tightly coupled IT and business processes. Integrating these legacy systems with newer technologies often requires significant resources and sometimes entirely new systems. Integrating a patchwork of legacy systems to use common data and support standardised processes can be extremely challenging.

9.2.4 Managerial Autonomy

IT system implementation is often driven by behavioural challenges rather than technical challenges. Even when implementing enterprise systems, managerial autonomy across different functions and business units can affect the development of such systems. Deciding which processes should be standardised and which should be customised has proved challenging, often as a result of the level of autonomy of managers affected by the changes brought about by the IT system. When managers have traditionally had a lot of autonomy and control over decision-making at the functional level, they may resist accepting a standardised firm-wide approach and hold on to customised, disparate systems that are not integrated with the rest of the firm's IT infrastructure.

> **Illustration 9.1 The Case of a Human Resource (HR) System and the Causes of Poor IT Performance**
>
> This case provides an illustration of issues around silos, tightly coupled and inflexible legacy IT systems and management autonomy in the context of a HR shared services implementation [3]. The shared services arrangement involved transforming the HR function across eleven government departments, replacing outdated IT systems with a single enterprise system, modernising payroll and HR processes and providing centralised administrative HR services from an outsourced shared services centre. It was a highly complex, large-scale shared services arrangement involving almost 30,000 users of HR services, ranging from senior management to clerical officer level. The underlying philosophy behind the transformation involved creating a shared services centre to handle routine queries and transactions, which would allow the retained HR function in the departments to focus on more strategic HR activities.
>
> Analysis by the project team of existing internal HR processes and systems revealed the following problems:
>
> - *Disparate systems*—51 systems were being used by the departments to maintain personnel data, along with the central HR systems. In addition, some of these systems were automated, whilst others were manual. Rather than interfacing all these systems into new payroll systems, it was felt that it would be more appropriate to replace them with a single HR enterprise system that all departments and corporate HR could access in the same way.
> - *Lack of consistency*—departments were interpreting HR policies and procedures in different ways, often as a result of high managerial autonomy at the departmental level. Although policies were developed at the corporate level, they were being applied differently by departments in areas such as special leave or sickness absence.
> - *Lack of a coordinated HR structure*—there was no coordinated structure for the delivery of HR services. Some departments were receiving HR services from another department, whilst pensions and external recruitment services were delivered at the corporate level.
> - *Ageing legacy systems*—much of the technical infrastructure supporting the delivery of HR services had become obsolete.

Table 9.1 Business issue and performance impact (included in shaded grey above)

Business issue	Performance impact
HR services provided through an obsolete technological infrastructure with a number of supplier delivery contracts due to expire	Higher maintenance costs Not exploiting advances in technology Ongoing disruptions to service delivery
Multiple data sources and lack of system integration	No single definitive source of HR data which was impacting service delivery Duplication of work as disparate systems and manual workarounds were used to support existing HR system Lack of accessible historical data due to presence of fragmented systems
Lack of ownership of personal data. Basic staff information was not fully accurate as staff did not always provide full details of changes in circumstances due to a perceived lack of ownership of individual staff records	Inaccurate personnel data led to errors in HR processing as data were out of date
Lack of common HR standards. There were inconsistencies using cumbersome coding structures and discrepancies in definitions	Inconsistent definitions led to distortion of similar information across departments. Staff time wasted in resolving the resulting queries that arose.
Labour-intensive and time-consuming recruitment processes were not exploiting more effective IT-enabled recruitment capabilities	Adversely affecting the ability to recruit the best people with appropriate competencies for the job
Need to match skills and competencies to jobs and improve career management and HR planning	Adversely affecting the ability to align career development with business objectives and match competencies to jobs

Table 9.1 summarises the problems with the arrangement and the impact on performance.
Source: McIvor, R., McCracken, M., and McHugh, M. (2011). Creating outsourced shared services arrangements: Lessons from the public sector. *European Management Journal*, *29*(6), pp. 448–461.

9.3 The Digital Core Concept

The concept of the digital core is often used in the context of digital transformation to highlight the infrastructure that firms need to take advantage of the opportunities that digital technologies offer. It shares some of the characteristics of an operational backbone, which is defined as the technology and business capabilities that ensure the efficiency, scalability, reliability, quality and predictability of core operations [4]. These capabilities can include access to a single authoritative source of information on finance, customers and products, a stable integrated supply chain, or back-office shared services for functions such as HR and finance. Common features of a digital core include the following:

- A 'single source of truth' for critical data, including customer, order and product data. Fragmented data are difficult to protect consistently in a privacy and security context. Data that are maintained and used by different functions in the firm can be centralised and combined in one central location, thus improving decision-making [5]. Seamless and transparent transaction processing can reduce unnecessary duplication of resources or systems and, thus, reduce costs. Streamlining processes that were performed in different departments are also regarded as an opportunity to redesign processes to be more customer-focused.
- Standardisation of back-office shared services in functions such as HR, finance and IT. Standardisation leads to reductions in duplicated processes and ensures a standardised and consistent delivery of services to customers. Standardisation for back-office shared services also allows the freeing up of management time to focus more on core competencies [6].

A digital core can provide both operational and strategic benefits in the form of cost reductions and customer satisfaction, as well as developing new products and services and the ability to integrate acquired companies. Firms with a digital core can easily automate repetitive processes to enhance speed and accuracy, and it allows firms to introduce new digital technologies to existing products and services.

9.4 Digital Maturity Frameworks and the Transition to the Digital Core

Digital maturity frameworks have been widely employed both in academia and in practice as a tool to understand the level of digital maturity by highlighting strengths and weaknesses in a firm's digital capabilities. It can also serve as a road map in the journey towards building a digital core and allow a firm to measure progress and benchmark its capabilities against competitors. Although it may not be formally articulated in a set of plans, it can underpin decisions relating to data, applications, IT infrastructure and management responsibilities in building a digital core. A digital maturity framework can also provide a road map for both short- and long-term investments in these areas.

There are common stages in transitioning towards different levels of digital maturity in building a digital core, as set out below [7].

Stage 1—Business silo

Firms develop IT applications to address the needs of specific functions, with little effort made to integrate applications and share data across the firm. Many firms are at this stage, where investments in IT are controlled by the IT function, and the impact is dispersed across the firm in an inconsistent manner. This type of disjointed approach makes it difficult to share and scale innovation across the firm, and the firm lacks the architecture and capabilities to exploit the potential of digital technologies [8].

Stage 2—Standardised technology. In this stage, firms focus on developing IT standards and a shared infrastructure. This leads to better management of IT and a focus on standardisation that helps improve efficiency and reduce duplication of data. Firms typically begin by launching pilots that bridge separate groups and share shareable data and technology resources to deploy digital technologies. There is an emphasis on functional managers working with IT specialists and data scientists to improve decision-making in their functional areas.

Stage 3—Optimised core. The focus here is on shared IT infrastructure and local applications through the development of enterprise systems and further sharing data across the firm. Moreover, significant attention is given to employing IT to further integrate disparate business processes and, where appropriate, use the cloud to consolidate disparate data across different systems. Firms have to deal with employee resistance by investing in training and encouraging employees to pursue opportunities for digital transformation in their functional areas.

Stage 4—Modularity. Whilst continuing to drive process and data standardisation, firms focus on reusable business process modules to link processes both internally and externally. Modular architectures tend to have IT-driven business processes and plug-and-play components, which aid flexibility and allow firms to grow more rapidly. From an operations perspective, the firm's capabilities are modular, and data are viewed as a strategic resource that can be shared and accessed by those in the firm who need it.

The transition through each stage of maturity can be an evolutionary process due to the challenges of removing silos, phasing out legacy systems and often the need for firms to address short-term IT needs rather than building long-term capabilities. Moreover, different business sectors are likely to be at different maturity levels as a result of the disruptive impact of digital technologies. For example, media and entertainment sectors are far more advanced than firms in sectors such as construction and energy.

> **Illustration 9.2 Cloud Computing and the Hold-Up Problem**
>
> Firms have been increasingly using cloud service providers for computing services such as data storage and analysis, email and social networking. Firms often benefit from lower costs and greater flexibility from service providers, as they no longer have to invest time and in-house resources in adding extra capacity to their existing internal hardware and software infrastructure. Cloud services are updated continually, accessible on any device and are often more secure against the threat of hackers. Crucially, these features of cloud services have allowed firms to quickly scale up and adapt their computing needs as their businesses grow.
>
> However, firms have encountered problems with some cloud service providers regarding price charging structures, tiered storage costs, unfavourable longer-term contracts and compliance with strict data regulations. Some of these problems have increased the potential costs of switching to other cloud service providers. This situation is similar to the hold-up problem in outsourcing, where the buyer in a trading relationship makes investments specific to the requirements of the supplier, which increases dependency and makes it difficult to switch to other suppliers. In the case of cloud services, the hold-up problem arises when suppliers accumulate large volumes of client data and introduce unforeseen data transfer fees, which make it difficult for firms to switch to other cloud providers.
>
> These developments have given rise to calls for regulation to force cloud service providers to allow firms to easily transfer data to other providers and adopt common standards around data storage and transfer. Of course, firms can reduce the risk of the hold-up problem by using more than one cloud service provider or retaining some critical data on internal systems.

9.5 The Importance of Modular Architectures in the Digital Core

The development of more modular architectures has become increasingly important in the context of building a digital core for digital transformation for the following reasons:

- Standardised interfaces between applications for services across the IT environment can facilitate better linkages both internally between functions and externally into the supply chain. The use of application programming interfaces (APIs) can facilitate the exchange of data between these applications.
- Standardised interfaces and plug-and-play capabilities can help firms quickly establish relationships with many customers and suppliers, with limited need to customise the integration of the processes involved.
- As many established firms move towards employing digital platforms as an integral part of their product and service offerings, modular architectures are increasingly required. For example, as many subsystems of a car have become digitised and connected through digital platforms, automakers have to establish more modular architectures that allow other firms in the automotive industry to develop and integrate new digital devices, services and content into the car.

The trend towards modular architectures is likely to continue, and potentially accelerate, through the development of new technologies and the needs of firms in digital ecosystems [9]. As many firms increasingly move away from product-based strategies towards platform-based strategies, they need to attract a range of players to the platform so that consumers can have access to a wide range of products. Modular architectures allow platform designers, complementors and users to quickly add, remove and update functions within digital ecosystems. Modularity can also reduce entry barriers for firms to join the ecosystem, provided they have the capacity to conform to the ecosystem standards, regardless of their location or position in the network.

9.6 Practices for Building a Digital Core for Digital Transformation

The previous analysis has highlighted the key stages of maturity in building a digital core, and transitioning through each stage can be complex, involving both technical and organisational challenges for established firms. Organisational culture and politics, along with fragmented and inflexible systems, can hinder the development of enterprise-wide capabilities. Although implementation can be a priority for many firms faced with disruption from digital technologies, it requires a significant investment in terms of time, people and financial resources. There are a number of key practices that can guide firms through the journey of building a digital core for digital transformation, as shown in Fig 9.1, and each of these is outlined below.

9.6.1 Process Improvement

Process improvement is a key element of developing a digital operating core, as firms often embark on a programme of redesigning and improving processes across different business functions to address the proliferation of fragmented IT systems and processes. A key aim in the redesign process involves standardising processes around best practices to reduce costs and to improve controls. Process improvement is a systematic effort to seek out

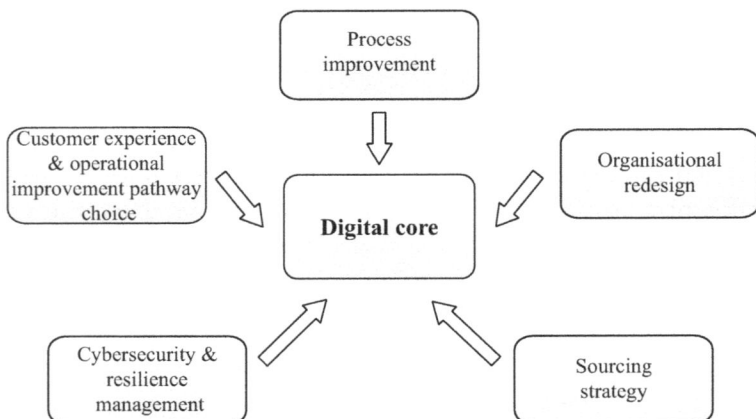

Fig. 9.1 Key practices for building a digital core for digital transformation

and apply new ways of working, and actively and repeatedly make process improvements [10]. Process improvement has its origins in the business process view, which is a structured approach to improving performance that involves the design and execution of a company's end-to-end business processes [11]. Process improvement is central to the process view, which involves constant efforts to improve performance and increase customer satisfaction. Organisations achieve process improvement through the deployment of business improvement techniques such as benchmarking, Six Sigma, process mapping, performance management and knowledge management.

How process improvement, standardisation and digital technologies are complementary Process improvement, standardisation and digital technologies are closely linked and complement one another in the context of developing a digital core, as evidenced by the following benefits:

- *Consistency*—standardisation involves creating uniform processes across a firm, which reduces differences in how tasks are performed, thus leading to more consistent outcomes. Process improvement is complementary to standardisation as it eliminates inefficiencies and bottlenecks, and employing digital technologies ensures consistency, with processes being performed in the same way regardless of location or time.
- *Performance management*—standardisation provides a baseline to measure performance and highlight areas for process improvement. Digital technologies ensure monitoring is straightforward, as activities and events can be tracked and analysed in real time, thus providing opportunities for testing and experimentation. Standardised processes are an important means of providing valid baselines for further improvements. For example, Six Sigma tools can be employed in a back-office services context to highlight any process inefficiencies and identify how best practices can be integrated to improve process performance.
- *Replication*—standardised and digitised processes also make it more straightforward to quickly replicate new, improved processes across different business units and locations within a firm, thus enabling scalability. For example, a firm with a standard, digitised customer acquisition process across different locations can rapidly scale up by ensuring that customers are acquired in a standard manner. This is particularly important, as a firm will be able to quickly sign up new customers effectively as the firm grows.
- *Enforceability*—digital technologies build in enforceability, as developers of a new process can ensure that the process is executed as intended [12].

Furthermore, it is not possible for staff in the firm to revert back to the old way of delivering the process, and it is possible to analyse whether people are embracing the new process when it goes live.

9.6.2 Organisational Redesign

Organisational redesign involves deciding where business processes should be performed. In a digital transformation context, firms often design structures to ensure staff are involved in high-value, high-touch processes that are close to customers so they can solve their specific needs. In contrast, standardised, low-touch processes are more likely to be automated via digital technologies. There is likely to be overlap between process improvement and organisational design, as processes have to be redesigned when differentiating between high-value and standard processes.

Shared services models provide an interesting illustration of the issues involved with organisational design when building a digital operating core. A shared services arrangement can specialise in back-office functions such as HR, finance and accounting (F&A), and IT, which then allows it to provide better service levels to users in the organisation. Shared services involve consolidating and standardising common tasks associated with a business function across different parts of the organisation into a single service centre [3]. These services are then provided by the service centre to other parts of the organisation.

Through transferring many administrative and transaction-oriented tasks into shared services centres, retained functions can take on a more strategic role and focus on more value-adding tasks [13]. For example, in the case of F&A, the retained function can focus on strategic issues such as budgeting, risk management and financial reporting, whilst the transaction-oriented tasks such as general accounting, accounts receivable and tax processing can be carried out in the shared services centre. Process improvement is often an important feature of shared services, where specialisation allows the operator of the shared services centre to drive improvements in both efficiency and service levels.

However, organisational redesign often involves redesigning and standardising back-office processes that are dispersed across different business units and locations, which can lead to challenges in the following areas:

- Organisational redesign impacts back-office functions with many employees and involves major organisational upheaval in the form of changes to complex functional structures and processes.
- Standardising processes with links to tightly coupled systems can be extremely time-consuming and expensive.
- Firms face challenges in enhancing the strategic value of the retained function. Traditionally, personnel in support functions operated in a transactional, clerical-type environment where there was little emphasis on driving improvement and enhancing the strategic value of the retained function.

9.6.3 Sourcing Strategy

Sourcing strategy involves deciding on the mix between in-house and supplier delivery provision when transitioning towards a digital operating core. Employing outsourced arrangements for both redesigning processes and providing the technical infrastructure has become an important vehicle for firms to leverage the specialist capabilities of suppliers.

Although outsourcing offers attractive features, including supplier performance improvement capabilities, better technology utilisation and cost savings through scale economies, it exposes organisations to supply market risk in the form of excessive dependence on a single supplier, knowledge loss, performance measurement difficulties and supplier opportunism [14]. These risks increase where requirements are difficult to specify, and there are frequent changes required to the contract. Firms attempt to pre-empt risk by adopting relational contracting arrangements, such as partnerships and joint ventures, which are characterised by trust, joint problem-solving and information sharing.

How standardisation drives outsourcing? Standardisation of business processes and parts of the technical infrastructure by a firm can facilitate outsourcing to specialist suppliers for the following reasons:

- Standardising a process means it can be performed successfully using a set of consistent and repeatable tasks. For example, when a customer places an order for a product from a company, there are a number of pre-determined steps and a sequence involved in processing the order. The consistency of the process means that it is straightforward to transfer to a supplier.
- Standardising processes also make it easier to compare in-house costs with those of sourcing the process from a supplier. Through outsourcing processes with standard requirements, suppliers can achieve economies

of scale and, in turn, reduce costs for their customers. Many processes, such as labour recruitment, payroll processing and debt collection are often performed in the same way by many firms.
- Digital technologies can allow the firm to implement standard interfaces with internal processes and those of suppliers, thus making it easier for firms to outsource. This means that responsibility and performance for the processes can be clearly handed over to the supplier.

Potential sourcing improvement options. When deciding on a sourcing strategy, firms are often faced with the choice of whether to improve their existing internal processes and related technologies internally or outsource and allow the supplier to drive improvement during the outsourcing contract. Typically, improvements are made in the following areas:

- Poorly defined processes may need to be redesigned in terms of process definition, structure and performance.
- Certain processes may offer significant improvement potential in terms of cost and service levels, and the firm has to decide whether this should be done in-house prior to transferring the process to the supplier.
- Improvements may be required in the technology infrastructure. For example, this can include application upgrades, system integrations or automation of certain processes.

There are a number of influences on the potential improvement options, including potential opportunism from the supplier, customer improvement capabilities, supplier improvement capabilities and customer outsourcing capability [15]. Each of these options is now outlined, along with the associated benefits and risks of each, as shown in Table 9.2.

- *Improve performance and retain internally*—rather than having to outsource, it may be possible to improve performance and retain the process internally. This option offers a number of benefits in the form of control over the process internally, attaining all the benefits of the improvement initiative and avoiding the risks of dealing with an external supplier. However, potential risks of retaining the process internally include failure to achieve the required performance improvements due to a lack of internal resources and skills, as well as failing to leverage the specialist capabilities of suppliers.
- *Improve performance internally prior to outsourcing*—it offers the customer a number of benefits, including retaining internal knowledge of process

9 Building a Digital Core for Digital Transformation

Table 9.2 Suggested conditions for each sourcing improvement option

	Improve performance and retain internally	Improve performance internally prior to outsourcing	Outsource and allow supplier to improve performance
Potential for opportunism from supplier	High potential for opportunism from outsourcing	Possible to reduce supplier opportunism by improving performance and re-designing the process. The improvement effort will create a better understanding of the process and allow the customer to better specify requirements to the supplier prior to outsourcing	Possible to manage the potential for opportunism by adopting an appropriate relationship strategy such as relational contracting which is characterised by trust, joint problem-solving and information sharing
Customer improvement capabilities	The customer has the capabilities and resource to improve performance in the process	Customer has the capabilities to improve performance prior to outsourcing. However, post-outsourcing the specialist capabilities of the supplier means it can deliver further performance improvement	Customer does not possess the capabilities or resource to improve performance. Suppliers can deliver significant performance improvement through greater experience and specialisation
Supplier improvement capabilities	External suppliers do not possess the required capabilities to deliver the required performance improvements	Although the customer has the potential to improve performance initially, suppliers possess stronger improvement capabilities to deliver further and sustained performance improvement over time	Suppliers have far superior process improvement capabilities

(continued)

Table 9.2 (continued)

	Improve performance and retain internally	Improve performance internally prior to outsourcing	Outsource and allow supplier to improve performance
Customer outsourcing capability	The customer has a lack of experience in managing outsourcing arrangements where significant performance improvement is required	Customer has a lack of experience in outsourcing arrangements where the supplier is responsible for driving all the improvement effort	Customer has extensive experience with complex outsourcing arrangements in areas such as formal contracting, relational contracting and implementing governance arrangements
Benefits	Avoid supplier opportunism potential associated with outsourcing. Customer obtains all the benefits from the performance improvement efforts	Customer can attain some of the benefits of the improvement efforts prior to outsourcing. Customer can reduce potential for supplier opportunism by redesigning and improving the process prior to outsourcing. Customer can leverage the superior capabilities of a supplier to further improve performance during the outsourcing relationship	Customer can focus scarce internal resource on areas where it can build stronger performance positions. Customer can access the superior process improvement capabilities of suppliers. Potential to build a strong relationship with the supplier and deploy supplier capabilities in other parts of the firm

improvements, deriving clearer requirements and performance measures for the supplier, and therefore reducing the level of dependence on the supplier in the outsourcing contract. However, the customer may often lack the necessary resources and process improvement capabilities to improve performance internally and therefore has to rely on the supplier for performance improvement.

- *Outsource and allow the supplier to improve performance*—this option allows the customer to benefit from reallocating scarce internal resources and accessing the specialist improvement capabilities of the supplier to enhance performance. In some cases, suppliers can deliver significant performance improvements. However, this option leads to greater dependence on the supplier, loss of important knowledge about the process and the need for significant experience and skills to manage the contract and relationship to ensure performance improvements are delivered.

9.6.4 Customer Experience and Operational Efficiency Improvement Pathway Choice

When embarking upon a major overhaul of IT infrastructure, there can be tension in the sequence between improving the underpinning IT infrastructure and enhancing the front-end, customer-facing applications. Radically changing back-office legacy systems and business processes may lead to a deterioration in service levels for customers. A digital transformation framework has been developed that is relevant for understanding and managing the tension between improving the back-office infrastructure and customer-facing applications [16]. This framework includes two dimensions that closely reflect this tension: customer experience and operational efficiency. Figure 9.2 outlines the categories based on the levels of transformation along each of these two dimensions.

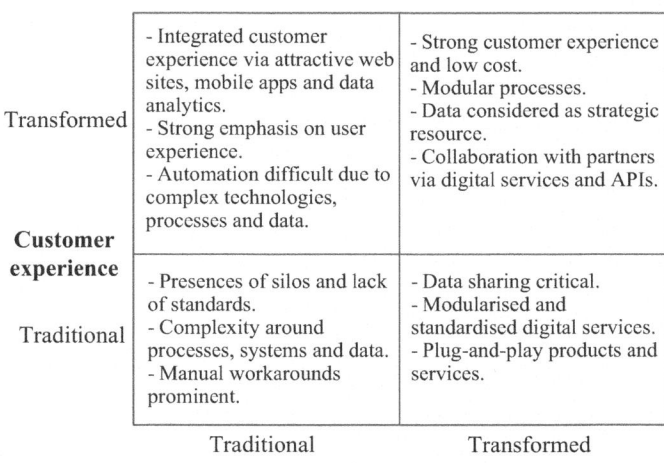

Fig. 9.2 The relationship between customer experience and operational efficiency [17]

This framework also considers transformation pathways based on the dimensions of customer experience and operational efficiency, and these are explained below.

Pathway 1: Standardise first. The primary focus here is on eliminating legacy systems and processes and building a platform mindset with API-linked business services that can be accessed across the firm. This can be a complex and time-consuming process and may mean pausing other projects. However, technologies such as cloud computing, APIs and better solution architectures can speed up the process and make it less disruptive.

Pathway 2: Improve customer experience first. This involves focusing efforts on improving processes that positively impact customer experience. This effort can focus on a number of developments concurrently to improve customer satisfaction, including developing new mobile apps, adding more functionality to web channels and automating call-centre services. Focusing on the customer experience dimension can lead to potentially higher customer satisfaction and increased sales. However, this pathway can add further complexity to already complex and inefficient systems and processes.

Pathway 3: Iterate between improving customer experience and operational efficiency. Pathways 1 and 2 can be difficult to separate in practice, and firms often embark on an approach that iterates between the two. This pathway involves alternating the focus between improving customer experience and operational efficiency. A firm might start by adding more functionality to its web channels, followed by standardising inefficient back-office processes.

Firms can also rapidly develop customer-facing applications whilst, at the same time, gradually replacing legacy systems. For example, it is possible to build a middleware interface to connect the front and back ends and allow improvements to be made simultaneously at the same time [18]. Over time, legacy systems can be replaced, ensuring they do not get in the way of focusing on improving customer-facing applications. The advantage of this pathway is that it consists of tightly specific projects, thus reducing the overall risk. However, iterating between different projects can lead to a lack of focus and confusion amongst employees due to changes in direction.

Illustration 9.3 The Case of Tourism Union International (TUI) and Customer Experience and Operational Efficiency

TUI, the German leisure, travel and tourism company, faced the challenge of managing the tension between improving customer experience and operational efficiency in its digital transformation journey. The firm's retail, telephone and online services were geographically and operationally separate, whilst its reservation legacy systems were outdated. The disruptive effect of pure online players, such as Expedia, on the travel agency business had made digital transformation a competitive imperative for TUI. Although it could have begun this transformation journey by overhauling its IT infrastructure, it decided against this course of action due to the risks associated with replacing complex and critical systems.

Consequently, TUI developed a plan to replace its technology over a three-year period, whilst at the same time developing digital solutions to improve the customer experience. The vision of the firm was to map out the ideal customer journey and learn from customers what they wanted from digital technologies. The front-end applications were connected to legacy back-end systems through a middleware interface. It then separated the back-end legacy system into modular subsystems and gradually replaced them, adding customer-facing applications at each stage. When TUI upgraded a component of the back end or the front end, it tested it in one market and then iterated the prototype to improve it before rolling it out to other business units.

Source: Furr, N., and Shipilov, A., 2019. Digital doesn't have to be disruptive: the best results can come from adaptation rather than reinvention. *Harvard Business Review*, 97(4), pp. 94–104.

9.6.5 Cybersecurity and Resilience Management

A key aspect of building an effective digital operating core is having practices in place to deal with cybersecurity. Cybersecurity has become more critical in an era where firms have significant numbers of network connections and human–device interactions occurring on a continuous basis, both inside and outside the firm, thus increasing the associated risks. Cybersecurity risk refers to the risk of financial loss, disruption or damage to the reputation of a firm due to a failure in its IT systems caused by external attacks.

Examples of cybersecurity risks include remote attacks on IT systems, unauthorised access to data on systems, phishing emails, system infiltration or damage through malware, and disruption or denial of service that prevents system access. These threats can lead to the risk of losing sensitive data and disruption in a firm's network systems and services. The level of cybersecurity risk is likely to vary across different business sectors. For example, the cybersecurity risk for an entertainment company is likely to be lower than that for a bank, a hospital or a government agency.

Despite the risks, many firms are not effectively addressing cybersecurity in several areas, including failing to make connecting via virtual private networks mandatory, prompting staff to regularly change passwords, performing mandatory software updates and regularly backing up data. However, customers expect their data to be secure and, in some cases, regard security as a key source of value and a potential differentiator. Therefore, firms need to protect their digital operating core by managing the risk of cyberattacks, and there are a number of practices that can be adopted to deal with these risks [19]:

> **Illustration 9.4 Cyber Meltdown at Marks and Spencer**
>
> Marks and Spencer, the UK clothing, food and home retailer, experienced a cyberattack that damaged its operations for months and potentially reduced its operating profit by up to £300 million. The cyberattack forced Marks and Spencer to shut down its online clothing operations, led to the theft of customer data and knocked £750 million off its market capitalisation.
>
> Cyber criminals gained access to its systems by manipulating staff into performing actions that compromised the security of its systems via a third-party supplier, after they were unable to bypass the firm's own cyber defences. The criminals fraudulently claimed to be an employee and tricked staff into changing passwords and resetting authentication processes, which allowed them to access the firm's systems.
>
> Marks and Spencer entered crisis management mode and brought in cybersecurity experts to deal with the attack. The firm warned that its ecommerce operations would be out of action for months as it had to cleanse its entire systems portfolio, which involved putting hundreds of applications and thousands of servers through a technological washing machine.
>
> The firm gave significant attention to keeping customers informed with frequent updates and apologies via social media and email channels, and it was open about the theft of customer data. It committed additional resources to its physical store network by increasing the number of staff at tills and store entrances by 75% and adding more capacity to its customer service hotline to allow customers to quickly resolve any queries. These human interactions were regarded as critical for attempting to maintain customer trust and loyalty to the brand.
>
> The cyberattack highlighted the risks for firms dependent on third-party suppliers for IT services, which led to insurers insisting on more disclosure regarding risk management practices and controls. When relying on third-parties, firms need to ensure access to systems is controlled and auditable, with clear rules on who is responsible for each element of cybersecurity. As other major retailers in the UK were targeted at the same time, this cyberattack is regarded as a wake-up call for all consumer-facing businesses.
>
> Source: Barrett, C. (2025, May 25). This is not just any cyber meltdown: will shoppers forgive M&S? *Financial Times* and Onita, L., and Harris, L. (2025, May 22). M&S undone by old-fashioned con: how retailer's cyber hell unfolded. *Financial Times.*

Distinguish between digital security and digital resilience. Digital security involves focusing on security measures such as developing firewalls, encrypting data, formulating clear user access privileges, securely storing data and implementing multi-factor authentication processes. Staff training is an important aspect of security and can involve the following [20]:

- *Compliance awareness*—training on the legal, regulatory and policy aspects of cybersecurity to ensure adherence to compliance standards and best practices.
- *Threat simulation*—hands-on tasks that replicate cyberthreats to improve awareness, vigilance and the need to respond.
- *Specialised instruction*—cybersecurity education customised to specific roles or functions to address specific risks, needs and operational protocols.
- *Incident response planning*—interactive workshops and security management sessions on specific scenarios to ensure effective crisis response and to develop resilience.

Digital resilience is a management issue and focuses on the ability of the firm to deal with cyber incidents and breaches, relating to how it conducts business in a digital environment. There should be plans for resilience and recovery in place that are tested regularly. Management should have a clear understanding of the cybersecurity risks the firm faces in terms of legal and reputational impacts, and they should have incident reporting and performance indicator mechanisms in place. Firms also must strike a balance between data accessibility and protecting customer data security, as there is often a trade-off between security and interactivity, thus affecting customer acquisition and retention. Although firms may be faced with the ongoing threat of managing security risks, prioritising resilience will allow them to deal with any breaches of security.

Leadership education. Both middle and senior managers need to be educated on cybersecurity risks and the security and resilience implications. This involves creating an awareness of the difficulties inherent in any cybersecurity strategy preventing all attacks and highlighting the need to keep the business running in the event of an attack. Senior management needs to have the knowledge to view cybersecurity as a firm-wide issue and be aware of the resource implications. For example, investments may have to be made in cloud computing security, safeguarding computer networks and preventing attacks on the connected devices on the IoT.

Use understandable language. Management should have access to cybersecurity expertise, and digital security experts, in turn, should be able to communicate in a way that is understandable across the business. For example, these experts need to present cybersecurity information at a level and in a format that is understandable by non-technical managers. Moreover, in some instances, cybersecurity risk management may have to be a regular feature of board-level meetings.

> **Illustration 9.5 Rapidly Developing AI Capabilities and Phishing Scams**
>
> Rapid developments in AI tools are being used by hackers to mount highly targeted cyberattacks on firms and individuals. The increasing availability of generative AI tools and the race to develop more sophisticated versions by technology firms have reduced the entry barriers for those involved in advanced cybercrime. These tools are allowing hackers to scrape a lot of information about a person for use in targeted phishing emails. More than 90% of cyberattacks begin with a phishing email, and they often bypass the email filters a firm has in place.
>
> AI bots can process large amounts of data on the tone and style of a firm or individual and analyse these features to develop a convincing phishing scam. These tools can also scrape data on the online presence and social media activity of an individual to determine issues they are most likely to respond to. This then allows hackers to generate highly sophisticated and customised phishing emails that can trick individuals into transferring funds or divulging confidential corporate information. The significant cost of a cyberattack means firms have to put ever-more-sophisticated tools and practices in place to combat the threat of attack.
>
> Source: Stacey, S. (2025, Jan 2). AI-generated phishing scams target corporate executives. *Financial Times*.

Discussion Questions

1. Undertake research on a well-known firm and analyse common causes of poor IT performance it faced, and how it then embraced some of the features of the digital core concept.
2. Select a process in a firm and analyse how the process could be redesigned and better integrated with other internal processes. Referring to Section 9.6.1, highlight how process improvement, standardisation and digital technologies deliver the benefits of consistency, performance management, replication and enforceability for the process.
3. In your role as a consultant for a large retail firm, outline the critical issues that the firm should consider when employing outsourcing to build a digital core.
4. Select a firm that has adopted a digital transformation strategy and undertake the following tasks: (i) referring to Fig 9.2, highlight examples of how the firm has improved customer experience and operational efficiency; and (ii) compare how one of its competitors has improved customer experience and operational efficiency.
5. Compare the cybersecurity risks faced by firms in the health and entertainment sectors. Highlight the specific risks around data security for each organisation and the potential strategies for mitigating these risks.

References

1. Tapper, J., & McKie, R. (2024), NHS cannot embrace AI until its basic IT systems are up to scratch. *The Guardian*, https://www.theguardian.com/society/2024/sep/15/nhs-cannot-embrace-ai-until-its-basic-it-systems-are-up-to-scratch.
2. McIvor, R. (2010). *Global services outsourcing*. Cambridge University Press.
3. McIvor, R., McCracken, M., & McHugh, M. (2011). Creating outsourced shared services arrangements: Lessons from the public sector. *European Management Journal*, 29(6), 448–461.
4. Ross, J. W., Beath, C. M., & Sebastian, I. M. (2017). How to develop a great digital strategy. *MIT Sloan Management Review*, 58(2), pp.7–9 and Sebastian, I., Mocker, M., Ross, J., Moloney, K., Beath, C. and Fonstad, N. 2017. How big old companies navigate digital transformation. *MIS Quarterly Executive*, 16(3), 197–213.
5. See Sebastian et al. (2017) in reference 4 above.
6. Paagman, A., Tate, M., Furtmueller, E., & De Bloom, J. (2015). An integrative literature review and empirical validation of motives for introducing shared services in government organizations. *International Journal of Information Management*, 35(1), 110–123.
7. The following references considers aspect of digital maturity relevant to building a digital core. M. Iansiti & S. Nadella. (2022). Democratizing transformation. *Harvard Business Review*, 43–49. See Ross et al. (2017) in reference 4 above. See Sebastian et al. (2017) in reference 4 above. Bradley, R. V., Pratt, R. M., Byrd, T. A., & Simmons, L. L. 2011. The role of enterprise architecture in the quest for value. *MIS Quarterly Executive*, 10(2), 73–80.
8. See Iansiti and Nadella (2022) in reference 7 above.
9. Sturgeon, T. J. (2021). Upgrading strategies for the digital economy. *Global Strategy Journal*, 11(1), 34–57.
10. Anand, G., Ward, P., Tatikonda, M., & Schilling, D. (2009). Dynamic capabilities through continuous improvement. *Journal of Operations Management*, 27, 444–461.
11. Hammer, M. (2002). Process management and the future of six sigma. *Sloan Management Review*, Winter, 26–32.
12. McAfee, A., & Brynjolfsson, E. (2008). Investing in the IT that makes a competitive difference. *Harvard Business Review*, 98–107.
13. See Paagman et al. (2015) in reference 6 above.
14. McIvor, R. (2016). An analysis of the application of process improvement techniques in business process outsourcing. *International Journal of Quality and Reliability Management*, 33(3), 321–343.

15. McIvor, R. (2013). Employing business improvement techniques to improve performance and reduce risk in services outsourcing. Institute of Chartered Accountants for Scotland Report, Edinburgh, https://icas-com.uksouth01.umbraco.io/media/jryby45g/employing-business-improvement-techniques-to-improve-performance-2013.pdf.
16. Weill, P., & Woerner, S. L. (2018). Is your company ready for a digital future? *MIT Sloan Management Review, 59*(2), 21–25.
17. This matrix has been adapted from Weill and Woerner (2018) in reference 17 above.
18. Furr, N., & Shipilov, A. (2019). Digital doesn't have to be disruptive: The best results can come from adaptation rather than reinvention. *Harvard Business Review, 97*(4), 94–104.
19. Rothrock, R. A., Kaplan, J., & Van Der Oord, F. (2018). The board's role in managing cybersecurity risks. *MIT Sloan Management Review, 59*(2), 12–15.
20. Abhari, K., Safaei Pour, M., & Shirazi, H. (2024). How to design a better cybersecurity readiness program. *MIS Quarterly Executive, 23*(4), 8.

10

Leading Change in Digital Transformation

10.1 Introduction

Digital transformation poses challenges to firms as it involves significant changes to processes, products, business models and, in some cases, the emergence of new competitors. Managing the change implications of digital transformation can be extremely challenging for firms, as the process occurs in an environment where digital technologies have accelerated the pace of change, leading to more disruption, uncertainty and complexity. These challenges are further exacerbated in the case of established firms that are encumbered by legacy systems, firm silos, resistance to change and firm politics.

Senior management in established firms believes they can remain successful by integrating digital technologies into their existing business models without fully appreciating the challenges involved. This view is often based on the erroneous assumption that business models, norms and practices that were successful in the past are likely to be successful in the future. Therefore, these firms are unwilling to experiment with new business models and change established ways of creating value for customers.

This chapter considers the key issues surrounding leading and managing the change implications of digital transformation. It highlights the importance of changing organisational structures, building employee collaboration, developing employee skills and capabilities, and breaking down barriers to change. Consideration is given to the change paths available to firms in their digital transformation journeys, based on factors such as the scope and speed of change required. Practices for embedding change in digital transformation are also presented, with particular attention given to the leadership capabilities required for driving change.

> **Learning Outcomes**
> - Understand the digital transformation contextual change factors, including scope, speed, preservation, cultural diversity, capability and capacity.
> - Understand the digital transformation change paths, including revolution, evolution and adaptation.
> - Understand how the contextual change factors influence each digital transformation change path.
> - Understand the key practices for embedding change in digital transformation, including recruitment, retention and skills development; organisational structure change; and driving change through leadership.

10.2 Leading Change in Digital Transformation

Leading change in digital transformation requires an understanding of both the firm and the business environment. Firm issues, such as the existing culture and acceptance of change amongst employees, and business environment issues, such as the pace of product and service digitisation, will influence the firm's approach to change. The experience and skills of employees can act as significant impediments to driving digital transformation.

10.3 Contextual Change Factors in Digital Transformation

A key aspect of leading change involves understanding the specific context of the firm and how it will affect change in digital transformation. The change kaleidoscope provides a useful framework for understanding some of the contextual features of change in digital transformation [1]. Some of the influences in this framework offer a valuable basis for understanding the actions that managers should take in managing the change implications of digital transformation. Each of these contextual change factors is now outlined.

10.3.1 Scope

Scope is essentially concerned with the level of change required for digital transformation. Useful indicators of scope include the impact of digital transformation across the firm, ranging from firm-wide to only one part of the firm, changes in relationships with customers and suppliers, or changes in the business model of the firm. Clearly, where all of these indicators are affected by the scope of digital transformation, it will involve significant change and complexity. This, in turn, will influence the level of resources and time that must be committed to driving the required change.

The case of CNH Industrial provides an example of a digital transformation project with significant scope [2]. The firm was committed to driving the digital transformation of the agricultural industry and intended to connect all the stages of farming via a digital platform with automation capabilities, value-added services, connecting customers with internal and external partners, and transitioning to a service-based business model. The project involved thirty employees, including managers from the commercial vehicles unit, industry-specific vehicles unit, as well as information technology, operations and other senior stakeholders.

10.3.2 Speed

Speed is concerned with assessing the time required to deliver the change associated with digital transformation. Much of this will be influenced by the pace of technology disruption in the business environment. For example, where the market share and profitability of the firm are in rapid decline as a result of the emergence of new digital competitors, there will be considerable urgency in the need to respond. However, a sense of urgency can serve as a useful basis for action and breakdown resistance amongst employees to embracing the required changes.

> **Illustration 10.1 The Big Bang and Long-march Approaches to Leading Organisational Change in Digital Transformation**
>
> Where there is a real need to act quickly, a firm may adopt a big bang approach to change, which involves top-down, managerial-led change, strict adherence to a timeline and performance indicators, major structural changes, and formal, directed communication. Such an approach to digital transformation is often adopted as extensive disruption means firms do not have the time to engage

with stakeholders, and the need for urgency makes buy-in from employees more likely.

However, digital transformation may have to be rolled out on a more phased basis for several reasons. In this case, a 'long-march' approach to change is more appropriate, which involves an incremental approach to change. Key aspects of the long-march approach include running the change programme over a number of years and gradually changing the culture and behaviour of employees.

The pace of change in the business environment brought about by digital technologies may not be overly disruptive, thus allowing firms to pursue a more incremental approach to change. Moreover, the culture and structure of the firm may mean that it has no choice other than to pursue a more gradualist approach to change. For example, this approach is common in public sector organisations where digital transformation is implemented on a phased basis due to the potential for significant employee resistance.

10.3.3 Preservation

Preservation refers to firms making decisions about preserving or discontinuing certain processes and divesting assets in digital transformation. For example, many retail banks have scaled back their branch networks in the transition to digital channels, and this has led to the redeployment of branch staff or the redundancy of staff.

As part of preservation analysis, firms have to identify tangible and intangible assets affected by digital transformation. Tangible assets include physical, human and financial resources, whilst intangible assets include employee skills and knowledge. Once firms have identified these assets, they have to decide which to preserve and which to discontinue. There are a number of important considerations associated with this analysis.

- The knowledge and skill sets of some employees may become redundant in a digital context. In this case, firms will have to consider upskilling certain staff through training and development activities. New staff with digital skills may have to be recruited, which will require investment.
- Where possible, the mindsets of staff will also have to be changed, as the factors that represented drivers of success in an analog context are no longer appropriate in a digital business context. The concept of unlearning is relevant in this context, which involves employees letting go of unhelpful behaviours or ways of thinking and embracing new ways of thinking. Enacting this type of change can be extremely challenging, particularly in environments with rigid cultures and strong resistance to change.

- The analysis may also highlight opportunities for complementing existing analog assets with digital assets. Firms have to balance the competing concerns of needing to align existing capabilities while also building new digital capabilities. For example, when adding digital services to their products, firms have to retain existing design capabilities for the hardware in the product, whilst at the same time relying on external firms for digital services.

10.3.4 Cultural Diversity

This is concerned with the level of cultural diversity between employees or employee groups impacted by the level of change associated with digital transformation. Increasing digitisation of processes is likely to lead to employee groups with different cultures having to cooperate with one another in a way that did not happen in the past. For example, established manufacturers that have embraced the IoT and integrated digital services into their products have had to foster collaboration between research and development (R&D) and IT functions, something which did not happen in the past. Cultural diversity in a digital transformation context can arise in the following areas:

- Younger and older staff groups can be a source of cultural diversity. As many fashion retailers have embraced social media channels to reach their customers, they have had to recruit Generation Z staff, individuals born between the mid-to-late 1990s and early 2010s, who better understand these technologies than their existing older employees, who are lagging technically. Firms have to manage this diversity carefully to ensure that each cultural group complements one another in creating value for customers.
- Integrating digital services into physical products requires more collaboration across functions and disciplines for manufacturing firms. This can create the challenge of integrating employees with different work practices and diverse cultural backgrounds. For example, the speed of software development is often quicker than traditional manufacturing processes, which means firms that integrate digital services into their products have to adapt their organisational structures and human resource policies.

Firms are often faced with the option of developing a change strategy to promote a uniform culture or tailoring it to the needs of each cultural group.

Using a change strategy to promote a uniform culture to limit any potential conflict may be appropriate in an environment where the level of disruption is low. However, the downside of this approach is that it may stifle the development of new ideas and different viewpoints on how best to implement digital transformation. An advantage of promoting diversity is that it may lead to the emergence of new ideas and encourage experimentation amongst employees with new business models.

> **Illustration 10.2 Managing Cultural Diversity Via Reverse Mentoring**
>
> Reverse mentoring is a useful approach for managing cultural diversity in digital transformation. This involves encouraging younger employees to share their knowledge and insights on contemporary digital technologies with their more senior, older colleagues. This can help more senior colleagues acquire technical knowledge, learn about current trends, understand the younger generation and expand their social networks. Younger employees can gain respect, mentoring skills and insights into the business whilst developing positive attitudes towards older people.
>
> As digital technologies play a more prominent role in firms, younger employees are in a strong position to share their technical knowledge and skills with older, less tech-savvy colleagues. Many of these younger employees are part of the digital native generation, who grew up when the internet was mainstream and had more exposure to social media platforms such as Instagram, TikTok and Facebook. As digital natives, they can encourage their more senior colleagues to employ contemporary digital technologies and help shift their thinking on the potential benefits. Exposing more senior colleagues to this knowledge through reverse mentoring can accelerate change towards digital transformation and foster more collaboration at different levels within the firm.
>
> Sources: Gadomska-Lila, K., 2020. 'Effectiveness of Reverse Mentoring in Creating Intergenerational Relationships'. *Journal of Organizational Change Management*, *33*(7), pp. 1313–1328; and Kaše, R., Saksida, T., and Mihelič, K.K., 2019. 'Skill Development in Reverse Mentoring: Motivational Processes of Mentors and Learners'. *Human Resource Management*, *58*(1), pp. 57–69.

10.3.5 Capability

This considers the capabilities the firm has for managing the required change for digital transformation. A firm will need different capability levels for certain types of change. For example, a firm may have experience in delivering operational changes, such as introducing a redesigned process into the business. However, it does not follow that this firm has the capability to deliver transformational change across the business. Capability for managing change has two levels:

- *Individual level* refers to the capability of employees and managers to deliver change. Influencing factors at the employee level include skills and attitudes towards change, as well as their experience in dealing with change. A firm may need to employ training and development programmes to enhance their change capabilities, as well as recruit new staff. The change capabilities of managers play a key role in digital transformation [3]. They need to be prepared to embrace the required change, and they should be able to empower and actively involve their employees in digital transformation projects.
- *Firm level* refers to the capability of the firm to deliver change and includes factors such as experience, culture and incentives for change. The level of experience with change at the firm level is an important influence on the scope of change that can be enacted. Where a firm has limited experience with radical change, it may have to follow a more incremental path in the change required for digital transformation. Of course, the firm can build up its experience through management development and recruitment initiatives.

10.3.6 Capacity

Capacity refers to how much resource the firm should invest in the change required for digital transformation in terms of finance, time and people, as outlined below:

- *Finance*—digital transformation can require financial investment in areas such as upgrading the technology infrastructure, redesigning office space, building new warehousing space and developing the digital skills and competencies of employees.
- *Time*—management time at both the senior and middle management levels will have to be committed to driving the change. A strong leader should be selected and given the time to commit to leading the digital transformation project. Middle managers should also be encouraged to drive the change, as well as manage their day-to-day jobs.
- *People*—this involves considering whether there are enough managers and digital specialists to commit to delivering the change. The change capabilities of these managers are a further issue to consider here.

The time frame over which the change is being delivered is also relevant, as incremental change approaches may require an on-going commitment of resources over a long time period, whereas a big bang approach to change will have a shorter, more sustained resource commitment.

10.4 Change Paths in Digital Transformation

The extent of change associated with digital transformation is likely to differ depending on the specific circumstances of the firm. For firms faced with an urgent need to digitally transform due to increasing digitisation and the emergence of new competitors, significant change across the business is likely to be required. Alternatively, for some firms not greatly impacted by digitisation, a gradual approach to change is more appropriate. There are three potential paths of digital transformation that firms can adopt, including revolution, evolution and adaptive. The contextual features of change already outlined are useful guides for selecting the most appropriate change path to take, as shown in Table 10.1.

These contextual change factors can act as enablers or constraints in the change paths. Where a firm has significant *capacity* in the form of finance, time and people, this can act as an important enabler for driving change through investing in new recruits and digital skills development.

At the same time, the *scope* and *speed* of change required can act as a considerable constraint to achieving the level of change needed. For example, firms may be under considerable pressure to rapidly transform but lack the *capacity* and *capability* to do so. Of course, firms can pursue practices to deal with these factors when embedding the change, and these will be considered later in Sect. 10.5. Each of the change paths in Table 10.1 is now outlined.

10.4.1 Revolution Change Path

In this change path, there is a high degree of urgency in pursuing digital transformation. This can be as a result of digital technologies rapidly disrupting the firm's business model and leading to new competitors entering the marketplace through new digital platforms. For example, established players in the film industry, such as Disney, have had to react to the emergence of new competitors, such as Apple and Amazon, by launching their own streaming platforms. This is an entirely different business model from releasing films in cinemas and then selling them through physical and digital channels.

Table 10.1 Contextual change factors and change paths in digital transformation

Contextual change factors	Revolution	Evolution	Adaptive
Scope	Significant change required across the firm, and with suppliers and customers. High level of complexity	Change is required across the firm, and with suppliers and customers	Change can be rolled out gradually across the firm, and with suppliers and customers
Speed	High degree of urgency required in driving the change and keeping pace with changes in the business environment	Required change can be delivered over time and aligned with changes in the business environment	Gradual speed of change driven by the overall strategy of the firm
Preservation	Need to discontinue certain processes and assets as a result of redundancy from digital disruption. Need to protect some existing capabilities, align with new digital resources and acquire new digital assets	Need to discontinue certain processes and assets as a result of redundancy from digital disruption. Protect some existing capabilities and align with new digital resources	Continue to focus on core processes and assets. Build up skills and knowledge of employees in application of digital technologies
Cultural diversity	Rapid transition to digital environment requires considerable culture change and fusing analog and digital cultures	Transition to digital environment requires gradual culture change and fusing analog and digital cultures	Limited effort required for managing cultural diversity
Capability	Significant attention must be given to rapidly enhancing the change capabilities at both the individual and firm levels	Some effort has to be given to enhancing the change capabilities at both the individual and firm levels	Some attention should be given to enhancing the change capabilities at the individual level
Capacity	Rapid and significant commitment of finance, time and people required. Sustained investment over time required to drive radical change	Significant commitment of finance, time and people required. Sustained investment over time required to drive change	Required commitment of finance, time and people driven by the overall strategy of the firm

The speed and scope of change required are key influences here and can be considerably greater than what the firm has been accustomed to. Innovative start-up businesses have displaced many established companies in a relatively short period of time and have expanded across industries and markets. This change path involves a fundamental shift in the firm's business model, strategy and culture. The firm needs to transform the existing employee mindset and culture and develop new ones suited for a digital context. It typically entails a firm-wide transformation that involves all levels of management.

Strong transformational leadership and a committed top and middle management team to digital transformation are required. This will involve a significant resource commitment in the form of finances and people, and this can include bringing in new individuals with digital skills and experience across the business.

Consider the example of many high-street retailers that have had to quickly adapt to the new digital landscape brought about by digital technologies [4]. For example, Nike has had to transition towards digital technologies as part of its digital transformation journey. This has involved creating a premium and seamless experience for customers and generating significantly more sales online. It has created its own sports ecosystem via its digital platform. Nike has moved away from primarily selling through retailers to directly selling to customers via its online channels. This has involved changing its organisational structures and investing heavily in digital technologies.

10.4.2 Evolution Change Path

The key distinction between this change path and the *Revolution* change path is the speed of change that must occur. In the *Evolution* change path, the firm must pursue significant change in digital transformation, but over time. Although there may be new competitors and digital technologies disrupting the marketplace, it is not leading to the rapid disappearance of established firms. This path involves a change in the firm's strategy and culture over time. The firm may need to let go of existing mindsets and cultures and develop new ones for a digital context. These changes will be broad in scope, impacting all business functions and altering relationships with customers and suppliers.

The *Evolution* change path can avoid the risks of embarking on too much change and encountering significant resistance. This change path shares some of the characteristics of the discovery-driven approach to digital transformation [5]. Gradually implementing digital transformation projects over time will allow the firm to learn from experience and gain the support of key stakeholders affected by the changes. By then moving quickly and demonstrating the potential benefits of these projects, it is possible to implement a wider digital transformation effort for the firm. Such an approach allows established firms to bring about the change required for digital transformation, whilst at the same time minimising the disruption to existing operations.

> **Illustration 10.3 The Evolutionary Change Path in Digital Transformation in the Automotive Industry**
>
> Some established car makers in the automotive industry provide an example of firms pursuing the Evolution change path. Digital technologies are bringing about changes in the automotive industry in the form of new competitors, more digital features in cars, new business models in the form of car-sharing schemes and direct selling from automakers to customers. This has led these car makers to pursue change in the following areas:
>
> - Automakers have had to change their view of customers and increasingly focus on learning more about customer lifestyles and values, as well as how they use their cars, to create new sources of revenue in the form of software upgrades and additional digital entertainment services.
> - These developments have led to changes in the traditional role of some functions in automakers. For example, rather than delivering historical reports to business users, the IT function has had to work with other business functions to develop data analytics capabilities in areas such as quality management and analysing customer product usage behaviour.
> - As automakers become more and more technology-oriented, the skills mix of many employees has had to change. With digital technologies now playing a significant role in the car, automakers have had to develop the technical skills of their employees, particularly in R&D, engineering, manufacturing and marketing.

10.4.3 Adaptive Change Path

In this change path, digital technologies are not disrupting the established rules of competition in the marketplace. Employing digital technologies can have a positive impact on firm performance, but any change is likely to be incremental and characterised by a low pace of change and a relatively narrow scope. An adaptive change path is appropriate when a firm is performing well and, at the same time, intends to improve further and adapt to gradual changes in the marketplace through employing digital technologies.

Firms in the construction and power generation industries fit into this category. Proactive firms in these industries can exploit the power of digital technologies to further improve firm performance. It is also possible for these firms to pursue digital transformation without radically changing the business model of the firm. Much of the digital transformation change effort is at the process level and involves embedding the necessary changes amongst affected employees.

Existing organisational structures can be gradually changed to allow for the greater diffusion of digital technologies, and many of these developments can be accommodated within the existing firm culture. Some upskilling will be required around technical skills, and senior management in the firm should enhance their awareness of the potential of digital technologies to improve their competitive position.

Many of the headlines around digital transformation have tended to focus on sectors such as technology, media, telecoms or retail, where new digital competitors have been most successful and traditional, established firms have struggled. However, there are many examples where established firms have pursued an incremental approach to digital transformation and achieved the benefits of less disruption to their existing business model. For example, the Italian utility Enel Corporation went through a successful digital transformation during the 2010s, which allowed it to incorporate new technologies into its manufacturing facilities and energy distribution processes, and to radically change its internal practices [6]. During this time, its business model remained stable, with any changes being invisible to customers or suppliers.

> **Illustration 10.4 The Adaptive Change Path and the Incumbent Advantage**
>
> The German metals distributor Klöckner provides an illustration of a firm that has pursued an incremental approach to change in digital transformation. Rather than creating a digital platform for the entire industry, the firm developed capabilities incrementally and, at the same time, benefited from the knowledge of employees in its core steel business. In the first two years, it digitised inefficient manual processes by creating an online shop, a contract portal, order transparency tools, and a parts-manager app. These projects allowed the firm to learn how to create a platform through which the firm and its customers could easily interact.
>
> Klöckner used its existing knowledge and databases of previous transactions with customers to develop rich insights, something new start-up firms in the industry struggled with. Start-ups are often led by technical experts who often lack in-depth knowledge of potential customers. Digital investments are more likely to be successful when firms know their customers. Klöckner focused on

> ensuring that every digital project helped customers communicate more easily and efficiently with the firm. This is consistent with a philosophy in which technology is viewed as an opportunity for the business rather than as an opportunity for technology.
>
> Source: McGrath, R. and McManus, R. (2021). Discovery-driven digital transformation. *Harvard Business Review*, Summer Special Issue, pp. 85–91.

10.5 Practices for Embedding Change in Digital Transformation

Firms can pursue a number of practices to embed the necessary changes required for digital transformation, and some of these key practices are now outlined.

10.5.1 Recruitment, Retention and Skills Development

Embedding change in digital transformation requires continuous investments in both digital and management competencies and skills through recruitment and retraining. A firm should have human resources practices in place to scan the labour market for new recruits that can augment and refresh its digital and management knowledge base, whilst at the same time encouraging skills development amongst existing employees.

Recruitment practices. An enduring challenge for firms when embarking on digital transformation is finding people with the right skills. Some studies have shown that it is not just about paying more or spending more on training but about recruiting people who can develop their skills and offering incentives to make this happen. There are a number of important practices for recruitment in a digital context [7]:

- *Look for potential, not credentials*—often, the life cycle of technology skills, such as programming languages, is around two years, making such technical skills rapidly redundant. Rather than focusing on technical skills, some firms have been paying more attention to recruiting people who are curious, flexible and quick to learn.
- *Value soft skills as much as technical skills*—IT development has evolved more towards finding problems and developing solutions rather than writing a specification and then coding it. Soft skills, such as teamwork

and communication skills, have become more important as digital transformation focuses on improving customer experience via digital technologies.
- *Consider teams, not individuals*—firms are increasingly focusing on people who are likely to be important contributors to teams. Selection of these people may not be driven by their academic and technical qualities alone but also considers those who have come through vocational training routes. Firms need a mix of people with these qualities to drive digital transformation.
- *Employee incentives for development*—once a firm has recruited a person, it must provide them with the opportunity and incentive to complete training courses during work hours or in their personal time to further their development.

Skills development. The level of uncertainty and change in the business environment means firms must continuously develop the skills of their employees. Many employees, regardless of their position in the hierarchy, now require a higher level of technical expertise than was necessary in the past. Rather than relying on their own firm for skills development, proactive employees have been reskilling to enhance their own career prospects. These employees are recognising the importance of taking up learning opportunities as a means of unlocking their potential [8].

However, firms need to invest in upskilling employees, as this should ensure employees are better equipped to deal with change in the context of digital transformation. There are a number of practices that firms can adopt in this context.

- *Employee-digital technology alignment*—this involves ensuring that employees are effectively trained to obtain the benefits that digital technologies offer. For example, there is little point in investing in an innovative AI application if employees are not sufficiently skilled to use it. Managers should also have the skills to use digital technologies as a means of improving their own decision-making. For example, where a firm invests in data analytics applications, managers must have the skills to develop meaningful insights from the data to improve firm performance.
- *Increasing importance of soft skills development*—soft skills development has become an important focus for firms, particularly for employees who are the most flexible and curious, and therefore more willing to learn. For example, in a digital context, it can be difficult to forecast which technical skills will be the most important in the future. Where a firm invests in

employees who are willing to learn, they can quickly upskill them in in-demand and contemporary technical skills.
- *Higher-level skills on management implications of digital technologies*—this involves training current employees to understand the potential of digital technologies in a range of business contexts. This should allow the firm to gain insights into environmental changes and be able to develop effective responses.

Vodafone provides an interesting example of a firm that developed employee capabilities during the digital transformation of its customer care services [9]. Rather than using a customer contact centre to answer customer calls, it designed conversational frameworks for a chatbot to handle customer requests. Vodafone employees were involved in training the conversational models to ensure accurate responses were provided to customer requests. This was achieved through a digital feedback process of continuous improvement in the accuracy and relevance of conversations, based on customer experiences. A neural network training unit was established to enable operators to use the new system, which resulted in the creation of new jobs.

Illustration 10.5 Generation Z and Soft Skills Development

Some firms have found that Generation Z employees lack soft skills such as time management, empathy and confidence in speaking on the telephone or giving presentations. The advent of social media and exposure to other digital media have changed the communication habits of Generation Z employees compared to earlier generations. Remote working and the increasing reliance on text messaging have meant that many young people are not prepared for the basics of working life and lack the skills that firms took for granted in the past. The lack of these soft skills and confidence can lead to anxiety and depression when young people struggle to cope in the workplace.

Firms, universities and government bodies have started to offer courses that address some of these issues. Some firms offer courses that teach their Generation Z employees how to answer the telephone and conduct themselves client meetings. Other courses include assessments on how to interact in person with others, how to spot fake news, how to stay safe on the internet, how to challenge racism, sexism and homophobia, and how to avoid scams. Research in the United States has shown that 85% of job success in the workplace comes from soft skills. This also poses challenges to traditional education systems, which have focused mainly on developing hard skills rather than nurturing young people to be mentally strong.

Source: Halliday, J. (2025, April 21). Thousands of 'digital natives' to be taught social skills, as employers say they are too afraid to speak on the phone. *The Guardian*. https://www.theguardian.com/society/2025/apr/21/gen-z-students-in-manchester-to-learn-soft-skills-such-as-empathy-and-time-management

10.5.2 Organisational Structure and Change

Traditional hierarchical firm structures often hinder collaboration both internally and across firm boundaries, which is a prerequisite for digital transformation. Therefore, new structures must be put in place to drive more collaboration and integration across functions to take advantage of the opportunities that digital technologies offer. Greater collaboration, cross-functional teams, the digital workplace, and hybrid working are some of the key drivers of structural changes, and these are explained below.

Increased employee collaboration. A key challenge in driving digital transformation is encouraging employees to escape from the constraints of existing structures, associated processes and roles. These constraints often hinder collaboration and knowledge sharing across the firm. A process-oriented approach can foster collaboration by developing an end-to-end mindset and rethinking ways of meeting customer needs, seamlessly connecting work activities and effectively managing across silos [10].

Therefore, senior management needs to dismantle any rigid areas of responsibility and develop project structures that foster cross-functional collaboration and complement existing structures. Consider the case of a manufacturing company developing data analytics capabilities. It will have to design structures to ensure collaboration between the technology domain, including data integration and technology infrastructure; the business domain, including business acumen; and the analytics domain, including the development of analytics models and visualisation [11].

Creating cross-functional teams. Cross-functional teams should be an integral part of any digital transformation effort for established firms [12]. These teams include employees from different functions, and they are accountable to the team leader and not their line managers. Working across functions can benefit the culture of the firm and encourage teams and employees to challenge thinking outside their own areas of expertise. Cross-functional teams are normally assessed against performance metrics at both the team and individual levels, and the work of these teams is supported by senior management.

> **Illustration 10.6 Cross-Functional Teams at CarMax**
>
> CarMax, the Virginia-based car retailer, has adopted cross-functional teams to drive digital transformation and has moved away from traditional planning approaches. As a result of rapidly changing technologies and customer expectations, it has had to organise into cross-functional teams, as single-functional teams cannot deliver quickly enough. For example, CarMax used a cross-functional team

to develop an omni-channel experience, which was a new approach to buying and selling cars online. This allowed customers to complete the entire car purchase from home and have the test drive delivered to their driveway.

Typically, each team had seven to nine members from any department but included a product manager, lead developer and user-experience expert. Each team was tasked with what they had to achieve rather than how to achieve it. Progress was closely monitored by considering how each team was tracking against objectives, the experiments completed and what they had learned. It was straightforward to conduct experiments digitally and quickly without incurring any significant risks. The performance of team members was monitored at both the team and individual levels. The move towards cross-functional teams changed the firm's mindset around technology planning, shifting the focus to product teams and business outcome goals. The involvement of top executives across departments helped leaders create a supportive environment.

Source: https://www2.deloitte.com/content/dam/Deloitte/lu/Documents/deloitte-digital/lu-accelerating-digital-innovation.pdf. Refer to pages 9–10.

The digital workplace and hybrid working. Firms are increasingly employing digital technologies to create new digital workplaces that breakdown organisation silos and segregated physical spaces. The digital workplace refers to the physical, cultural and digital arrangements that simplify working life in complex, dynamic and often unstructured working contexts [13]. These digital workplaces can be an important driver of change in the digital transformation journey, particularly in the area of increasing employee engagement and sharing knowledge and ideas across the business. There are three levers that enhance digital and physical communication:

- *Systems*—this involves employing the latest technologies, such as videoconferencing and internet of things sensors, to enable work activities required for innovation, the delivery of integrated customer experiences and collaboration with other employees.
- *Social*—this uses social media platforms to accelerate collaborative work and generate new ideas.
- *Space*—this redesigns physical areas to include flexible meeting and learning spaces, supporting collaboration and fostering new interpersonal connections.

The trend towards hybrid working has also become an important element of the digital workplace. Employees have been able to achieve greater flexibility, and, in many cases, firms have also been using hybrid working as a tool to attract, retain and motivate people. However, firms must be careful in balancing the flexibility and cost benefits with the need to build a collaborative culture necessary for digital transformation. This involves balancing the time employees spend doing hybrid work whilst spending time in the office to establish and develop social relationships and engage in creative tasks. The following four categories of work tasks can differentiate between those that should and should not be performed remotely [14]:

- *Individual procedural tasks*—these tasks can be performed without interacting with each other and include data entry or claims processing tasks. Supervision can be difficult for these tasks in a remote-working context.
- *Focused creative tasks*—these require little teamwork and are easily supported by technology. Examples include writing code or designing a brochure. These tasks can be straightforward to transition to hybrid working.
- *Coordinated group tasks*—these involve regular meetings that can be standardised yet still require human interaction. These tasks are more difficult to undertake remotely, although communication technologies can facilitate the process.
- *Collaborative creative tasks*—these are important drivers of innovation and can include highly social interactions in areas such as product development and creative problem-solving tasks. The collaborative nature of these tasks makes them difficult to accomplish via remote working and can potentially have negative consequences for culture and innovation.

Illustration 10.7 Digital Transformation: Changing Organisational Structures and the Impact on the IT Function

The trend towards increasing digital transformation has posed significant challenges to the IT function in many established firms. Many firms have inflexible legacy systems that are difficult to change and require people with technical skills to work collaboratively with the rest of the business. At the same time, many IT departments have lacked the ability to drive the required changes and have primarily focused on 'keeping the lights on'. However, digital transformation requires a capable IT function that builds trust with the rest of the business, which means IT specialists must deliver business value with every technology innovation. Therefore, IT leaders must be strong communicators and able to make technological choices that balance innovation and address technical debt.

In a manufacturing context, the prominence of the IoT has led to the involvement of the IT function in the design and manufacture of products. Although R&D possesses strengths in developing and combining mechanical and electrical components, they often lack the capabilities to integrate software into products and understand the data management implications over the life cycle of the product. Therefore, R&D and the IT function have to collaborate on a continuous basis, which has led to various organisational structures emerging. For example, some firms have been embedding IT specialists in R&D departments, whilst other firms have been establishing cross-functional design teams with IT specialists, whilst having separate reporting lines.

Firms such as AUDI have been enhancing the capabilities and profile of the IT function within their business. Previously, the IT function in AUDI acted primarily as a support unit responsible for providing IT support services to business units and was not involved in the design process for new car models. As a result of digital transformation, AUDI developed the capabilities of the IT function and encouraged cross-functional IT initiatives where business units actively collaborate with IT. The firm developed organisational structures that ensured digitisation efforts were highly interwoven and integrated across business units rather than being confined to separate organisational silos.

Sources: Davenport, T.H. and Redman, T.C., 2020. 'Digital Transformation Comes Down to Talent in 4 Key Areas'. *Harvard Business Review*, 2(6); Dremel, C., Wulf, J., Herterich, M.M., Waizmann, J.C., and Brenner, W., 2017. 'How AUDI AG Established Big Data Analytics in Its Digital Transformation'. *MIS Quarterly Executive*, 16(2), pp. 81–100; Porter, M.E. and Heppelmann, J.E., 2015. 'How Smart, Connected Products Are Transforming Companies'. *Harvard Business Review*, 93(10), pp. 96–114.

10.5.3 Driving Change Through Leadership

Leadership has a critical role to play in driving the change required for effective digital transformation. Many senior executives fail to appreciate that success involves integrating people, technology, processes and data. There are a number of key leadership characteristics for implementing change in digital transformation, as outlined below:

- *Communicate a strategy and vision*—leadership involves creating a strategy and vision that is transparent to affected stakeholders and communicated from the strategic level to the operational level. Employees at the operational level must understand the strategy and vision, as well as what is expected of them [15]. Leadership from senior management is important for articulating this vision and aligning it with the required investments in resources. This should help ensure that the digital strategy and vision receive the required level of support throughout the firm.
- *Develop digital capabilities amongst leaders*—leaders often lack the required digital capabilities to drive digital transformation, and in many established firms, leaders are tied to the firm's values, history and practices that are no longer the key drivers of success in a digital context. Leaders need to understand why digital technologies are important and how they can

transform their business. Although appointing a chief technology or digital officer can be an important enabler, it is not sufficient, and leaders need to develop their own digital capabilities. This can involve leaders joining the executive boards of digital firms and spending time with technology specialists, including venture capitalists, new digital start-ups and digital professionals in their own firm. Part of this effort could involve technology leaders being invited onto the board of the firm, and each leader in the firm should be encouraged to undertake digital training.

- *Assemble the correct team*—no one leader can possess all the knowledge and capabilities required for digital transformation. Therefore, a strong leader has to assemble and manage the correct team and talent. A key feature in the war for talent is leadership [16]. Although a shortage of digital talent is a key challenge, the more important challenge is finding the leaders who can manage the technical specialists and get them to work as a team with functional managers to outperform their peers. The correct team with a strong leader can be the single most important driver for guaranteeing success with digital transformation. Leadership should involve aligning the capabilities of the team with the objectives of digital transformation.
- *Data-driven leadership*—leaders need to understand the importance of data and why it is a key driver of change for digital transformation [17]. As data are an important aspect of digital transformation, it should be accurate, and therefore, there is an onus on leaders to ensure that data are captured and analysed correctly. Data can be used by leaders to evaluate the effectiveness of the digital transformation journey during implementation and serve as an impetus for action. Leadership will involve convincing many staff in the firm to take on new roles, such as data customers and data creators, which means thinking through and communicating the data they need currently and post-digital transformation [18].
- *Building a digital culture*—effective leadership involves ensuring that the culture of the firm is aligned with the digital transformation strategy [17]. This could involve developing a mindset that fosters openness and promoting empathy, positivity and inclusivity, which leadership needs to transfer from the strategic to the operational level. Getting buy-in from the firm requires a form of leadership that brings freshness and new ideas and enthuses the entire firm.
- *Leading cross-functional collaboration*—leadership in digital transformation involves collaborating both functionally and cross-functionally, and gaining support and participation from employees at all levels within the firm. This should include giving everyone the opportunity to propose ideas and allowing everyone to voice their opinions on digital transformation

opportunities and risks. Leaders should adopt a firm-wide perspective and encourage different functions to work together to address problems. Consider the common issue of a lack of system integration and its negative impact on digital transformation efforts. This problem often arises due to organisational structure and political influences that are difficult to change. However, functions such as operations and finance often perceive this as a technical matter and, therefore, the responsibility of the IT function. Leadership, however, involves motivating these technical and business functions to collaborate in addressing these challenges.

> **Discussion Questions**
>
> 1. Referring to Sect. 10.3.3 and the *Preservation* contextual change factor, select two firms from different business sectors that have embarked on digital transformation and analyse how their tangible and intangible assets were impacted by digital transformation. Highlight some of the challenges the firms encountered.
> 2. Referring to Sect. 10.3.4 and the *Cultural diversity* contextual change factor, analyse how two firms from different business sectors could employ reverse mentoring to drive organisational change in digital transformation. Highlight the benefits and challenges for each firm in the process.
> 3. Referring to Sect. 10.4.1, select a firm that has pursued a *Revolution* change path in its digital transformation journey and critically assess how it has driven organisational change. Highlight examples of how it dealt with the challenges around the contextual change factors in Table 10.1.
> 4. Referring to Sect. 10.5.1, research a firm of your choice and critically assess how it has embedded change in the digital transformation journey through the *Recruitment, retention, and skills development* practices.
> 5. Referring to Sect. 10.5.2 and the *Digital workplace and hybrid working* section, select a firm you are familiar with and carry out the following tasks: (i) analyse how it has employed digital technologies to develop the digital workplace; and (ii) highlight examples of work in this workplace that would fit into the categories of individual procedural tasks, focused creative tasks, coordinated group tasks and collaborative creative tasks.

References

1. Balogun, J., & Hope Haiey, V. (2008). *Exploring Strategic Change*, Prentice-Hall, 3rd Edition.
2. Correani, A., De Massis, A., Frattini, F., Petruzzelli, A. M., & Natalicchio, A. (2020). Implementing a digital strategy: Learning from the experience of three digital transformation projects. *California Management Review*, *62*(4), 37–56.

3. Gfrerer, A., Hutter, K., Füller, J., & Ströhle, T. (2021). Ready or not: Managers' and employees' different perceptions of digital readiness. *California Management Review*, 63(2), 23–48.
4. Volberda, H. W., Khanagha, S., Baden-Fuller, C., Mihalache, O. R., & Birkinshaw, J. (2021). Strategizing in a digital world: Overcoming cognitive barriers, reconfiguring routines and introducing new organizational forms. *Long Range Planning*, 54(5), 102110.
5. McGrath, R., & McManus, R. (2021). Discovery-driven digital transformation. *Harvard Business Review*, Summer, Special issue 85–91.
6. See Volbreda et al. (2021) in reference 4 above.
7. Kavanaugh, J., & Ravi Kumar, S. (2021). How to develop a talent pipeline for your digital transformation. *Harvard Business Review*, Summer, Special issue, 134-136.
8. Frankiewicz, B., & Chamorro-Premuzic, T. (2021). Digital transformation is about talent, not technology. *Harvard Business Review*, Summer, Special issue, 134-136.
9. See Correani et al. (2020) in reference 2 above.
10. Davenport, T. H., & Redman, T. C. (2020). Digital transformation comes down to talent in 4 key areas. *Harvard Business Review*, 2(6).
11. Dremel, C., Wulf, J., Herterich, M. M., Waizmann, J. C., & Brenner, W. (2017). How AUDI AG established big data analytics in its digital transformation. *MIS Quarterly Executive*, 16(2), 81–100.
12. Kane, B. G. C., Palmer, D., Phillips, A. N., Kiron, D., & Buckley, N. (2019). Accelerating Digital Innovation Inside and Out. *MIT Sloan Management Review and Deloitte Insights*, 60471.
13. Dery, K., Sebastian, I. M., & van der Meulen, N. (2017). The Digital Workplace is Key to Digital Innovation. *MIS Quarterly Executive*, 16(2), 135–152.
14. Trevor, J., & Holweg, M. (2022). Managing the new tensions of hybrid work. *MIT Sloan Management Review*, 64(2).
15. McCarthy, P., Sammon, D., & Alhassan, I. (2024). The characteristics of digital transformation leadership: Theorizing the practitioner voice. *Business Horizons*, 67(4), 411–423.
16. See Davenport and Redman (2020) in reference 10 above.
17. See McCarthy et al. (2024) in reference 15 above.
18. See Davenport and Redman (2020) in reference 10 above.
19. See McCarthy et al. (2024) in reference 15 above.

Correction to: Digital Transformation

Correction to:
R. McIvor, Digital Transformation, Palgrave Executive Essentials,
https://doi.org/10.1007/978-3-031-99258-2

Figure 6.2 (p. 142): In the originally published version, the box at the bottom right of Figure 6.2 was incorrectly labelled. It should have read "organisational structure alignment" to match the text. The corrected figure has since been incorporated.

Illustration 7.4 (p. 164): The title of Illustration 7.4 had incorrectly ended with a question mark. The question mark has now been removed.

The updated version of these chapters can be found at
https://doi.org/10.1007/978-3-031-99258-2_6
https://doi.org/10.1007/978-3-031-99258-2_7

Glossary

Algorithm is a set of rules to follow to complete a task or solve a problem that can be programmed into a software routine.

Algorithmic transparency refers to the extent to which the factors influencing the decision or recommendation from an algorithm are evident to the users.

Analog relates to non-digital aspects of a firm including face-to-face contact, people engagement in offline activities, and creating and delivering physical products and services.

Application programming interface (API) is a set of rules and protocols that link applications, allowing them to communicate and share data.

Big data refers to large and diverse collections of structured and unstructured data managed by a firm, and is characterised by the 3 V's of volume, velocity and variety.

Business case describes a business problem and outlines a proposal on how it should be overcome.

Business model explains how a firm creates value for customers and captures value for the firm, reflecting issues such as the architecture of the firm's value proposition, market segments, revenue model and cost structure.

Business model canvas is a framework for mapping the components of a business model and identifying ways it might be improved through for example, the use of digital technologies.

Business model transformation involves employing digital technologies to re-define current business models and create new value for customers.

Business model innovation involves reconfiguring how a firm operates, involving strategic choices that owners and managers can make as it involves defining how the firm interacts with other players and customers in its ecosystem.

Glossary

Business process a collection of activities across different business functions that create an output such as processing a customer order.

Chatbot a digital application that stimulates and responds to human conversation and questions, allowing humans to interact with the application as if it were a real person

Cloud computing refers to a network of remote servers hosted on the Internet to store, manage, and process data; and includes functions such as email, storage, data backup, data retrieval etc.

Codification the extent to which tasks associated with a process can be described completely in a set of written instructions.

Data-driven culture refers to a culture where data is shared across a firm and is recognised as a valuable resource and key driver of digital transformation.

Data analytics refers to the practice of using techniques to analyse and acquire intelligence from data to allow firms to make data-driven business decisions.

Data network effects occurs when data generated by users of a product or service increase the value for other users on a digital application.

Deliberate view of strategy involves a rational, analytical approach that identifies the optimal strategy prior to strategy implementation.

Design thinking is a solution-focused and user-centric approach to innovation and is a powerful tool for quickly testing whether an idea or solution can deliver real value to users.

Digital disruption refers to the disruptive impact of digital technologies on issues such as the competitive landscape, the product and service creation and delivery process and customer behaviour.

Digital innovation refers to the practices and processes involved in employing digital technologies to create new and improved products and services on an ongoing basis.

Digital platform refers to an online infrastructure that facilitates interactions and transactions between individuals, firms and third parties.

Digital transformation involves employing digital technologies to transform processes, products and business models, and leads to a holistic change in the operations and structure of the firm.

Digital data stream refers to the transmission of digital representations of events such as when a customer tweets about a purchase or where a customer made a purchase.

Digital twin allows product designers to create virtual replicas of physical products and then use data to mirror the functionality of the product when it is in operation.

Digital workplace refers to the physical, cultural and digital arrangements that simplify working life in complex, dynamic and often unstructured working contexts.

Disruptive innovation occurs when a product or service is targeted at an overlooked market or customers by established firms, and over time the product or service starts to attract the attention of more profitable customers in more upmarket segments.

Ecosystem refers to a network of relationships between firms, customers, suppliers, government agencies, academic institutions, new startups and even competitors, who are involved in creating specific products or services.

Economies of scale occurs when the unit costs of creating and delivering a service decrease, as volume increases.

Emergent view of strategy refers to strategy that emerges from a process of experimentation, learning, and adaptation during implementation.

Enterprise system a set of applications capable of integrating and managing business functions and operations for an entire, multi-site organisation.

Generative AI an AI application such as ChatGPT that can create types of images, text, videos and other media in response to user prompts.

Generativity refers to digital technology applications that create outcomes and behaviour beyond what was envisaged in the initial design stage.

Intellectual property refers to the rights given to a creator for the exclusive use of a creation over a certain time period, and can include patents, copyrights, trademarks, and trade secrets.

Internet of things involves connecting devices such as cars to the Internet and to other connected devices, all of which collect and share data about the way they are used and the environment around them.

Legacy systems older information technology applications that may be still capable of meeting the needs of the firm, although they may require updating to meet the future needs.

Machine learning a branch of AI that involves developing algorithms to interpret, process, and analyse data to solve business problems.

Modularisation involves breaking down large and complex business processes into component modules and activities so that firms can specialise in certain modules and activities.

Network effects occurs when each new user joins a digital application or platform, thus making it more attractive for current users to remain and other new users to join.

Omni-channel refers to a single, unified customer experience across a range of digital touchpoints including social media, mobile apps and websites.

Opportunism involves a supplier shirking on responsibilities agreed in the contract with the customer in outsourcing contracts.

Organisational structure refers to the roles, responsibilities, and reporting relationships in a firm.

Outsourcing refers to the use of external suppliers to provide products or services previously provided by internal business functions.

Power refers to the ability of individuals or groups to persuade or force others into taking certain actions.

Process transformation involves employing digital technologies to transform business processes to create customer value through improving how transactions are processed, how decisions are made, how existing customers are dealt with, and how new customers are attracted.

Process mapping involves creating a visual map of workflows within a process with the aim of improving process performance and delivering value for customers.

Product transformation involves employing digital technologies to transform products through embedding digital functions that provide additional services and create value for the customer.

Radio frequency identification (RFID) a technology that uses radio waves to identify and tracks objects such as inventory or vehicles in a supply chain.

Servitisation refers to the process of creating value by adding services to products and developing service-oriented business models in a manufacturing context.

Shared services involves consolidating and standardising common tasks associated with a business function such as human resource across different parts of the organisation into a single services centre.

Six Sigma an improvement programme for eliminating waste and improving performance in business processes. Statistical and scientific methods are at the heart of Six Sigma, both in developing an optimum process specification, and reducing defects in the process to almost zero.

Social media refers to websites and applications that are designed to allow people to share content quickly, efficiently, and in real-time via apps on electronic devices.

Social technologies digital technologies such as email and social media that enable social interactions and communication.

Standardisation the extent to which the tasks in a process can be executed using a set of consistent and repeatable steps.

Tacit knowledge knowledge that is based on subjective and experiential learning that is highly personal and difficult to formalise.

Unbundling involves breaking down large, complex processes into smaller, and in some cases, modularised processes.

Index

A

Accenture, 160
Adaptable products, 143
Adaptive algorithm, 86
Adaptive change path, 242
Add-on business model, 68
AirBnB, 10, 20, 25, 31, 34, 36, 47–48, 135–137, 155, 180
Algorithmic AI, 84
Algorithmic bias, 93
    proxy bias, 94
    selection bias, 93
    temporal bias, 94
Algorithmic transparency, 93
Algorithms
    adaptive, 86
    fixed, 86
    reinforcement algorithms, 86
Alibaba, 11, 36, 42, 47, 51, 177, 190
Amazon, 10, 29, 31, 38, 42, 45–46, 50, 55, 82, 114, 177, 190
Amazon, Apple and Google, 70
Anti-competitive practices, 46
Apple, 19, 29, 31, 33, 35, 38, 45–47, 51, 55, 68, 82–83, 129, 135, 183–184
Application program interfaces (API), 215
Artificial intelligence, 1
    autonomy capabilities, 87
    business value, 98
    categories of, 82
    data quality and availability, 97
    employee engagement, 100
    ethics implications, 98
    employee implications, 101
    explanation feature, 100
    how it transforms process and product capabilities, 90
    learning capabilities, 88
    risks of application, 92
    the impact on the legal profession, 92
    task augmentation, 96
    task automation, 96
Asos, 180, 195
Asset sharing, 163
AUDI, 249
Audio analytics, 122
Augmented reality, 3
Autonomy, 87

B
BASF, 37
Bayer, 37
Best Buy, 20, 188
Big data, 111
  variety, 111
  velocity, 111
  volume, 111
Biometric AI, 83
Blockchain technology, 3
BMW, 37, 183
Boohoo, 180, 195
Bosch, 60
Boston Consulting Group, 160
Business analytics, 110
Business intelligence, 110
Business model, 153
  value capture, 155
  value creation, 155
  value delivery, 155
Business model canvas, 165
  impact of digital technologies, 166
Business model innovation, 153, 158
  barriers to employing digital technologies, 164
  complementarities, 160
  design thinking, 168
  digital technologies as drivers of, 162
  digital technologies as drivers of at Uber, 164
  efficiency, 160
  lock-in, 160
  novelty, 159
  the business model canvas, 165
Business model transformation, 25–26
Business silo, 213
Business strategy, 176

C
Capability-based view, 40, 183
CarMax, 247

Cath Kidston, 195
Challenges of digital innovation, 140
Change kaleidoscope, 232
Change paths in digital transformation, 238
  adaptive, 239, 242
  evolution, 239–240
  revolution, 238–239
ChatGPT, 81–82, 97
Circular economy, 88
Closed innovation, 143, 145–147
Cloud computing, 3, 5, 214
CNH Industrial, 233
Complementarities, 160
Concept drift AI, 94
Contextual change factors in digital transformation, 232
  capability, 236–237
  capacity, 238
  cultural diversity, 235
  preservation, 234
  scope speed, 233
Continuous product design, 9
Conversational AI, 83
Coopetition, 180
Covariate shift AI, 94
Creativity, 132, 137
Crockett and Jones, 197
Crowdsending, 48
Crowdsourcing, 48
Culture, 147
  building a digital culture, 251
  data-driven, 22
  fusing cultural differences, 22
Culture change, 21
Customer cocreation, 163
Customer network approach, 8
CVS, 134
Cyber security, 18, 225
  digital resilience, 226
  digital security, 226

Index

D

Daimler, 37
Dark data, 126
Data
   competing on, 11
   driven leadership, 250
   structured, 111
   unstructured, 111
Data analytics, 2, 9, 78, 110
   audio analytics, 122
   descriptive analytics, 119
   diagnostic analytics, 119
   predictive analytics, 119
   prescriptive analytics, 120
   product-in-use data analytics, 144, 145
   text analytics, 121
   video analytics, 122
   the time dimension, 113
   tools for social media, 123
   tools for unstructured data, 121
Data anonymisation, 127
Data availability, 97
Data cleansing, 116, 118
Data management challenges, 115
Data masking, 127
Data networks effects, 114
Data ownership, 78
Data Privacy, 78, 127
Data quality, 18, 98, 116
Data quality assessment, 116
Data security, 78
Data warehousing, 116, 118
Debenhams, 195
Deep learning, 84, 121
Deere and Company, 145
Deliberate, 177
Deliberate strategy, 177, 202
Descriptive analytics, 119
Design, 132–133, 135–138, 144–146, 148–151
Design thinking, 168, 170
   benefits, 169

DHL, 66
Diagnostic analytics, 119
Digital automation, 13
   customer contact, 13
   customisation, 13
   knowledge intensity, 13
   regulatory issues, 13
Digital capabilities, 186
   distinctive digital capabilities, 188
   necessary digital capabilities, 187
Digital capabilities, 185
Digital capability analysis, 183
Digital capability development, 23
Digital core, 208
   customer experience and operational efficiency pathway choice, 223
   modular architectures, 215
   organisational redesign, 218
   process improvement, 217
   sourcing strategy, 219
Digital data streams, 112
Digital disruption, 178, 179
Digital footprints, 8
Digital innovation, 131–132, 134, 138, 140–141, 143–144, 146–150
   adaptable products, 143
   challenges, 140
   organisational culture, 147
   organisational structure, 149
   product-in-use data analytics, 144
   the role of data, 138, 140
Digital maturity frameworks, 212–213
Digital platform, 10
   anti-competitive practices, 46
   contradictory impacts of, 37
   disintermediation, 49
   external value creation, 36
   failure, 44
   key elements of, 35
   multi-homing, 49
   risks for firms dependent on, 44
   strategy, 39
   strategies for reducing threats, 50

types of, 30
versus value chain firms, 38
value creation, 41
value measurement, 44
Digital platform strategy, 39
  capability-based approach, 39
  industry positioning approach, 40
Digital platforms, 7
Digital resilience, 227
Digital resources, 183
  distinctive digital resources, 187
  financial resource, 185
  human resource, 185
  necessary digital resources, 187
  technical resource, 185
Digital technologies, 1, 2
  as drivers of business model innovation, 162, 164
  design, 136
  employee augmentation, 12
  employee substitution, 11
  entrepreneurship, 6
  innovation, 133
  productivity, 4
  scale, 4
Digital transformation, 14–15, 20
  challenges of, 16
  change paths 10-5, 238
  contextual change factors, 232
  culture change, 21
  digital capability development, 23
  framework for understanding, 20
  ineffective technology infrastructures, 18
  leadership, 23
  pressures for localisation, 18
  recruitment practices, 243
  resistance to change, 16
  resource constraints, 17
  skills development, 244
  structural changes, 22

Digital transformation strategy, 175
  break-out strategy, 190
  embed and sustain strategy, 194
  enhance and exploit strategy, 197
  evaluation and adaptation, 199
  implementation, 199
  incremental development strategy, 196
  organisational learning, 203
  the link with business strategy, 176
Digital twins, 136
Digital workplace, 246–247
Disintermediation, 49
Disruptive innovation, 156
Distinctive digital resources, 187

E
EBay, 11, 19, 29, 33
Ecosystem, 35, 159
Efficiency, 160
Emergent strategy, 177
Employee augmentation, 12
Employee engagement, 105
Employee substitution, 11
  knowledge intensive tasks, 12
  physical tasks, 11
Enel Corporation, 242
Enterprise systems, 209
European Union, 7, 19
Expedia, 10
Experimentation, 134, 168
Explanation feature, 100
External value creation, 36

F
Facebook, 29, 31, 34–36, 43, 47, 114, 123–124
Fat-Face, 195
Flexible working, 12

G

Gap, 196
Generation Z, 235, 245
Generative AI, 81, 92, 96–97, 101, 137
    judgement integration, 102
    intelligent interrogation, 102
    reciprocal apprenticing, 102
Generative AI tools, 102
Generative design, 88
Gig workers, 12
Google, 11, 29, 31, 36, 38, 44, 46, 50, 84, 114, 129, 167, 180
Gucci, 19

H

Hapag-Lloyd, 177
Harley davidson, 12
Heidelberger druck, 62
Hybrid working, 12, 247

I

Imitability, 183
Implementation, 199
Incremental innovation, 135
Industry convergence, 180
Industry positioning approach, 40
ING, 177
Innovation, 132
    incremental, 135
    radical, 135
Innovation platforms, 31, 41
    value creation, 155
    digital technologies, 133
Instagram, 29, 123, 203
Internet of things, 55, 131
    applications in healthcare, 64
    capabilities of, 58
    data considerations, 78
    how it impacts competition, 75
    how it transforms customer relationships, 62
    how it transforms supply chains, 65
    impacts on business functions, 60
    implementation challenges, 71
    key building blocks, 57
    privacy and security implications, 69
    servitised business models, 67
    technical considerations, 76
    the power of, 56
    value capture for firms, 73
    value creation for customers, 73
IoT applications in healthcare, 64
IT poor performance causes, 208

K

Kaggle, 32
Klöckner, 242
Kodak, 158
Konecranes, 61
Kroger, 198

L

Leadership, 23, 149
    digital innovation, 148
    digital transformation, 23–24
    driving change, 249
Legacy systems, 209–210
Lego, 8, 193
LinkedIn, 29, 123

M

Machine Learning, 85–86
    reinforcement algorithms, 86
    supervised algorithms, 85
    unsupervised algorithms, 86
Made.com, 195
Maersk, 66, 198
Marks and Spencer, 226
McKinsey, 160

Merck Group, 38
Meta, 47, 127, 129
Microsoft, 31, 38, 46
Mobile device technologies, 2
Modular architectures, 215
Modularity, 213
Moore's Law, 3
Morrisons, 198
Multi-homing, 49

N

National Health Service (NHS), 207
Natural language processing, 84, 121
Necessary digital resources, 187
Negative network effects, 45
Netflix, 97, 120, 136
Network clustering, 47
Network effects, 11, 32, 34, 36
Neural networks, 84
Next, 195
Nike, 29, 137, 240

O

Ocado, 198
Open innovation, 146
Operational backbone, 212
Organisational change, 233
   big bang approach, 233
   long march approach, 233
Organisational culture, 147
   building a digital culture, 251
   data-driven, 22
   fusing cultural differences, 22
Organisational learning, 199, 203
Organisational redesign, 218
   challenges, 218
Organisational structure, 149, 246
   greater employee autonomy, 22
   more flexible organisational structures, 22
   outward looking orientation, 22
   physical workspace redesign, 22
Outsourcing, 219
   standardisation, 219

P

Personalisation, 163
Phishing scams, 228
Process improvement, 216
Process transformation, 24–26
Procter and Gamble, 29
Product and service co-design, 8
Product transformation, 24–26
PWC, 160

R

Radio-frequency identification (RFID), 64–65
Radio Shack, 17, 190
Rarity, 183, 186
   See also capability-based view
Reiss, 196
Resilience management, 225
Reverse mentoring, 236
Revolut, 10
Robotic AI, 84
Robotic process automation, 84
Rolex, 197
Rolls-Royce, 67
Rule-based expert systems, 84

S

Sainsbury, 39
Samsung, 135
Schindler, 9
Scope, 233
Sears, 190
Sentiment analysis, 122, 124
Servitised business models, 67
Shared services, 210, 218
Sharing business model, 68

Siemens, 37
Silos, 209, 214
Six Sigma tools, 217
Social media, 1–2
    data analytics tools, 120
Soft skills development, 244, 245
Solution-oriented business model, 69
Sourcing strategy, 219
Spotify, 114
Standardisation, 212, 217
    outsourcing, 219
    process improvement, 216
Starling, 10
Structured data, 111
Sustainability, 9

T

Tesco, 40, 188
Tesla, 38, 144
Text summarisation, 122
Topshop, 17, 195
Toyota, 61, 183
Transaction platforms, 31, 42
    value creation, 41
TUI, 224–225

U

Uber, 19, 34, 47, 164, 180
UberEats, 170
Udaan, 51
Unstructured data, 111
    data analytics tools, 118
UPS, 66
Usage-based business model, 68, 163

V

Value, 180, 182–183
    See also capability-based view
Vodafone, 245
Volkswagen, 37
Volvo, 146

X

X, 123

Y

YouTube, 123

The manufacturer's authorised representative in the EU is Springer Nature Customer Service Centre GmbH, Europaplatz 3, 69115 Heidelberg, Germany. If you have any concerns regarding our products, please contact ProductSafety@springernature.com

Printed and bound by CPI Group (UK) Ltd, Croydon, CR0 4YY
20/04/2026
02093316-0001